Study Guide

for use with

The Legal & Regulatory Environment of Business

Thirteenth Edition

O. Lee Reed
University of Georgia

Peter J. Shedd
University of Georgia

Jere W. Morehead
University of Georgia

Robert N. Corley
University of Georgia

Prepared by
O. Lee Reed
University of Georgia

 **McGraw-Hill Irwin**

Boston   Burr Ridge, IL   Dubuque, IA   Madison, WI   New York   San Francisco   St. Louis
Bangkok   Bogotá   Caracas   Kuala Lumpur   Lisbon   London   Madrid   Mexico City
Milan   Montreal   New Delhi   Santiago   Seoul   Singapore   Sydney   Taipei   Toronto

McGraw-Hill Irwin

Study Guide for use with
THE LEGAL & REGULATORY ENVIRONMENT OF BUSINESS
O. Lee Reed, Peter J. Shedd, Jere W. Morehead, Robert N. Corley

Published by McGraw-Hill/Irwin, an imprint of The McGraw-Hill Companies, Inc., 1221 Avenue of the Americas, New York, NY 10020. Copyright © 2005, 2002, 1999, 1996, 1993, 1990, 1987, 1984, 1981, 1977, 1973, 1968, 1963 by The McGraw-Hill Companies, Inc. All rights reserved.

1 2 3 4 5 6 7 8 9 0 VFM/VFM 0 9 8 7 6 5 4

ISBN 0-07-296405-7

www.mhhe.com

The McGraw-Hill Companies

PREFACE

For many studying *The Legal and Regulatory Environment of Business*, this will be the first law-related course. As it is a reading-intensive course, the text authors felt that a guide to help direct student reading and study in an unfamiliar subject area would be helpful. The publisher agreed, which led to development of the following text supplement.

Most student study guides are prepared by someone other than a text author. However, as lead-author of *The Legal Environment of Business*, I am proud to bring to bear on the study guide knowledge gained from research and writing of the text. I believe that students will benefit more from a text author's personal attention to this important guide than if its preparation were left to someone substantially unfamiliar with the writing of the text.

The guide does not replace a thorough reading of the text, but if used to focus effort and measure content mastery, it can make a very valuable tool. Each study guide chapter corresponds to a text chapter. It contains an outline which summarizes principal points of each chapter, using the same section headings found in the chapter. Major terms and concepts appear in boldface to highlight them. Significant points are italicized.

Following the outline are completion exercises, true-false selections, multiple-choice problems, and a discussion. At the end of the study guide are answers to the various exercises. Also included is a suggested development for the discussion. Careful attention to the exercises and discussion should aid self-measurement and exam preparation significantly.

Woodrow Wilson noted, "Every citizen should know what law is, how it came into existence, what relation its form bears to its substance, and how it gives to society its fibre and strength and poise of frame." For the business professional whose decisions are heavily influenced by legal considerations, an understanding of the legal and regulatory environment of business is especially important. This study guide, used in conjunction with its text, can make a significant contribution to that understanding.

O. Lee Reed

Table of Contents

Chapter
1

Law as the Foundation of Business

This chapter examines law as a foundation for business practice in the private market system. The three concepts that establish the foundation are:

1. Law
2. The rule of law
3. Property

The chapter also examines basic classifications of law, outlines the sources of law in our legal system, and explains the judicial process and judicial review. It explores the enforcement of law and legal sanctions such as money damages, and it introduces the topic of corporate governance, an important topic throughout the book.

PROPERTY, THE FOUNDATION OF THE FUNCTIONING MARKETPLACE

I. Why nations are prosperous or poor is an issue of great importance. There are differing theories about why some nations are prosperous while others are poor.

    A. **Dependency theory** asserts prosperous nations exploit the resources and labor of poor nations through trade, causing poor nations' poverty. Exploitation is not an important cause of general poverty, however, as prosperous countries invest and trade more with each other than with poorer nations, and international trade makes up only a small fraction of the economies of even the poorest nations.

    B. Superior natural resources do not account for poverty or prosperity, as illustrated by wealthy Japan which has few and poor Russia which has many.

    C. Education and technology alone do not account for differences between prosperous and poor nations. Advantages from this kind of development are more a result than a cause of wealthy economies.

    D. The private market seems to be superior to any state planning system in terms of flexibility and coordinating power for producing new resources. In these ways the private market promotes the economic growth that creates wealth. However, this is only a partial truth. Not all private markets successfully promote wealth, as those in Russia illustrate.

1

E. The key to a successful, wealth-creating private market is having an adequate legal system. Law itself is a necessary foundation for the private market in the prosperous modern nation.

II. **Law** is the most significant of the formal social forces that hold together societies.

A. Law is understood by everyone as being intended to tell members of society what they can or cannot do.

B. Even strangers to a society can observe formal laws. Interpreters of the rules, such as lawyers and judges, can help them.

C. A simple definition of law has two parts.

1. *Law is made up of rules.*
2. *These rules are laid down by the state and backed up by enforcement.*

D. Law is a formal social force: laws come from the state and are usually written down and accessible.

E. To maintain order in society, adequate enforcement institutions such as courts and the police are a necessary part of the legal system. Written laws mean little unless they can be promptly and fairly enforced.

F. *Without fair and neutral enforcement institutions, the certainty and trust necessary for complex long-term business arrangements are absent.* People spend much time guarding their resources rather than developing them.

III. The **rule of law** goes beyond the concept of legal commands backed up by force. Under the rule of law, laws are *generally and equally applicable*, applying to all or most members of society and to various groups in the same way.

A. The fact that, under the rule of law, law applies to lawmakers as well as to the rest of society, gives lawmakers (for instance, legislators) an incentive to make laws that benefit everyone.

B. In today's international business environment, more and more voices are calling for the rule of law. It is a cornerstone of the order necessary for a flourishing private market.

C. The rule of law is an ideal, rather than a complete fact, in even the most democratic nation. Special interest groups attempt to persuade lawmakers to favor their interests, and it is not always clear what it means to apply laws generally and equally.

D. In a democracy well-educated voters who understand the importance of the rule of law can hold to account lawmakers who favor special interests.

IV. The concept of **property** represents the establishment of an exclusive legal right in resources. Through the law of property individuals and business organizations possess, use, and transfer private resources.

    A. Inadequate property law means that individuals must personally guard their resources. There is then little incentive to develop resources, since they may be seized by the state or by others.

    B. The *right of property* is not the same as the *resources* that property guarantees. In a legal sense, "my land" is not the same as "my property."

    C. Property can be thought of as *ownership*. That means owners can exercise their right of property by excluding others – usually including the state itself – from the resources that property protects. The police or courts can be called upon to keep others from interfering with an owner's resources.

    D. Enforcement of property under the rule of law gives people the incentive to develop the resources they own. This assists the poor as well as the wealthy.

    E. Recognition of the right of property provides a basis for the private market and modern development. Countries with strong property systems have the highest national incomes. A strong system of property law creates the maximum condition for national prosperity, and a weak property system almost guarantees national poverty.

V. Property can be thought of as the central concept underlying Western legal systems. Most of the topics in this book relate to the exclusionary right of property.

    A. Property, in its broadest philosophical sense, includes an ownership of individual constitutional and human rights in ourselves that excludes the state from interfering with these rights. We call these rights "liberty," but liberty and property in this sense have almost identical meanings. The modern understanding of human rights began with the concept of property, as set forth from sources like John Locke and the framers of the U.S. Constitution.

    B. It is as important for business students to understand the broad legal concept of property and its foundational role in the marketplace as it is to understand technical business subjects.

CLASSIFICATIONS OF LAW

This section examines several major classifications of law, which will be useful in organizing the necessary vocabulary of legal terms and concepts.

VI. Common Law and Civil Law are the world's two major legal systems.

    A. **Common Law,** taken from the English legal system dating to the eleventh century, emphasizes the role of judges in determining the meaning of laws and how they apply.

        1. The United States and many other former British colonies also have common law systems.

        2. In the United States, judges can determine the meaning of the Constitution and can declare void the legislation of Congress and the acts of the president.

        3. Common law continues its development today, as judges' decisions become part of the body of law.

        4. At the heart of the common law legal system is **stare decisis**. Stare decisis refers to the following of prior judicial opinions as a basis for applying law to present cases.

    B. **Civil Law** refers to legal systems that de-emphasize the role of courts in the creation and interpretation of law. In Civil Law the legislature plays a greater role in specifying legal rules and determining their meaning. The majority of the world's nations follow a Civil Law legal system.

VII. Whether under Common Law or Civil Law, legal rules can be divided into areas of public and private law.

    A. **Public law** concerns those matters that involve the regulation of society in general rather than the interaction between individuals. Examples of public law include constitutional law, administrative law, and criminal law.

    B. **Private law** encompasses the legal problems and relationships between individuals. It is traditionally separated into three areas:

        1. *Property law* recognizes the individual's exclusive rights in both tangible and intangible resources.

        2. *Contract law* covers when agreements concerning an owner's transfer of all kinds of resources can be enforced.

        3. *Tort law* addresses when one can recover damages from another for injuries not related to breach of agreement.

VIII. Law can also be divided into civil law and criminal law.

    A.   **Civil law** cases typically involve a request for damages or other relief that does not involve punishment of the wrongdoer. Note that this meaning of "civil law" is quite different from that found in VI. (B) above.

    B.   **Criminal law** involves a representative of the people attempting to have a wrong against society punished by the court system. Criminal law is divided into

        1.   *Felonies*, which are punishable by fines and by more than one year of imprisonment, and

        2.   *Misdemeanors*, which are punishable by fines and up to one year imprisonment.

IX. Another important distinction in law is between substance and procedure.

    A.   **Substantive law** defines rights and duties. It governs the legal relationship of people with each other or between people and the state. Rules of law governing property, contracts, and torts are examples of substantive law.

    B.   **Procedural law** provides the machinery for enforcing the rights and duties governed by substantive law. It deals with the method and means by which substantive law is made and administered, for example the time allowed for parties to sue each other or the rules of law governing the process of a lawsuit.

    C.   Note that judicial procedures involve the conduct of lawsuits and appeals and the enforcement of judgments. These procedures are different between civil trials and criminal trials.

SOURCES OF LAW

In order to evaluate a legal issue, attorneys must consider various sources of law. "Sources of law" refers to where attorneys actually look for the rules of law. Sources of law include constitutions, legislation, administrative law, and case law.

X. The highest laws of the nation are the federal constitution and the state constitutions.

    A.   The **U.S. Constitution** establishes the federal government, and its amendments guarantee basic rights and liberties to the people. All powers not specified in the federal constitution are retained by the states. The U.S. Constitution identifies what the federal government can do.

B.   A state's constitution provides a structure for the state government and also guarantees various rights and liberties to the people. The state constitutions tell the state governments what they can do.

C.   Attorneys look closely at constitutional sources of law to determine if a regulation or legislation that affects you violates your constitutional rights. If your rights are violated, the laws violating them are void.

XI.   The second most important source of law, after the constitutions, is the formal written law known as legislation. **Legislation** is created and adopted by our elected representatives in the legislative branch of government.

A.   Legislation at the federal or state level is usually referred to as a **statute** or **act**. Laws passed by local governments are called **ordinances**.

B.   Collections of legislation are called **codes**. In business one of the most important codes is the **Uniform Commercial Code**.

C.   How courts interpret the meaning of legislation is called **statutory construction**.

XII.   **Administrative regulation** is a major source of law, affecting almost every business activity to some degree at the federal, state, or local level.

A.   Legislative bodies authorize the creation of administrative agencies to provide clarity and enforcement of a legal area.

B.   Administrative agencies, such as the Environmental Protection Agency, regulate business activities through the adoption of rules and regulations.

XIII.   Case law, or the decisions of judges, is an extensive source of law. It is the vast collection of judicial interpretations of the meaning of all sources of law, including common law.

A.   The written decisions of judges, called **opinions**, interpret the meaning of the law and are published in volumes known as "reporters." These opinions apply to the law in particular cases.

B.   A *case citation* is similar to a bibliographic reference in that it points to the location of the published opinion.

C.   Published opinions include the reasoning behind judicial decisions in particular cases. The opinions then become **precedents** for future cases involving similar facts and legal issues.

D. If you know a case citation, you can easily find the case in a library or through computer databases. Keyword searches through law digests can also find case precedents on given topics.

E. The law doctrine of **stare decisis** means that, when possible, judges follow the precedents set by judges in prior, similar cases. Greater deference is given to precedent in areas of private law, such as contracts, than in the area of constitutional law.

F. The advantages of stare decisis in case law are:

1. Stability of legal issues in many areas, such as contracts
2. Certainty and predictability in the law
3. Expediency
4. Foreknowledge of the legality of individual conduct

G. There are disadvantages to the doctrine of stare decisis and the system of common law, though they do not outweigh the advantages. Disadvantages are:

1. The sheer volume of judicial decisions necessitates large amounts of research on the part of many lawyers, leading to much time and expense.
2. Conflicting precedents are frequently discovered, requiring additional time and expense to determine the precedents most applicable to a particular case.
3. Much of the time, no precedent is found in case law.
4. Judges will often comment on matters not necessary to the decision reached. These judicial expressions are called **dicta**; and they lack the force of a judicial settlement, though they do carry weight to the extent that the court is knowledgeable about the subject matter.
5. Case law is subject to change. A precedent may be changed or reversed, particularly if social forces and circumstances change; although judges are reluctant to reject a precedent, believing that unfair or out-moded precedents will be changed by legislation.
6. Each of the fifty states has its own body of common law, as well as the common law created by the federal legal system. These bodies of law often conflict. To address this problem a body of law, called **conflict of laws**, has developed. This body of law determines which state's substantive law is applicable to a given question when more than one state is involved.

LEGAL SANCTIONS

Legal sanctions are vital to the rule of law and the legal system. **Sanctions** secure obedience to the law.

A legal sanction may benefit society generally, or criminally punish someone, or benefit someone wronged by another, as an award of damages. In the latter case, the sanction is called a **remedy**. There are various legal situations calling for sanctions or remedies.

XIV. Sanctions for criminal conduct are designed to protect the public and to deter persons from wrongful conduct.

    A. Because a crime is a public wrong against society, criminal cases are brought by the government on behalf of the people.

    B. Punishment for criminal wrongdoing may include:

        1. Death
        2. Imprisonment
        3. Fine
        4. Removal from office
        5. Disqualification from holding any office and from voting.

XV. Remedies for *breach of contract* apply in situations where one party to a contract fails to do what he or she agreed to do. Much litigation, especially in the federal courts, involves one corporation suing another for breach of contract.

    A. The usual remedy for a breach of contract is a suit for dollar damages, called **compensatory damages**. The objective is that the wronged party be in as good a position as he or she would have been in had the contract been performed. They do not, however, usually include attorney's fees.

    B. **Consequential damages** may be awarded when the breaching party knew or had reason to know that special circumstances existed that would cause the other party to suffer additional losses.

    C. If a breach by one party is serious enough, the other party may be permitted to *rescind* (cancel) the contract and recover what was given to the first party.

    D. A decree of **specific performance** may be issued, ordering the other party to actually perform the bargain as agreed.

XVI. Non-contractual remedies come from the civil areas of torts. A **tort** is a civil wrong other than a breach of contract committed against persons and their property. It is different from a crime, which is a wrong against society, though the same act may be both a crime and a tort.

A. Tort liability is based on two premises:

    1. In a civilized society, persons will not intentionally injure others or their private resources.
    2. All persons will exercise reasonable care and caution in their activities.

B. **Intentional torts**, which arise from *intentional* wrongful behavior, include assault and battery, libel, slander, trespass, and invasion of privacy.

C. **Negligence** is the field of tort liability that arises from *unreasonable* behavior. It is the failure to exercise the degree of care the law requires.

D. The objective of **compensatory damages** in a tort case is to fully compensate the plaintiff for a proven loss or injury caused by the intentional or negligent conduct of another.

E. There may be **punitive** or exemplary damages awarded, in addition to compensatory damages. They are designed to punish wrongful conduct and to deter others from such conduct in the future. These damages often bear little or no relationship to the actual damages sustained.

XVII. Both federal and state statutes impose a variety of sanctions for violating the statutes or regulations of administrative agencies. These sanctions are similar to those imposed for criminal conduct, breach of contract, or tortuous conduct.

A PROPERTY-BASED LEGAL SYSTEM AND CORPORATE GOVERNANCE

A. Property problems arise when one person harms another's resources or takes them without permission or authorization. These problems certainly arise in a **corporation**, a business that is chartered by the state to do business as a legal person. Much of the business in the United States is transacted through corporations.

B. The legal owners of corporations are the shareholders who have stock in the business. They elect the board of directors who legally run the business and who often hire managers to be in charge of day-to-day operations. These directors and managers, who control the resources, are the agents of the shareholders, who own the resources.

C. **Corporate governance** in its narrow sense refers to the legal rules that structure, empower, and regulate the agents of the corporation and define their relationship to the owners. Corporate governance rules protect the property interest the owners have in the corporation.

D. The complexity of corporations allows managers to abuse their control of corporate resources in a way that benefits themselves in ways that impair or even destroy the corporation's value to the shareholders. They may raise their own incomes by manipulating the books to inflate profits and conceal debts or they may engage in insider trading, or otherwise take advantage of business opportunities that rightfully belong to the corporation and its shareholders.

E. Corporate governance, in its *larger sense*, refers to how corporations are limited by the rule of law to ensure that they recognize the equal right of all other owners in our property-based legal system. Corporate governance includes questions of how the law protects all of us from injury-causing products, harmful pollution, destructive competition, and certain employment discriminations.

COMPLETION EXERCISES

1. _____ is made up of rules laid down by the state and backed up by enforcement.

2. An exclusive legal right in resources is termed _____.

3. _____ and _____ are the world's two major legal systems.

4. _____ emphasizes the role of judges in determining the meaning of laws and how they apply.

5. Property law, contract law, and tort law are generally termed _____ law.

6. _____ provides the framework for enforcing the rights and duties of substantive law.

7. The highest laws of nations come from their _____.

8. The following of prior precedents by judges is called _____.

9. A civil wrong other than a breach of contract is called a _____.

10. The legal rules that in their narrow sense structure, empower, and regulate managers and directors of business organizations is termed _____.

TRUE-FALSE SELECTIONS

1. _____ The rule of law requires that laws be generally and equally applicable.

2. _____ In legal significance, "property" refers to a legal right and not to a piece of land or a widget one owns.

3. _____ Criminal law is divided into felonies and misdemeanors.

4. _____ According to your outline, the lack of education and available technology is the primary cause of poverty in the world.

5. _____ Laws passed by local governments are generally termed "statutes."

6. _____ The written decisions of judges are called "opinions."

7. _____ Published opinions become precedents for future cases.

8. _____ The usual remedy for a breach of contract is compensatory damages.

9. _____ A corporation is considered a legal person.

10. _____ Intentional torts arise from unreasonable behavior.

MULTIPLE CHOICE PROBLEMS

1. Select the most *incorrect* statement.

    a. Law is the most significant of the formal social forces that hold together societies.
    b. The rule of law refers to legal commands backed up by appropriate sanctions.
    c. The key to initiating a wealth-creating private market is an adequate legal system of property law.
    d. Without fair and neutral enforcement of law, the certainty necessary for complex, long-term business arrangements is lacking.

2. In a legal sense, property can be thought of as (select the most *incorrect* statement):

    a. One's resources.
    b. Ownership.
    c. The central concept underlying Western legal systems.
    d. A necessary framework for modern business.

3. The advantages of stare decisis in the common law include all of the following *except*:

    a. Foreknowledge of the legality of individual conduct.
    b. Certainty and predictability in the law.
    c. Dicta in many judicial decisions.
    d. Stability of legal issues in many areas, such as contracts.

4. In a lawsuit for breach of contract, a party might seek all of the following remedies *except*:

    a. Exemplary damages.
    b. Compensatory damages.
    c. Consequential damages.
    d. Specific performance.

5. Punishment for criminal wrongdoing may include all of the following *except*:

    a. Death.
    b. Mutilation.
    c. Imprisonment.
    d. Disqualification from holding office.

DISCUSSION ANALYSIS

Discuss reasons given for why some nations are wealthy and others are poor.

Chapter
2

The Ethical Basis of Law and Business Management

Because ethical values underlie much law, it is important for business students to know about the nature and sources of ethics as well as the problems of achieving an ethical business organization.

This chapter explores ethics and law in relation to the current concern over the behavior of business people. It examines two principal approaches to ethics and four sources of ethical values. It also considers the problems faced in achieving an ethical business organization and suggests strategies for implementing corporate ethics. Finally, it examines the moral implications of property as an exclusive private sphere of resources to which the community and the state have no legal claim.

I.   In our diverse society, there are few shared ethical values to guide behavior. Diversity fosters concern over values. There are several contributing factors to this concern:

    A.   Both the educational system and the family have declined as sources for ethical teaching.

    B.   Increasing economic interdependence in a marketplace-dominated society promotes concerns about business ethics.

    C.   The role of the news media continues to increase, making us more aware of business decisions, as what was once private is now exposed to public scrutiny.

    D.   There is evidence in society at large that certain values are declining.

II.   In the last century government has become increasingly active in regulating business.

    A.   Business leaders, seeking to limit further governmental regulation, increasingly tend toward self-regulation to encourage ethical conduct.

    B.   Federal law encourages self-regulation by reducing criminal fines for legal violations in companies that have taken specific steps to self-police ethical/legal conduct.

III.   Ethics and morality are separate though related terms, which are often used interchangeably.

    A.   The values that guide our behavior through our sense of right and wrong are our **morality**. Shared moral values promote social cooperation and foster trust and acceptance of others. Shared moral values are important in business, both within a company and among companies. Internationally, businesses often face problems when they do business with nations with different moral values.

    B.   **Ethics** is a formal system for deciding what is right and wrong and for justifying moral decisions. It involves a rational method for examining our moral lives, something that is necessary for a meaningful life.

    C.   The end result of ethical examination is what philosophers call **the good**. The good may be defined as those moral goals and objectives we choose to pursue. It defines who we are. Leading a good life involves more than having the "good life" of material possessions.

IV.   Ethics and law have similar or complementary purposes, serving to promote social cooperation and guide conduct. There are, however, differences, with ethical behavior encouraging a higher moral standard.

    A.   The legal system is an institution of the state; ethical systems are not.

    B.   The motivation to observe ethical codes comes from within, but the motivation to observe the law comes from outside the individual in the form of state sanctions.

    C.   Law sets only the minimum standard acceptable to a society. Ethical systems involve a broad-based commitment to proper behavior.

    D.   A commitment to ethical values is superior to mere observance of the law in ensuring responsible business behavior. Legal rules can never be specific enough to regulate all business actions and lawmakers may lack either the information or the consensus to act in the face of potentially harmful business actions.

TWO SYSTEMS OF ETHICS

The two systems that dominate thinking about morality in Western civilization are *formalism* and *consequentialism*. Most people adopt elements of both systems in making ethical choices. It is important to understand how your own values and moral beliefs have been influenced by these two systems.

V. **Formalism** (also called **deontology**) is an approach to ethics that affirms an absolute morality. A particular act is either always right or always wrong. Lying, for example, is always wrong, and that wrongness does not depend on the situation.

    A. The ethical focus of formalism is on the worth of the individual. The rights of individuals should not be infringed.

    B. The formalist thinker Immanuel Kant emphasized a consistency, which he called the **categorical imperative**. It is your duty to act toward others the same way you wish to be treated. You must have a good intent, and your actions must be ethically consistent. This is similar to the Golden Rule: "Do unto others as you would have others do unto you."

    C. Many business choices can be framed in terms of formalist ethics. In other words, if something is wrong when others do it, can it possibly be right for you to do it?

    D. John Rawls writes about **social contract theory**, in which formalist thinking is applied to business and personal ethics. This theory is based on contract (agreement), not on duty. Rawls suggests *a veil of self-ignorance*, behind which we assume we do not know our status of wealth, age, gender, race, etc. We examine ethical questions without self-knowledge, and thus without self-interest. This enables us to fairly evaluate issues. Social contract theory is especially valuable in international business, in the absence of much law. Rawls proposed two ethical principles:

        1. Everyone is entitled to certain equal basic rights, including liberty, freedom of association and personal security.
        2. Although there may be social and economic inequalities, these inequalities must be based on what a person does, not on who a person is, and everyone must have an equal opportunity for achievement, an equal place at the starting line.

VI. **Consequentialism** (also called **teleology**) is concerned with the moral consequences of actions rather than with the morality of actions themselves. Lying, for example, is not unethical in all situations. It is the consequences, or end results, of lying that must be evaluated for their ethical implications. The loss of trust or harm done by lying makes it unethical.

    A. Consequentialism focuses on the common good, rather than on individual rights. If actions increase the common good, they are ethical. The converse is also true.

    B. **Utilitarianism** is the dominant form of consequentialism. For utilitarians, the end essentially justifies the means. However, to determine the ethical course of action, one must first consider all reasonable courses of action to determine which course has the greatest utility, or usefulness, to the common good.

C. Business ethics tend to focus more on consequentialism than on formalism. Statements such as "ethics are good for business" illustrate this point. The primary goal of business is to produce a profit; profit is the good. Cost-benefit analysis and values-based management are other consequentialist approaches to business.

D. The **Protestant ethic**, with its religious formalism, was a boon to capitalism. The religious basis of the Protestant ethic, however, has been eroded by rising wealth and the encouragement of mass consumption. The emphasis on hard work, success, and rational planning continues, but without the original absolute moral values. Business actions are justified by their usefulness in accomplishing the goal of profit.

VII. Formalists and consequentialists can reach the same conclusion for an ethical course of action, but they use a different evaluation process.

SOURCES OF VALUES FOR BUSINESS ETHICS

There are at least four sources of values for business ethics:

Legal regulation
Professional codes of ethics
Organizational codes of ethics
Individual values

VIII. Legal regulation of business illustrates application of society's ethics to business practice.

A. In our society ethical values frequently become law, and legal regulation can reflect society's ethical values.

B. It is also the case that legal regulations can influence society's view of what is ethical. The 1964 Civil Rights Act had this effect on people's views about sex discrimination.

C. Legal regulation is a significant source of values for business ethics. Many business and professional organizations look to the law when drawing up their codes of ethical conduct. At least five major ethical rules can be drawn from the law:

1. Respect for the liberty and rights of others is required by the law and is often found in ethical codes. Respect for individual rights is also historically connected to the legal concept of private property.

2. The law requires that good faith be demonstrated in various economic and other transactions. *Good faith* can be defined as acting with an honest intent. Bad faith is dishonesty in intent.

3. *Due care* is an ethical concept that derives from society's expectations about how fair and reasonable actions are. Courts weigh punishment in negligence cases in terms of a balance: on the one hand is the likelihood the defendant's conduct will cause harmful consequences, and the seriousness of those harmful consequences; and on the other hand is the effort required to avoid the harmful consequences. *Due diligence* is another way of saying "due care." It is often used in determining the liability of corporate boards of directors and the punishment in white-collar crime.

4. *Honoring confidentiality* is a legal requirement that appears in agency law generally and in t he professional-client relationship in particular. In addition to not telling others of a confidence, an agent must in many instances not act on the confidence related by a principal. Insider trading is a violation of this legal and ethical value.

5. Avoiding *conflicts of interest* is another ethical value flowing from the law, especially from agency law. This value means that no one can "serve two masters." No agent or employee of one principal can secretly work for another whose interest competes with that of the first principal. In public service, no judge or administrative regulator can make a decision involving a company in which he or she owns stock, as that would interfere with his or her ability to make an unbiased decision.

IX. Another important source of business ethics comes from the historic tradition of the professional codes of ethics in professions such as law and medicine.

    A. Professions such as law and accounting have ethical codes or rules of professional conduct that are adopted by the professional organizations. They are not laws, although they are enforced by the organizations themselves with the use of sanctions for noncompliance.

    B. Because the state will likely regulate these professions if they do not do so themselves, it is appropriate to term their ethical codes **self-regulation**.

X. There are few industrywide codes of ethics, so many businesses have adopted ethical codes at the individual organization level.

    A. Nearly all large corporations now have their own codes of business ethics, often called codes of conduct.

B. The Business Roundtable has identified a general list of topics that organizational codes should cover. These include:

1. Fundamental honesty and adherence to the law
2. Product safety and quality
3. Health and safety in the workplace
4. Conflicts of interest
5. Fairness in selling/marketing practices
6. Financial reporting
7. Supplier relationships
8. Pricing, billing, and contracting
9. Trading in securities/using inside information
10. Payments to obtain business/Foreign Corrupt Practices Act
11. Acquiring and using information about others
12. Security
13. Political activities
14. Protection of the environment
15. Intellectual property/proprietary information

C. Some companies provide only general guidelines in their ethical codes. Other companies spell out their expectations for employees' behavior in considerable detail. Many codes contain both general statements of shared ethical values and more specific applied examples of these values.

D. A majority of organizational codes of business ethics provide sanctions for their violation, up to and including employee termination. These codes can appropriately be called self-regulation.

E. An important issue in determining the value of business ethical codes is whether companies pursue ethical self-regulation with enthusiasm and commitment or whether the codes are mere window dressing to satisfy the government and the general public.

XI. The ultimate source of ethical values for business decision making is individual values. Only you can make your behavior ethical. There are five questions that you can ask yourself to help guide you through personal and business decisions:

A. Have I thought about whether the action I may take is right or wrong? Ignorance and thoughtlessness often lead to unethical behavior.

B. Will I be proud to tell of my action to my family? To my employer? To the news media? The less proud you are to share your decision with others, the more likely your decision is to be unethical.

C. Am I willing for everyone to act as I am thinking of acting? This question encompasses a major principle of ethical formalism. A negative answer almost always indicates an immoral action.

D. Will my decision cause harm to others or to the environment? In answering this question you may have to weigh potential harms against benefits to the common good.

E. Will my actions violate the law? The law provides only minimum standards for behavior, but they are standards that should be observed. If you believe a law itself is morally wrong, you may ethically disobey it only if you are willing to make public your disobedience and accept the consequences for it.

XII. Corporate life presents ethical problems and obstacles that private life does not.

A. The emphasis on corporate profit sometimes conflicts with ethical responsibility. How a profit is made becomes less important than that it is made. This can be especially true when responsibility for profit making is decentralized. A local manager may be expected to achieve profit goals that are difficult or impossible to achieve ethically and legally.

B. Individuals in groups may feel a diminished sense of responsibility for decisions made and actions taken. "I did it because everyone else did it" and "I just followed orders" are typical rationalizations for unethical behavior in corporations and other groups.

C. In many large corporations top managers effectively possess and control vast resources they do not own. It may be easy to manipulate the resources in their own interest and difficult for others to find out that they have done so. In other words, managers may be in an ideal position to infringe on the property interest of the corporate owners.

XIII. Despite the obstacles to ethical corporate behavior, certain steps can be taken to promote business ethics in corporate life.

A. Top management must act as a role model for values it wishes corporate employees to share. Corporate employees are very sensitive to the values of top corporate management because the employees' advancement prospects are tied to their ability to fit in with management. This means they will model their values after the actual values of top management, not management's professed values, if those differ from the values management models.

B. Openness in communication is essential to ethical corporate decision making because of the complexity of information required to evaluate the implications of many business decisions. Without complete and open communication, information crucial to making an ethical decision may be lacking.

    C.   **Stakeholder theory** is a consequentialist ethical philosophy, which maintains that ethical corporate behavior depends on managers who recognize and take into account the various stakeholders whose interests the corporation impacts. This system goes beyond corporate governance, which focuses on the *legal* responsibilities of managers to society and to the investor-owners of the corporation. Stakeholder theory suggests that ethical corporations, through their managers, must behave responsibly and ethically toward all stakeholders, which includes owners/investors, employees, the community, even society itself.

XIV.   A business that does not act ethically severs itself from society, from the good, and ultimately from its own source of support. The Spanish journal *Boletin Circulo* writes that business ethics are rewarding in four ways:

    A.   Profits and business ethics are not contradictory. Some of the most profitable businesses have also historically been the most ethical.

    B.   An ethical organizational life is a basic business asset that should be accepted and encouraged. The reverse is also true. Unethical behavior is a business liability.

    C.   Ethics are of continuing concern to the business community. They require ongoing reevaluation. Businesses must always be ethically sensitive to changes in society.

    D.   Business ethics reflect business leadership. Top firms can and should exercise leadership in business ethics.

XV.   Although many have argued that it is immoral for individuals to control and profit from property that the community may need, there are powerful arguments in defense of the morality of the law of property that is the foundation of private enterprise.

    A.   Considerable evidence exists that the more resources that can be put under the legal system of property the less wastefully those resources will be treated. People are more careful with their own resources than with resources that are common to all.

    B.   Adequate property in resources maximizes total wealth in society. It provides incentives to production and innovation. Societies that recognize property flourish more than societies that do not in almost all areas.

    C.   Enforcing the legally exclusive right to resources protects the resources of the poor at least as much as those of the rich because the poor are less able to guard their resources without those legal protections.

D. Acquisitiveness and territoriality appear to be very important parts of human nature, connected to personal survival and reproduction. The legal recognition of these aspects of our nature, which allows us to keep what we acquire but also prevents us from acquiring it by force, fraud, or theft, is called "property."

E. Supporters as well as critics of property acknowledge that there are moral questions about the distribution of resources. These moral questions include the legitimacy of the original acquisition of resources, how voluntary an exchange of resources is, and society's responsibility to its weak, old, young, and sick members.

PROPERTY AS A SYSTEM OF PERSONAL ETHICS

Once you understand property as a "right" rather than a "thing," you appreciate how property can be the basis for a system of personal ethics in business. Property is a system of law enforced by the state but the values underlying this system are moral ones. Property provides an ordering of relations between people, in terms of internal resources as well as external resources. Each person must respect the equal right of others to what is proper to them. The rule of law and property are fundamental not only to the structure but also to the values of the private market and of ethical behavior in the business community.

COMPLETION EXERCISES

1. As a term ethics is often used interchangeably with _____.

2. The two systems that dominate thinking about morality in Western civilization are _____ and _____.

3. Deontology affirms a(an) _____ morality.

4. Kant's emphasis on ethical consistency is called the _____.

5. Consequentialism, or teleogy, is concerned with the moral _____ of actions rather than with the morality of the actions themselves.

6. The dominant form of consequentialism, which is also the moral basis for economics, is called _____.

7. An ethical theory that maintains managers should take into account all those persons impacted by business activity is called _____ theory.

8. The ethical codes of the professions are called _____

9.   When one "serves two masters," one has a(an) _____ .

10.   In law, acting with an honest intent is termed _____ .

TRUE-FALSE SELECTIONS

1.   _____   According to your outline, both the educational system and the family have declined as sources for ethical teaching.

2.   _____   Ethics and law have similar, complementary purposes.

3.   _____   The "veil of ignorance" is associated with Immanuel Kant.

4.   _____   Deontology holds that the end justifies the means.

5.   _____   "Due care" is an ethical concept about society's expectations regarding how reasonable actions are.

6.   _____   Nearly all large corporations now have their own codes of ethics.

7.   _____   The less proud you are to share your decision with others, the more likely your decisions is to be unethical.

8.   _____   Top management should act as a role model for values it wishes corporate employees to share.

9.   _____   Profits and business ethics are contradictory.

10.   _____   Individuals in groups often feel a diminished sense of responsibility for decisions made and actions taken.

MULTIPLE CHOICE PROBLEMS

1.   "What's good for General Motors is good for the United States" reflects what general ethical view?

    a.   Formalism
    b.   Consequentialism
    c.   Deontology
    d.   Social contract theory

2. John Locke believed that property reflected natural law and that ultimately the right of ownership came from God, making the right of property an inherent moral principle. This belief reflects what general ethical view?

    a. Teleology
    b. Formalism
    c. Utilitarianism
    d. Consequentialism

3. The emphasis by religious colonists who helped settle New England on hard work, planning, and success has come to be called the

    a. Categorical imperative.
    b. Social contract theory.
    c. Puritan or Protestant ethic.
    d. Utilitarianism.

4. One of the questions you can ask yourself to promote ethical business decisionmaking is "Will my decision cause harm to others or to the environment?" This ethical approach is most accurately termed:

    a. Utilitarianism.
    b. Formalism.
    c. Social contract theory.
    d. Hypernorm theory.

5. For a judge or administrative regulator to make a professional decision regarding a company in which he or she holds stock constitutes:

    a. A conflict of interest.
    b. A breach of fiduciary duty.
    c. A breach of due diligence.
    d. Negligence.

DISCUSSION ANALYSIS

Is it ethical to file share copyrighted material such as music? Discuss using the ethical systems of this chapter.

Chapter 3

The Court System

This chapter, which describes our court system, is divided into three parts:

1. Personnel of the court system
2. Organization of the court system
3. The power of judicial review

PERSONNEL

I. Judges and justices operate our court system.

    A. Trial judges determine applicable rules of **law**.

        1. In non-jury trials, judges also determine facts.
        2. Trial judges are the main link between the law and the people.

    B. Justices sit on **appellate courts**, or **courts of appeals**. They decide **appeals**, giving reasons for their decisions.

        1. Justices' reasoned decisions become *precedent*, part of our body of law under stare decisis.
        2. Justices' opinions affect the future of law and society as a whole, not just the litigants, so they must consider the societal impact of their decisions.
        3. In reviewing appeals, justices are concerned with issues of *law*, not issues of *fact*, which are normally resolved at the trial court level by the jury.
        4. Judges and justices have *judicial immunity*. Their official acts cannot place them at risk from legal actions against them personally, even if their actions are malicious or exceed authority.

II. Jurors are the fact-finding body.

    A. The right to a trial by jury is constitutionally guaranteed, in both criminal and civil (over $20) cases. A trial jury is also called a **petit jury**.

B. Historical traditions concerning juries are changing.

   1. Juries may consist of 12 or fewer persons, sometimes as few as six.
   2. Some states are eliminating the requirement of unanimity among jurors.
   3. Jurors in some jurisdictions become more actively involved in trials by taking notes, discussing trials in progress, even questioning witnesses.

C. Long, complex cases present difficulties, as many jurors cannot afford to participate.

III. Lawyers represent parties to a lawsuit (plaintiff and defendant) by presenting evidence, points of law, and arguments to the juries and judges.

A. Ethical conduct is required of lawyers due to their triple capacities of *counselor*, *advocate*, and *public servant*.

B. Courts can sanction lawyers for unprofessional conduct.

C. *Attorney-client privilege* protects confidentiality of communications between lawyers and their clients.

   1. In *Munson v. Tenneco Packaging Co.* the federal 11th Circuit Court of Appeals upheld (agreed with) the trial court's reprimand of the plaintiff's attorney who had – without evidence – accused the defendant's attorney in formal court documents of racism.

D. The two major courts systems in the United States are the federal courts and the 50 state courts. The systems (except for a few states) all have three levels: **trial courts**, **appellate courts**, and **supreme courts**.

IV. State courts are created by and governed from three sources: *state constitutions*, *state legislatures*, and their own *rules of procedure*.

A. In **trial courts**, parties file lawsuits or complaints to protect their property rights or redress a wrong.

   1. The **trial court** determines both the facts and the law in a case.
   2. More than 95% of all complaints are resolved at the trial level.

B. Parties to litigation are entitled to an appellate review of the case, subject to the requirements of procedural law.

1. Most states have two levels of **appellate courts**: **courts of appeal** (intermediate courts) and the state **supreme court**. Some states have only one level, usually called the **supreme court**.

2. **Appellate courts** are primarily concerned with questions of law.

C. **Small-claims courts** handle much of the litigation between businesses and customers.

1. Lawyers are not usually required and sometimes may not be allowed.

2. There is usually a dollar limitation to suits that may be filed.

V. Federal courts have been established and limited by Congress. They have power in four basic areas:

A. **Federal question cases** concern questions of law arising from the Constitution or federal statutes. They are civil actions, which may or may not be suits for damages. They may involve matters based on federal laws or issues of constitutional rights.

B. **Diversity of citizenship** cases are decided in federal court when all the plaintiffs are from different states than all the defendants.

1. Corporations that incorporate in one state and do business in another complicate the determination of eligibility of a case for **diversity of citizenship** status.

2. Each claim under **diversity of citizenship** must meet a jurisdictional amount requirement of more than $75,000.

3. **Diversity of citizenship** jurisdiction is designed to protect nonresidents against state court bias.

C. Federal courts also decide disputes among the states.

D. Federal courts also decide disputes when the United States is a party in a lawsuit.

E. There are three main levels of federal courts:

1. *District courts* are the **trial courts** of the federal judicial system.

a. Every state has at least one district court, as does the District of Columbia.

b. Federal litigation begins at the district court level.

c. District courts have **subject matter jurisdiction** – the power to try cases – over all federal litigation.

> d. The **Federal Rules of Civil Procedure** detail the procedures to be followed in federal court litigation. These rules are strictly enforced by the courts.

> 2. There is a congressionally established **appellate court** system at the federal level.

>> a. There are 12 **Court of Appeals** (12 circuits).
>> b. There is a special **Court of Appeals** for the Federal Circuit, which hears appeals of administrative decisions as well as appeals from special U.S. courts.

> 3. The U.S. **Supreme Court** is established by the Constitution. There are nine justices appointed for life by the President who decide cases.

THE POWER OF JUDICIAL REVIEW

Judicial review is the courts' most significant power. Courts may use this power to declare legislation unconstitutional, and thus void. Courts may also declare actions taken by the executive branch unconstitutional. Though the Constitution does not expressly give the judicial branch this power, it has been in use since the case of *Marbury v. Madison* in 1803.

VI. The **Supreme Court** hears only cases involving major constitutional issues or interpretation of federal law.

> A. A losing party in the **Courts of Appeal** must file a petition for **writ of certiorari**, that is a request to file an appeal; and four of the nine justices must vote to take the case.

> B. **Judicial review**, the power to review the acts of the other branches of government and declare them unconstitutional, is the most significant power of the courts. This power makes the judiciary the overseer of the government.

> C. Note that judicial review is applied only in specific cases before the Supreme Court. The Court does not "automatically" examine the constitutionality of everything Congress or the President does.

VII. **Judicial restraint** is the philosophy that prevents the courts from assuming preeminence among the three branches of government.

> A. **Judicial restraint** is often practiced by those who believe that the judiciary should not overrule an act of Congress unless absolutely necessary to the decision of a case and that litigation should not be an agent of social, economic, or political changes.

B. *Strict constructionists* want to adhere to the intentions of the Framers of the Constitution. They believe arguments about constitutionality of legislation should be resolved in favor of the statute.

C. **Judicial restraint** jurists are deeply committed to precedent. They tend to accept trial court decisions if there is a reasonable basis for them.

VIII. **Judicial activism** is the use of the court system to help correct perceived wrongs in our society.

A. Activists assert that the political system is too slow and unresponsive to effect necessary change in a timely manner.

B. **Judicial activists** believe the Constitution should be interpreted within the context of contemporary society, a belief sometime referred to as constitutional relativity.

C. Activist courts tend to be more results conscious and to rely less on precedent.

D. A court may use existing statutes and precedents, if those exist.

E. A court may refuse to apply existing case law or declare a statute unconstitutional.

F. The nature of the judicial process, i.e., how judges go about determining the law, varies by case and by court. Justice Benjamin Cardozo lectured about judicial process:

1. First the judge must extract the *underlying principle* of a precedent and then determine the path along which that principle is to continue its *direction of development*.
2. Logic, particularly *analogy*, must be applied in determining the principle's path.
3. *History*, often in the form of precedent analysis, helps illuminate the path.
4. *Custom or trade practice* plays an important role in the development of law that concerns business.
5. Even jurists have *psychological processes* which influence them and which are influenced by *society and social interests*.

COMPLETION EXERCISES

1. In a trial a judge determines applicable rules of _____, and the jury decides the _____.

2. A judge cannot be held liable for official acts because of the doctrine of _____.

3.   A trial jury is also called a(an) _____.

4.   The two levels of appellate courts found in most states are the _____ and the _____.

5.   In a federal court, issues of law arising from the Constitution, federal statutes, and federal regulations are called _____.

6.   The power (or jurisdiction) of a federal court over cases when all plaintiffs and defendants are from different states is called _____.

7.   The power of courts to declare unconstitutional the acts of the other branches of government is called _____.

8.   A request to file an appeal with the Supreme Court is called a petition for _____.

9.   Judges who think that the Constitution is relative to the times in which it is interpreted are sometimes known as _____.

10.   Justice Cardozo wrote that judges relied on history, custom, psychological processes, and _____ in making their decisions.

TRUE-FALSE SELECTIONS

1.   _____   In a trial the jury normally determines the facts of the case.

2.   _____   At the appellate level the judges (or justices) determine the facts of the case.

3.   _____   Judges can be sued for making legal mistakes or acting maliciously.

4.   _____   Petit juries are constitutionally required to have 12 jurors.

5.   _____   Some states have eliminated the requirement of unanimity among jurors.

6.   _____   Attorneys usually cannot divulge what clients tell them because of the attorney-client privilege.

7.   _____   Small-claims courts handle much of the litigation between businesses and customers.

8.   _____   Each diversity of citizenship plaintiff must meet a jurisdictional minimum claim of $75,000.

9.   _____   There are 15 federal Courts of Appeal.

10. _____ Judges who are extremely reluctant to declare legislation unconstitutional believe in "judicial restraint."

MULTIPLE CHOICE PROBLEMS

1. Select the *incorrect* statement about judicial review.

    a. Judicial review came from the case of *Marbury v. Madison*.
    b. The Constitution expressly gives judges the power of judicial review.
    c. Federal judges can declare unconstitutional an act of the President.
    d. Congress cannot legislate limits to the power of judicial review.

2. Select the most *incorrect* statement about judicial activism and restraint.

    a. Judicial activists are more likely to declare prison conditions unconstitutionally "cruel and unusual."
    b. Judicial restraintists are more likely to be committed to stare decisis.
    c. Judicial restraintists are more likely to believe in "strict construction."
    d. Judicial activists are more likely to resolve the constitutionality of legislation in favor of the statute.

3. Select the *incorrect* statement. Ethical conduct is required of lawyers due to their capacities of:

    a. Counselor.
    b. Judge.
    c. Advocate.
    d. Public servant.

4. Approximately what percentage of complaints are resolved at the trial level and thus not appealed?

    a. 65 percent.
    b. 75 percent.
    c. 85 percent.
    d. 95 percent.

5. Select the *incorrect* statement.

    a. Lawyers are not usually required to represent litigants in a small claims court.
    b. Appellate courts are primarily concerned with issues of law.
    c. State courts decide controversies between or among states.
    d. Federal litigation begins at the district court level.

Chapter 3

DISCUSSION ANALYSIS

Discuss what it means to say that federal courts have only limited power to decide cases.

Chapter 4

The Litigation Process

This chapter describes the **litigation process**, or how lawsuits work. First, it identifies and defines the terminology used to describe the parties who are adversaries in lawsuits. It continues with discussions of when a party has the right to file a lawsuit, when a court has power over the parties, and when a class-action, or multiple-party, lawsuit might be filed. Finally, the procedures of litigation are discussed, from pretrial procedures, through trial procedures, to posttrial issues.

TERMINOLOGY OF LITIGATION

I.   Special terminology describes the parties to litigation.

    A.   The **plaintiff** files the lawsuit. In federal courts and in most states, all persons may join in one lawsuit as plaintiffs if the **cause of action** (legal basis for the lawsuit) arises out of the same transaction or series of transactions and involve common questions of law or fact.

    B.   In a civil case, the party sued is known as the **defendant**. Plaintiffs may sue as defendants all persons who are necessary to a complete determination or resolution of the lawsuit. The term **defendant** is also used for the person against whom a prosecutor files criminal charges.

    C.   If a **defendant** alleges that other parties need to be present in order for a complete determination to be made, the defendant may bring in those other parties as **third-party defendants**. This is most often done in order to pass on any potential liability to the third-party defendant.

    D.   A **defendant** who wants to sue the **plaintiff** files a **counterclaim**. The defendant then becomes known as the **counterplaintiff** and the plaintiff becomes the **counterdefendant**.

    E.   The party who appeals a trial court result is the **appellant**. This party is usually listed first in a published decision of an appellate court, even if the appellant was the defendant in the trial court. Usually, the appellant has a right to have an intermediate appellate court hear and decide the appeal.

F. In an appeal, the party who was successful at the trial level is called the **appellee**. This party is usually listed second in an appellate court decision.

G. A party who is dissatisfied with the appellate court's decision must petition (or ask) the Supreme Court to grant **certiorari** (or agree to hear the case). This party has no right to have the Supreme Court hear and decide the issues. If a petition for certiorari is filed to the Supreme Court, the party initiating the petition is the **petitioner**. The other party becomes known as the **respondent**.

II. In order to have a trial court decide a dispute, the **plaintiff** must establish **standing to sue**. This requirement is designed to present the issues in sharper focus by defining the nature of the *adversarial relationship* between plaintiff and defendant. Standing to sue *does not depend* upon the merits of the plaintiff's contention of illegality on the part of the defendant. It simply requires that two conditions be met:

A. The plaintiff must allege that the litigation involves a case or controversy with a connection to the law. There must be an allegation of a legal wrong.

B. The plaintiff must allege a personal stake, a personal legal position, in the resolution of the controversy. This prevents abstract legal questions of potentially wide public significance – questions that are best left to legislative or administrative bodies – from being brought into court for resolution when the plaintiff is not directly affected.

C. In *Friends of the Earth v. Laidlaw Environmental Services*, the U.S. Supreme Court ruled that the plaintiff showed "injury in fact" and thus had standing to sue by showing that its members' "recreational, aesthetic, and economic interests" were directly affected by the defendant's water pollution.

III. For a court to hear and decide a case, it must have **subject matter jurisdiction**, the legal power to hear a case.

A. Some state trial courts have *general subject matter jurisdiction*, the ability to hear any type of case.

B. *Limited jurisdiction* is the legal power to hear only certain types of cases.

C. Jurisdiction may be limited by subject matter, by amount in controversy, or by area in which the parties live.

D. A court with limited jurisdiction may be named according to the subject matter with which it deals. Traffic courts and juvenile courts are examples of courts limited by subject matter.

IV. In addition to subject matter jurisdiction, a court must have **personal jurisdiction** over the parties to the lawsuit. This gives the court legal power or authority over the parties themselves.

A. Personal jurisdiction over the plaintiff is obtained when the plaintiff files suit, indicating voluntary submission to the court's power.

B. Power over the defendant is usually obtained by the service of a **summons**, a notice to appear in court.

1. Service of a summons may be upon the defendant in person; or it may be valid if served upon a household member above a certain age, if another copy is mailed to the defendant's home.
2. **Service of process** is the delivery of a summons by publication of a notice and by mailing a summons to the defendant's last known address.
3. **Long-arm statutes** enable states to serve a summons beyond their borders, as long as the defendant is provided with *due process* of law. That means the defendant must have certain minimum contacts with the state. A typical long-arm statute allows a state court to obtain jurisdiction over a defendant if the defendant:

a. Has committed a tort within the state.
b. Owns land within the state that is the object of the lawsuit.
c. Has entered into a contract within the state or transacted the business that is the subject of the lawsuit within the state.

4. In *Toys "R" Us; Geoffrey, Inc. v. Step Two, S.A.; Imiginarium Net, S.L.*, the federal Court of Appeals for the 3rd Circuit reversed the district court's decision that it had no jurisdiction over a Spanish company, even though its web site did not "purposefully avail" itself of customers in the state (NJ) where the case was brought. The appellate court ruled that the plaintiff should be allowed to show other evidence of minimum contacts, such as the fact that the Spanish company's president attended an annual toy fair in the U.S.

C. Personal jurisdiction is obtained differently in the case of criminal defendants. It is obtained by *arrest*. If the arrest is made in a state other than the one in which the crime was committed, the governor of the state in which the arrest was made must decide whether to turn over the prisoner to the state which requests the prisoner. The process of requesting and transporting the prisoner from state to state is called **extradition**.

D. A defendant can choose to submit voluntarily to a court's authority, even if personal jurisdiction could not otherwise be obtained by the court.

V. A **class action suit** is one in which plaintiffs file suit on their own behalf and on behalf of all other persons who may have a similar claim. Examples of categories of persons who may be included in class action suits are: all consumers of a named product or service and all shareholders of a named corporation.

A. Including a large number of people in a single suit is often profitable for the lawyer who brings the suit. It is more feasible than filing multiple suits involving the same issue, since any individual member of the class is unlikely to have a sufficient financial interest to warrant litigation.

B. Federal courts have sought to discourage **class-action suits**:

1. All members of the class who can be located must be given individual notice of the action.
2. Plaintiffs must pay all court costs of the action.
3. If a trial court denies class-action status, the denial cannot be appealed; only a final decision of the lawsuit itself can be appealed.
4. If a class-action suit is in federal court because of diversity of citizenship, the claim of *each member* of the class must meet the jurisdictional amount of $75,000.

C. Although the federal courts used to routinely approve proposed settlements of class-action suits, they have more recently become less likely to approve them.

1. Any proposed settlement of a class-action suit in federal courts must meet high standards for fair and equitable terms.
2. Before a settlement can be approved, the class certification requirements for trial must have been met.

PRETRIAL PROCEDURES

This section explores questions surrounding the pretrial phase of litigation. How does a lawsuit begin? How are issues presented to a court? What steps can each side take to protect itself and to maximize its position?

VI. **Pleadings** are the legal documents that are filed with a court to begin the litigation process. They specify the parties to the lawsuit, bring into focus the issues to be resolved, give notice of each party's contentions, and set the boundaries of the litigation.

A. A plaintiff files a **complaint** with the court clerk.

1. The complaint contains allegations about the defendant as well as a statement or request of the relief sought.
2. A **summons** is issued by the court clerk and delivered by a court official to the defendant, along with a copy of the complaint.

3. The summons contains the date by which the defendant must respond to the complaint, often within 30 days.

B. The defendant must usually respond with a written pleading, called an **answer**.

1. The answer will either admit or deny each allegation in the complaint.
2. The answer may also contain affirmative defenses designed to defeat the plaintiff's claim.
3. If the answer contains causes of action the defendant has against the plaintiff, those statements are called *counterclaims*.
4. If the defendant does not respond in any way, the court may enter an order of default and grant the relief sought by the plaintiff.

C. If the defendant's answer contains one or more counterclaims, the plaintiff must reply, admitting or denying each allegation.

VII. The process of **discovery** is designed to ensure that prior to the trial each side is fully aware of all facts of the case and of the intentions of the parties. It minimized the role of skill of counsel by shining a light on the relative merits of the controversy. It also narrows the issues in dispute and thus encourages settlement of the lawsuit. There are several methods of discovery, requiring client and lawyer to work closely.

A. **Interrogatories** are written questions presented to the opposing parties. They must usually be answered and are often attached to the respective pleadings.

B. After interrogatories are answered, either party may ask the other to produce specific documents important to the lawsuit's outcome. This is called **request for production of documents**.

C. The most expensive method of discovery, and the most revealing, is the taking of **depositions**. In depositions, lawyers orally ask questions of possible witnesses and receive oral responses. A court reporter records the answers and a written transcript is prepared. Each side then has a permanent record of the witnesses' anticipated testimony.

D. At the end of discovery, either party may request the other to admit that certain issues presented in the pleadings are no longer at issue. This **request for an admission** may narrow the issues in dispute and make a *settlement* more likely.

VIII. The scope of discovery is usually interpreted broadly. If one party objects to another party's discovery, the party objecting will seek a judge's opinion. Most judges rule that if the information sought in discovery will lead to evidence admissible during the trial, the information is discoverable and the objection is overruled. Even if there is no abusive discovery – and there sometimes is – the cost of discovery can be high for several reasons:

A. The time spent researching and compiling documents can be significant.

B. Attorneys' fees for time spent advising clients and generating documents may be high.

C. The delay in reaching the conclusions of the case imposes costs.

D. Discovery also burdens the resources of the judicial system when disputes must be resolved.

E. In *Chudasama v. Mazda Motor Corp.*, the federal Court of Appeals for the 11th Circuit reversed a district court ruling that granted a default judgment (one that does not focus on the legal or factual issues of the cause of action) against the defendant. The appellate court ruled that the district court abused its discretion. Both parties to the lawsuit had made entirely unreasonable discovery demands on the other, and the district judge had failed to control the attorneys. The appellate court ordered the case reassigned to a different trial judge.

IX. During the pretrial phase, there are a number of motions that may be filed by one or the other of the parties. A **motion** presents the argument that there are no factual questions about the dispute, only questions of law for the judge to resolve.

A. A defendant, instead of answering the plaintiff's complaint, may file a *motion to dismiss for failure to state a cause of complaint*. This motion argues that, even if everything in the complaint is true, the plaintiff has failed to plead some essential element of a valid claim and is not entitled to the relief sought.

B. A defendant may move to dismiss a suit for reasons that as a matter of law prevent the plaintiff from winning the suit. The defendant may allege a lack jurisdiction for the court, a lack of standing to sue, or say that the time limit for action has expired; the latter ground is usually referred to as the **statute of limitations**.

C. A motion for a **judgment on the pleadings** asks the judges to decide the case based solely on the complaint and the answer.

D. A motion for **summary judgment** asks the judge to base a decision on the pleadings and additional evidence. Usually the additional evidence takes the form of sworn statements called **affidavits**. The judge may then also conduct a hearing and allow the lawyers to argue the merits of the motion. If there is no question of material fact, the judge will decide the legal issues and rule in favor of one party over the other.

X.   Either on a motion by a party or their own accord, judges may terminate the litigation process upon determining that a complaint is totally lacking in merit. Such a complaint is known as a *frivolous* complaint. It can be difficult, however to determine what is a frivolous complaint until evidence is presented in the case. Rule 11 of the Federal Rules of Civil Procedure authorized fines against parties and their attorneys for filing frivolous lawsuits. Most states have a similar rule.

THE TRIAL

A trial normally involves the presentation of evidence to a jury to determine the facts in dispute. After the evidence is presented, the judge explains applicable law to the jury. The jury deliberates and renders a verdict, and the judge decides whether to enter a judgment based on the jury's verdict.

The stages of a trial are:

- Voir dire – parties and their attorneys select jury.
- Attorneys present opening statements.
- Plaintiff presents evidence through witnesses.
- Defendant moves for directed verdict.
- Defendant prevents evidence through witnesses.
- Attorneys present closing arguments.
- Court instructs jury on the law.
- Jury deliberates and makes a decision (verdict).
- Losing party files posttrial motion.

XI.   **Voir dire** means "speak the truth," and is the process by which jurors are selected. Prospective jurors are summoned into the jury box for voir dire examination by the court and often by the attorneys as well. Jurors are sworn to answer questions truthfully.

       A.   The aim of voir dire is to determine jurors' qualifications and ability to be fair and impartial.

       B.   A juror may be excused from the case because of a bias for or against one of the parties. That is called an **excuse for cause**.

       C.   Both plaintiff and defendant are entitled to a certain number of **peremptory challenges**, for which no cause or reason need be given to excuse a prospective juror. The number of peremptory challenges varies by court, by type of case, and may vary even between the parties. Peremptory challenges are sometimes employed in discriminatory ways and are the subject of controversy.

D.   In *J.E.B. v. Alabama ExRel. T.B.*, the U.S. Supreme Court ruled in a paternity and child support lawsuit that the parties could not strike potential jurors solely on the basis of gender.

XII.   There are a number of other steps common to trials:

A.   Attorneys present *opening statements*. These are designed to present the facts each side expects to prove and the witnesses they expect to call to make the proof.

B.   The plaintiff presents evidence to establish the truth of the allegations made in the complaint. If the defendant believes the plaintiff has not proven each allegation, the defendant may make a motion for a **directed verdict**.

C.   After all the evidence is presented, the lawyers for the plaintiff and the defendant summarize the evidence in **closing arguments**. They try to convince the jury, or judge if there is no jury, what the outcome of the case should be.

D.   The judge acquaints the jury with the law applicable to the case. These are the **jury instructions**. They are designed to bring together the facts and the law so that a verdict can be rendered.

XIII.   The term **burden of proof** has two different meanings, depending on the context in which it is used. It is applied differently in different types of cases.

A.   Burden of proof may mean the responsibility of a party alleging certain facts to come forward with evidence to prove those facts. Usually, the plaintiff has the burden of proof.

B.   Burden of proof may also refer to what is also known as the *burden of persuasion*. This means that the party alleging a fact must be persuasive as to its factuality.

C.   In criminal cases the burden of proof is described as **beyond a reasonable doubt**. If, in the jury's opinions, a reasonable person could entertain a reasonable doubt about the defendant's guilt, the jury may not convict the defendant.

D.   Civil cases have two different standards for burden of proof.

1.   **Preponderance of evidence** means there is more evidence on one side than the other. There may be only slightly more evidence. In most civil lawsuits, the plaintiff must meet this burden of proof.
2.   The **clear and convincing proof** standard requires more evidence than the *preponderance of evidence* standard but not as much as the *beyond a reasonable doubt* standard. In a few civil lawsuits, the plaintiff must prove the facts by this standard of proof.

XIV. Once the jury has determined the facts of a case and applied the law, as instructed by the judge, the jury renders a decision, a **verdict**. Then one of several things may happen.

    A. The judge usually accepts the verdict. Then a **judgment** is entered in favor of the party that won the verdict.

    B. However, the party that is dissatisfied with the verdict may file a posttrial motion seeking a **judgment notwithstanding the verdict**. This motion is sometimes – but not often – granted if the judge finds that reasonable persons viewing the evidence would not reach the conclusion the jury reached.

    C. The dissatisfied party may file a *motion for a new trial*. This may be granted if the judge is convinced that a legal mistake was made during trial. The motion for a new trial is rarely granted, and it is from the ruling on this motion that the losing party often appeals.

POSTTRIAL ISSUES

The most important posttrial issue is: how can a disappointed litigant obtain a review of the trial judge's rulings, i.e., appeal the rulings. Then, if the judgment is final, how can the victorious party collect the dollar damages awarded? Finally, can the same subject matter be relitigated?

XV. Each state has its own appellate procedures and determines the jurisdiction of its various appellate courts, often called reviewing courts, or courts of appeal.

    A. Courts of appeal look at the record of the proceedings in the lower court. They determine whether prejudicial errors occurred or an erroneous decision was made, i.e., they determine if trial judges (lower court judges) made legal mistakes.

    B. Each party to the suit files a written **brief**, which presents its position and arguments for reversing or affirming the lower court's decision.

    C. The reviewing court (appellate court) may also hear **oral arguments**, in which the attorneys present their positions and are questioned by the court.

    D. The justices take an initial vote and then one justice, along with staff, prepares an opinion. If the opinion is approved by a majority of the justices, it is adopted. Those who disagree may prepare a dissenting opinion.

    E. If the review took place in an intermediate court, the losing party may petition the highest court in the system for a writ of certiorari.

F.   Courts of appeal are, for the most part, not allowed to disturb factual findings unless they are clearly erroneous. Determining the weight and credibility of the evidence is the function of the trial court, and an appellate court cannot simply substitute its interpretation of the evidence for that of the trial court. There are no juries at the appellate court level.

XVI.   After the resolution of a lawsuit, the losing party may not voluntarily pay the amount of the judgment to the judgment creditor. There are tow main ways the court (judge) can assist in enforcing the decision:

A.   The judgment creditor can request the judge to order the **execution** of the judgment or decree. An execution of a judgment occurs when a court official – usually the sheriff – seizes some property of the judgment debtors (defendant), sells it at public auction, and applies the proceeds to the creditor's claim.

B.   The judgment creditor can also ask the judge to order garnishment of the debtor's salary or wages. Garnishment is a method of enforcement in which a portion of the judgment debtor's wages is paid to the court by the debtor's employer. The court in turn pays the creditor.

XVII.   Once a court decision has become final, it is said to be **res judicata**. That means either that the case has been finally decided on appeal or that the time for appeal has expired. There can be no new proceeding on the same cause of action (legal basis for the lawsuit), in the same court or any other court. Res judicata brings disputes to a conclusion.

COMPLETION EXERCISES

1.   Taking disputes to court is termed _____.

2.   The _____ files the lawsuit.

3.   The party sued is known as the _____.

4.   A defendant who wants to sue the plaintiff files a _____.

5.   The party who appeals the trial court result is the _____.

6.   At the Supreme Court if one party is the "petitioner," the other party is the _____.

7.   The requirement that a plaintiff must be directly and adversely affected by what the defendant did is called _____.

8. For a defendant in a case to sue another defendant requires the filing of a _____.

9. The court's legal power over the plaintiff and defendant is known as _____.

10. A notice to appear in court is called a _____.

TRUE-FALSE SELECTIONS

1. _____ Long-arm statutes enable states to serve a summons beyond their borders.

2. _____ The process by which the governor of one state obtains a prisoner held in another state is called "extradition."

3. _____ Federal courts have generally encouraged class action lawsuits.

4. _____ Pleadings are the legal documents used by the judge to instruct the jury.

5. _____ The defendant usually responds to the service of process by filing an answer.

6. _____ The process of discovery ensures that prior to the civil trial each side is fully aware of the facts of the case.

7. _____ Depositions are written questions presented by the opposing parties to each other and to witnesses.

8. _____ The motion for a summary judgment argues that the plaintiff has failed to plead some essential element of a valid claim.

9. _____ A sworn statement introduced as evidence is called an "affidavit."

10. _____ The judge's instructions to the jury are termed the "voir dire."

MULTIPLE CHOICE PROBLEMS

1. The plaintiff or the defendant can excuse a prospective juror and give no reason through the:

    a. Challenge for cause.
    b. Peremptory challenge.
    c. Closing argument.
    d. Verdict.

2.   In a criminal case, the burden of proof is:

    a.   Burden of persuasion.
    b.   Preponderance of evidence.
    c.   Clear and convincing proof.
    d.   Beyond a reasonable doubt.

3.   Select the most *incorrect* statement:

    a.   The jury's decision is called the verdict.
    b.   The judge usually accepts the jury's decision.
    c.   On appeal the parties' written arguments are called "briefs."
    d.   The appellate jury can order writs of execution and garnishment.

4.   Select the most *incorrect* statement.

    a.   Appellate judges who disagree with the majority opinion are called "dissenters."
    b.   The losing party at the Court of Appeals has a right to have the Supreme Court review the case.
    c.   To satisfy a monetary judgment, the judge can order the sheriff to seize the defendant's corporation stock.
    d.   To satisfy a monetary judgment, the judge can order the defendant's employer to pay a large part of the defendant's wages or salary to the court for the plaintiff.

5.   Select the most *incorrect* statement:

    a.   The primary purpose of the trial is to determine the facts of a case.
    b.   In some jurisdictions, jurors take notes and question witnesses.
    c.   Diversity of citizenship protects nonresidents against state-court bias.
    d.   The Federal Rules of Civil Procedure detail the substantive law to be followed in federal litigation.

DISCUSSION ANALYSIS

How does judicial activism and judicial restraint relate to the power of judicial review? Discuss.

Chapter
5

Alternative Dispute Resolution System

It is neither feasible nor desirable to litigate every dispute that arises in business. Litigation is costly financially and emotionally. In business it can also destroy a valuable relationship. To help avoid this harm, a number of alternatives to litigation have developed. These are known as alternative dispute resolution (ADR) systems.

Litigation does not prevent the use of ADR systems. It is common to employ ADR systems during the pretrial process. ADR systems may also be used as an alternative to litigation.

ADR systems may be agreed to in a contractual relationship between parties before a dispute arises. Disputing parties may also agree to use an ADR technique after the dispute arises, even if their original agreement contained no reference to dispute resolution.

This chapter discusses several ADR systems. In order, the are:

Negotiated settlements
Mediations
Arbitrations
Other alternatives

NEGOTIATED SETTLEMENTS

To negotiate a settlement refers to ending a dispute through discussion and agreement. There are two very different styles of negotiation.

I.   In **positional bargaining** each party states its respective expectations. Often the difference between these two positions is so wide that the parties are unlikely to reach a negotiated settlement. This is often the instinctive negotiation method of disputing parties, but there is a better method of negotiation.

II.   **Principled interest-based negotiations** contain seven elements that should become the focus of negotiators. Focus on these elements can help remove some of the barriers created by position-based negotiations. The seven elements are:

A. Clear **communication** can help the parties become joint problem solvers. Without communication, the parties are likely to continue blaming one another.

B. Effective communications should include the benefits to each party of a continued **relationship**. This can be an opportunity to maintain or even to enhance the existing relationship.

C. The **interests** of the disputing parties may not be mutually exclusive. Communication of these interests may help the parties realize that a continuing relationship is in their mutual best interests.

D. The disputing parties should brainstorm possible **options** or solutions to their dispute. Both parties should agree that an option mentioned is not necessarily a proposal for compromise. In this way it is possible that both parties can improve their positions.

E. **Legitimacy** can be achieved by applying accepted standards to the topic negotiated. It is not sufficient for the parties to state unsupported propositions; the propositions must be legitimized.

F. Both parties must understand that their **alternatives** to the negotiating process are less attractive than the negotiations. The desirable result of any negotiation is to agree on an outcome that is better than both parties' alternatives.

G. Any successful negotiation must conclude with each party making a realistic **commitment** that can be put into practice. An initial commitment that assists the process of negotiation is for the parties to agree that they will continue to meet and focus on the seven elements. If the conclusion of negotiations is not a settlement, then it might be an agreement to use another ADR system.

MEDIATION

When negotiations between disputing parties fail, the process of mediation is an alternative to litigation. **Mediation** is the process by which a third person, called a **mediator**, attempts to assist disputing parties in resolving their differences. A mediator *cannot impose a legally binding solution on the parties*, but as an unbiased and disinterested third party, a mediator is often able to help the parties understand a dispute and thus avoid litigation.

Parties may agree to mediation as part of a contract made before a dispute arose, or a trial judge may require the disputing parties to submit to the mediation process before a complaint can be litigated formally.

If mediation is successful, there is no need for judicial review of the mediation process. If it is not successful, the parties may continue to litigate or utilize another ADR technique.

III. Mediation has both advantages and disadvantages.

    A. The basic advantage of mediation over litigation and arbitration is that the disputing parties retain full control over the resolution of the controversy. They decide how much time and effort to put into the mediation process. If progress is being made, mediation can continue, or even expand into other areas of dispute. If it is not helping, either party can stop the process at any time.

    B. The fact that the parties control the mediation process can also be a disadvantage. There is no enforcement mechanism that ensures the parties will mediate in good faith. Sometimes the parties fail to agree even on who will be the mediator. Also, there are no standard training or licensing requirements for mediators.

IV. The odds for successful mediation increase greatly when the mediator follows some basic procedures:

    A. The mediator makes an opening statement, explaining the procedures of mediation and any rules that need to be specified.

    B. All parties to the dispute make a statement about their views, in the presence of each other and the mediator.

    C. The mediator attempts to establish open communication between the parties to shift their focus from "wrongs done in the past" to "how business can be conducted in the future."

    D. The mediator may decide to meet with each party privately. This private meeting is called a **caucus**. The parties may then meet together again; or the mediator may act as a shuttle diplomat, going back and forth between the parties. It is especially important during these caucuses that the mediator win the confidence of each party to the dispute.

    E. The final step to a successful mediation is the writing of the agreement and its signing by the parties. This agreement may be a legally binding contract.

ARBITRATION AND ITS PROCEDURES

Arbitration is a much more formal ADR. Disputing parties submit that dispute to a neutral third party, called an **arbitrator**, and authorize this person to make a decision by which the parties must abide. The act of referring a matter to arbitration is called **submission**. **Voluntary arbitration** is an agreement by the parties to use this ADR. Generally, once the parties have submitted to arbitration, they cannot withdraw and resort to litigation. A statute or a court may also require the parties to submit to **mandatory arbitration**.

The arbitrator conducts a hearing. Both parties present evidence and argue their positions, then a decision known as an **award** is handed down in writing. The award is valid as long as it settles the entire controversy and states which party is to pay the other a sum of money.

V.   *Submission by contract* occurs if the parties enter into an agreement to arbitrate an existing or future dispute.

    A.   In this case, submission occurs when one party serves on the other a demand to arbitrate.

    B.   Submission usually must be in writing and within a stated time period, usually six months after the dispute arises.

    C.   In the absence of a statute, the rights and duties of parties to a submission are described and limited by their agreement. They are not required to arbitrate any matters other than those previously agreed to. A court may determine whether a particular matter falls within the previous agreement.

    D.   Issues submitted to arbitration may be questions of fact, or law, or both. When a court decides whether or not a dispute falls within a previous agreement of arbitration, the court decides only that question, not the basic issue between the parties.

    E.   In *AT&T Tech., Inc. v. Communications Workers*, the U.S. Supreme Court reversed the decision of the federal court of appeals. The Supreme Court ruled that whether or not an employer had to arbitrate a certain dispute with a labor union under an arbitration clause in a contract was an issue of law for a court to decide. It was not an issue for an arbitrator to decide.

VI.   Arbitrators generally are chosen by the disputing parties. A provision in the agreement to arbitrate or in the statute that requires arbitration describes how the arbitrator is selected.

    A.   One reason arbitration is preferable to litigation is the use of an expert to resolve the dispute. In labor-management relations, for example, arbitration is quick and efficient and minimizes disruption in the workplace. Parties in workplace disputes choose arbitrators based on their knowledge of the "common law of the shop" and expect the arbitrator to look beyond strictly legal criteria to other factors that bear on dispute resolution, such as the effect of a particular result on the productivity and morale of the shop.

    B.   It is common to use one arbitrator, who is considered objective and impartial. There are no licensing requirements an arbitrator must satisfy, however often this person is chosen from a list of qualified persons. It is also common for each party to choose one arbitrator and for these two persons to then choose a third.

C. The limits to arbitrators' authority to decide has also been a topic of controversy and litigation. In *Howsam v. Dean Walter Reynolds, Inc.*, the U.S. Supreme Court stated that the meaning of an arbitration clause which stated that no dispute over 6 years old could be arbitrated was a "gateway procedural dispute" to be resolved by the arbitrator, not by a court.

VII. Generally arbitrators must disclose their findings only if the applicable statute, arbitration agreement, or submission requires them to do so.

A. *The U.S. Supreme Court favors a broad scope of the arbitrators' authority.* Parties are generally bound by the arbitrators' award because the parties themselves have agreed previously by contract to abide by the arbitrator's award.

B. *An arbitrator's award will be enforced by the courts as if it were a judgment of the court.* Only when fraud or other inappropriate action by the arbitrator can be shown will a court reverse an award granted in a voluntary arbitration proceeding.

POPULARITY OF ARBITRATION

Over the past eighty years, arbitration has become the most commonly used ADR system. The Federal Arbitration Act has played a particularly important role in creating a positive perception of arbitration.

VIII. There are several reasons to use arbitration.

A. The primary reason to use arbitration is to provide a relatively quick and inexpensive resolution of disputes.

B. Arbitration also helps ease congested court dockets.

C. Adversaries may be more likely to preserve their business relationship, as arbitration is a private proceeding with no public record available to others.

D. It is an advantage of arbitration that disputes are submitted to experts for solutions.

IX. The **Federal Arbitration Act** (FAA) of 1925 and its revision and reenactment of 1947 changed public policy perceptions of arbitration and led to its preference over litigation.

A. The FAA covers any arbitration clause in a contract that involves interstate commerce. The law prohibits the states from refusing to enforce such agreements. The federal policy favoring arbitration frequently conflicts with state laws favoring litigation as the means to resolve a dispute. The Commerce Clause and the

Supremacy Clause of the U.S. Constitution are often used to set aside such state laws that deny arbitration of certain disputes.

B.   In *Wright v. Universal Maritime Service Corp.*, the U.S. Supreme Court ruled that a general arbitration clause in a collective bargaining contract between the employer and the union did not require an employee to use arbitration in a claim brought under the Americans with Disabilities Act when the act granted specific rights to sue. The Court did suggest a "clear and unmistakable waiver" would give up the right to litigate.

X.   A growing number of states have adopted statutes that require **mandatory arbitration** for certain types of disputes. These statutes require arbitration before disputants are allowed to litigate. These cases are usually presented to a panel of three arbitrators, and the costs of arbitration are paid by the parties involved.

A.   Mandatory arbitration statutes cover only a few types of cases, such as claims involving a small amount of money (e.g., under $15,000) or issues arising out of divorces. Such arbitration is required only if one party has demanded a jury trial, as a judge hearing the case is assumed to be as efficient as an arbitrator.

B.   Mandatory arbitration requires less time than litigation, however it is often eight months from the time the claim is filed until the hearing. Discovery procedures take place during this time, usually by interrogatories rather than by deposition. Arbitrators have the power to determine the admissibility of evidence and to decide the law and the facts of the case.

XI.   The larger growth in the number of arbitration cases comes, not from the increase in mandatory arbitrations, but from disputing parties agreeing to arbitrate (voluntary arbitration). This trend will continue only as the goal of an efficient and affordable alternative to litigation is achieved. In *Green Tree Financial Corp. v. Larketta Randolf* the Supreme Court reversed the decision of the court of appeals. It ruled that when the arbitration agreement did not specify how the arbitration expenses would be paid, it was up to the party seeking to invalidate arbitration to prove that for that party the arbitration would be "prohibitively expensive."

XII.   There is limited judicial review (or appeal of) an arbitrator's award.

A.   Voluntary arbitrations are generally not reviewable because the parties have agreed by contract to accept the arbitrator's findings.

1.   If the scope of an arbitration clause is in doubt, the clause is interpreted in favor of arbitration.
2.   *Erroneous rulings or erroneous findings of fact are not grounds for setting aside an award* because the parties have agreed to accept the arbitrator's view

of the law. Only an award that would require the parties to commit a crime or violate the law can be rendered void.

3.   If an arbitrator acts *fraudulently* or *arbitrarily* or if a decision is against public policy, an award may be set aside, but the public policy must arise from laws and legal precedents, not merely opinions of the court.

B.   Note that unlike voluntary arbitration, *mandatory* arbitration may be constitutional only if ultimate judicial review is available. A **de novo judicial review** is one in which the court tries the issues anew as if no arbitration had occurred.

C.   The Federal Arbitration Act controls most business arbitrations. Section ten of the federal act provides that under judicial review an award may be vacated or set aside on any one of four grounds:

1.   If it was procured by "corruption, fraud, or other undue means," with "undue means" requiring some type of bad faith.

2.   If the arbitrators were obviously partial or corrupt, meaning that an arbitrator lacked the ability to consider evidence and to reach a fair conclusion.

3.   If arbitrators have been guilty of misconduct, such as communicating with a party or a witness without the knowledge or consent of the other party or accepting gifts from a party during the proceedings or committing an egregious evidentiary error.

4.   If arbitrators exceeded their power by attempting to resolve an issue that is outside the scope of the arbitration agreement.

OTHER ALTERNATIVES

Arbitration is less time consuming and expensive than litigation, but it is not a simple process. There are some additional ADR techniques that utilize aspects of the litigation process and avoid even the costs of arbitration.

XIII.   Mediation can be utilized in conjunction with other dispute resolution systems.

A.   Parties in the middle of heated litigation can agree to mediate just one issue. That may help the remaining issues proceed in a more efficient manner.

B.   Laws can encourage parties to be creative in utilizing ADR systems. The Magnuson-Moss Warranty Act, for example, provides that if a business adopts an informal dispute resolution system to handle complaints about its product warranties, then a customer cannot sue the manufacturer or seller for breach of warranty without first going through the informal procedures.

XIV. In recognition of the jury's fact-finding role, attorneys sometimes use a technique called a **mock trial**. They assemble a group of citizens, present their evidence, and the group deliberates and makes findings. This is like to a dress rehearsal, and is a "reality test" for the disputing parties. It often provides incentives to the parties to engage in mediation.

XV. A **minitrial** is designed to turn a lawsuit back into a business problem. Lawyers present the central issues in a dispute to the top executives of the disputing companies. The executives then meet with each other to negotiate and seek a settlement. Minitrials are successful; they avoid lengthy trials, reduce legal costs, save management time for productive pursuits, and achieve satisfactory settlements.

COMPLETION EXERCISES

1. ADR systems present alternatives to _____.

2. One can often avoid the need for formal dispute resolution through successful _____.

3. In _____ each party states its respective expectations.

4. A(An) _____ is a third party who assists two disputing parties with non-legally binding recommendations.

5. A(An) _____ is a non-judicial third party who gives a legally binding decision to resolve a dispute.

6. _____ arbitration usually occurs after the parties agree to it by contract.

7. An arbitrator's award can be enforced through a _____.

8. The congressional statute that requires that state courts honor voluntary arbitration agreements in interstate commerce is the _____.

9. Required arbitration is called _____ arbitration.

10. The arbitrator's written decision resolving the dispute of the parties is called the _____.

TRUE-FALSE SELECTIONS

1. _____ If the parties to a mediation sign an agreement at the end, that agreement is usually legally binding (can be enforced in court).

2. _____ The Supreme Court usually favors a narrow scope of the arbitrator's authority.

3. _____ An arbitrator's award can likely be successfully appealed to a court if the arbitrator is legally mistaken in the award.

4. _____ An arbitrator's award can likely be successfully appealed to a court if a party can show arbitral corruption or fraud.

5. _____ Mandatory arbitration usually involves small claims.

6. _____ Mock trials and minitrials are generally more expensive than litigation.

7. _____ The Magnuson-Moss Warranty Act encourages the use of ADR systems.

8. _____ A mediator's private meeting with a party to a dispute is called a "caucus."

9. _____ An arbitrator's private meeting with one party without the knowledge of the other is called "arbitral misconduct" and is grounds for successful appeal to a court.

10. _____ Mandatory arbitration would be unconstitutional if the states did not allow for de novo judicial review.

MULTIPLE CHOICE PROBLEMS

1. All of the following are advantages of arbitration over litigation *except*:

   a. The right to appeal.
   b. Takes less time.
   c. Nonpublic.
   d. Not as expensive.

2. The act of referring a disputed issue to arbitration is termed:

   a. Awarding
   b. Submission
   c. Referencing
   d. Res ipsa loquitur

3.   Dispute resolution based on clear communication, interests that are not mutually exclusive, legitimacy, commitment, and the benefits of continued relationship is termed:

    a.   Positioned bargaining.
    b.   Voluntary arbitration.
    c.   Mandatory arbitration.
    d.   Principled interest-based negotiation.

4.   What types of arbitration contracts does the Federal Arbitration Act cover?

    a.   Non-consumer contracts.
    b.   Mandatory contracts.
    c.   Contracts in interstate commerce.
    d.   Only labor contracts.

5.   An ADR system under which each side presents the central issues in a dispute to the top executives of the disputing companies, the allows them to negotiate, is called the:

    a.   Mock trial.
    b.   Mini-trial.
    c.   De novo trial.
    d.   Petit jury trial.

DISCUSSION ANALYSIS

Discuss the advantages and disadvantages of arbitration when contrasted with litigation.

Chapter
6

The Constitution and Business

This chapter focuses on how the federal government's power to regulate business is created and how this power limits the extent of regulation by state and local governments. It also covers how the federal government's authority to regulate is restricted or limited by what we call constitutional protections.

BASIC CONCEPTS

The Constitution contains four concepts or clauses that are of great significance to the regulatory environment of business. They are the *separation of powers* concept, the *Supremacy Clause*, the *Contract Clause*, and the *Commerce Clause*.

I.   In our federal government, the powers of government are separated both horizontally and vertically. The horizontal division separates the power and function among the three equal branches of government – the legislative, the executive, and the judicial. The vertical aspect of **separation of powers** is **federalism** or dual federalism, referring to governmental powers at both the federal and state levels.

   A.   In a federal system there are two levels of government – a federal level and a state and local level. Each has a separate and distinct role to play.

   B.   The federal government recognizes that is was created by the states. The Tenth Amendment reserves some powers to the states and to the people.

   C.   On the other hand, state government may not limit the exercise of powers granted by states to the federal government.

II.   The U.S. Constitution makes it clear in the **Supremacy Clause** that federal law is supreme over a state law or local ordinance. The Constitution is supreme under all laws.

   A.   *If a state law conflicts with a federal law, the state law is invalid*, whether or not the conflict is intentional. The courts decide if a conflict exists.

   B.   The concept of **preemption** applies if a state law attempts to regulate the same activity that is regulated by a federal law or federal agencies' rules and regulations.

The state law is then deemed unconstitutional. The issue of federal preemption can be complex, however, because often a federal law will expressly preempt one area of regulation while allowing state and local regulation in other areas.

C.   In *Geier v. American Honda Motor Co., Inc.*, the U.S. Supreme Court ruled that the Federal Motor Vehicle Safety Standard 208, which only required auto manufacturers to equip their 1987 vehicles with passive restraints, preempted a state common law tort action which sought to hold the defendant liable for failing to have a driver's side airbag.

III.   The **Contract Clause** of the Constitution is in Article I, Section 10. It says: "No State shall … pass any … Law impairing the Obligation of contracts."

A.   This clause applies only to the states, not to the federal government, which frequently enacts laws and adopts regulations that affect existing contracts.

B.   This limitation on state action impairing contracts has not been given a literal application. As a result of judicial interpretation, some state laws that affect existing contracts have been approved, especially when the law is passed to deal with a specific emergency situation.

THE COMMERCE CLAUSE

The **Commerce Clause** of the Constitution, which gives the federal government the power to regulate business activity, is in Article I, Section 8. It states, "Congress shall have Power … to regulate Commerce with foreign Nations, and among the several States, and with the Indian Tribes."

This clause has been interpreted as creating at least four areas of government regulation of business. They are:

Regulation of foreign commerce
Regulation of interstate commerce
Limitation on state police power
Limitation on state taxation

IV.   The power to regulate foreign commerce exists *exclusively* in the federal government, and it extends to all aspects of foreign trade. The federal government can allow commerce with restrictions or even prohibit foreign commerce entirely. A state can regulate activities related to foreign commerce only if such activities are conducted entirely within the state's boundaries, such as a state tax or retail sales that include sales of foreign-made goods.

V.   The phrase in the Commerce Clause of the Constitution that grants the federal government the power to regulate commerce "among the several States" has led to extensive litigation. Federal regulation of commerce is appropriate if it aids or in any way affects interstate commerce. The power of Congress over commerce is very broad.

VI.   State and local government authority arises from a concept known as **police powers**. These powers require state legislation and regulation to protect the public's health, safety, morals and general welfare. Business activity is regulated by the state under the power conferred by the phrase "general welfare."

   A.   There are limitations on state powers over commerce because of the commerce clause. These limitations reflect the **dominant commerce clause concept**.

       1.   Internal matters where uniformity on a nationwide basis is essential are *exclusively* federal. The states may not regulate such subjects. Airport regulation is an example. The width of railroad tracks is another.
       2.   Matters that are exclusively within the state's power are intrastate activities that *do not have a substantial effect on interstate commerce*. It is becoming more and more difficult to find a business activity that is truly exclusively local and does not affect interstate commerce.
       3.   Joint regulation by federal and state governments is possible. There are three subparts to this area:

           a.   Federal preemption exists when Congress has shown by express language or by comprehensive regulation that it intends to exercise exclusive control over the subject matter.
           b.   Dual compliance, or compliance with both state and federal regulation, is required if it is possible to comply with both.
           c.   The Commerce Clause invalidates state laws imposing an **undue burden** on interstate commerce. Courts weigh the burden of a law against the benefits to determine if it is an undue burden. .
           d.   The Commerce Clause also prohibits discrimination against interstate commerce in favor of intrastate commerce. In *So. Carolina Bell Telephone Co. v. Alabama*, the U.S. Supreme Court ruled that a franchise tax that Alabama assessed on foreign corporations (but differently on in-state ones) unconstitutionally discriminated against interstate commerce.

VII.   Because taxation is a primary form of regulation, taxes imposed by state and local governments are subject to the limitations imposed by the Commerce Clause.

   A.   Taxation distributes the cost of government among those who receive its benefits; therefore interstate commerce is not exempt from state and local taxes. The commerce clause ensures that a taxpayer engaged in interstate commerce only pays its fair share of state taxes.

B.   **Apportionment** formulas allocate the tax burden of an interstate business among the states entitled to tax it. The Commerce Clause requires the states to use reasonable formulas when more than one state is taxing the same thing.

C.   To justify a tax, there must be sufficient contact, connection, tie, or link between the business and the taxing state. This connection is called the **nexus**. If the business benefits from the state's roads, police and fire protection, well-educated labor poor, or any other services, the tax has a sufficient nexus. In cases involving property taxes, the term *taxable situs* is used in place of nexus.

D.   In *Hunt-Wesson, Inc. v. Franchise Tax Bd. Of California*, the U.S. Supreme Court ruled that it violated the Commerce Clause for California to deny a deduction of reasonable business expenses to the income that California taxed on an interstate company. The denial of the deduction was the same thing as an additional tax on income outside California's jurisdictional reach.

REGULATION AND BASIC FREEDOMS

The First Amendment to the U.S. Constitution establishes these freedoms:

Freedom of religion
Freedom of speech
Freedom of the press
Freedom of assembly
The right to petition the government for a redress of grievances

We usually think of these as personal rights; however there are very important aspects of these freedoms relating to economic opportunity and business activity. Four ideas to keep in mind are:

1.   Basic constitutional rights are not absolute.
2.   Cases involving the Bill of Rights almost always require courts to strike a balance either between some goal or policy of society and the constitutional protection involved or between competing constitutional guarantees.
3.   Constitutional guarantees exist to protect the minority from the majority, no matter how unpopular the minority might be.
4.   Constitutional rights vary from time to time and may be narrowly interpreted during emergencies such as war or civil strife. They are constantly reapplied and reexamined.

VIII. The First Amendment contains two clauses guaranteeing freedom of religion through the separation of church and state.

    A. The **Establishment Clause** says Congress shall make no law "respecting an establishment of religion."

    B. The **Free Exercise Clause** says Congress shall make no law "prohibiting the free exercise" of religion. Most business-related freedom of religion cases involve this clause.

IX. The First Amendment states that "Congress shall make no law … abridging the freedom of … the press." The publishing business is the only organized private business given explicit constitutional protection. Essentially, the press is authorized to provide organized scrutiny of government.

    A. The press is not free to print anything it wants without liability. Rather, freedom of the press is usually construed to prohibit **prior restraints** on publications, restraints that prohibit publication altogether. The press still has liability for publishing anything that is illegal or libelous. The courts have also allowed the Federal Communications Commission to uphold the public's interest in responsible broadcasting by, for example, censoring "filthy" words on television.

    B. A major area of litigation involving freedom of the press is **defamation of character**. The tort theory known as **libel** is used to recover damages as a result of printed defamation of character. In an issue of public interest and concern, such as when the person involved is a public official or figure, the plaintiff seeking damages must prove actual **malice** in order to recover. *Actual malice* includes knowledge that the printed statements are false or a reckless disregard for whether or not they are true. If the plaintiff is not a public figure, there is liability for libelous statements without proof of malice.

X. **Freedom of speech**, sometimes referred to as freedom of expression, covers both verbal and written communications. It also covers conduct or actions considered **symbolic speech**. Freedom of speech is not absolute, but it exists for thoughts many of us hate; and it recognizes that there is no such thing as a false idea. Freedom of speech exists to protect the minority from the majority.

    A. In the 1970's the Supreme Court began to recognize that free **commercial speech** – i.e., speech, such as advertising, by business – was essential to the public's right to know. Today, freedom of speech protects corporations as well as individuals, since corporations may add to the public's knowledge and information. Freedom of speech may not be as extensive as the right of an individual; however a government cannot limit commercial speech unless it misrepresents a product or service.

B.   In *Sec. Of Health and Human Services v. Western Sts. Medical Center*, the U.S. Supreme Court ruled that certain Food and Drug Administration rules prohibiting the advertising of compounded drugs violated the freedom of speech.

C.   The **overbreadth doctrine** holds that even when the government can regulate speech – such as when it defrauds or threatens others – regulation is unconstitutional if it regulates too broadly. For instance, it would be unconstitutional to prohibit all advertising of prescription drugs because some advertising might misrepresent the drugs.

THE FOURTEENTH AMENDMENT

The Fourteenth Amendment to the Constitution states "No state shall make or enforce any law which shall abridge the privileges or immunities of citizens of the United States; nor shall any state deprive any person of life, liberty or property, without due process of law, nor deny to any person within its jurisdiction the equal protection of the laws." Two of this amendment's provisions are of special importance to business – the Due Process Clause and the Equal Protection Clause.

XI.   The **Due Process Clause** cannot be narrowly defined. It describes fundamental principles of liberty and justice; and, simply stated, means "fundamental fairness and decency." It means that *government* may not act in a manner that is arbitrary, capricious, or unreasonable; and it restricts only government, not individuals or businesses. It probably arises in more litigation than any other constitutional phrase.

A.   **Procedural due process** cases are concerned with whether proper notice has been given and a proper hearing has been conducted. Such cases often, though not always, involve procedures established by statute.

B.   **Substantive due process** issues arise when property or other rights are directly affected by governmental action. *If there is no governmental action involved, due process requirements do not arise.* The constitutional requirement of due process does not, for instance, apply to a private employer.

C.   In *State Farm v. Campbell*, the U.S. Supreme Court ruled that assessing a defendant $145 million in punitive damages when compensatory damages were only $2.6 million "was an irrational and arbitrary deprivation of the property of the defendant" and thus violated due process of law.

D.   Judges have also used the due process clause of the Fourteenth Amendment to "incorporate" or "carry over" the Bill of Rights and make these constitutional provisions applicable to the states. Originally, the Bill of Rights applied only to prohibit *Congress* from denying free speech and other rights.

XII. A great deal of constitutional litigation centers on the equal protection clause. Almost any state or local law can be challenged under this clause, as no law treats all persons equally. But the equal protection clause does not always deny states the power to treat different persons in different ways. The ethical idea embodied in the clause is that law should not treat people differently without a satisfactory reason. Equal protection cases run the whole spectrum of legislative attempts to solve society's problems, dealing with school integration, voting requirements, rights of aliens, and many more. Courts use three distinct approaches in deciding cases using the clause to challenge state and local laws:

A. The traditional, or **minimum rationality** approach, usually results in the challenged law and its different classifications *not* being found to be a violation of equal protection if it has a *rational* connection to a *permissible* state end. A permissible state end is one not prohibited by another provision of the Constitution. The classification must have a reasonable basis. *These laws often involve economic issues or social legislation such as welfare laws.*

B. The **strict scrutiny** test will result in a finding of denial of equal protection unless the classification is necessary to achieve a *compelling* state purpose. The law must serve important governmental objectives and the classification must be substantially related to achieving these objectives. The strict scrutiny test is used if the classification involves either a *suspect class* or a *fundamental constitutional right.*

1. A *suspect class* is one that commands extraordinary protection from the political process of the majority; for example, classifications directed at race, national origin, and legitimacy of birth are clearly suspect, and the judiciary strictly scrutinizes laws directed at them.

2. If a classification unduly burdens or penalizes the exercise of a constitutional right, it will be found unconstitutional unless it is found to be necessary to support a *compelling* state interest. Among the rights included under strict scrutiny are the right to vote, the right to travel, and the right to appeal.

3. In *Adarand Constructors, Inc. v. Pena*, the U.S. Supreme Court ruled that "all racial classifications, imposed by whatever federal, state, or local government actor, must be analyzed by a reviewing court under strict scrutiny."

C. Some cases fall between the minimum rationality and strict approaches. These cases use what is sometimes called **quasi-strict scrutiny** bests because the classifications are only partially suspect or the rights involved are not quite fundamental. For example, classifications directed at gender are only partially suspect. Such classifications are unconstitutional unless they are *substantially* related to an *important* government objective.

Chapter 6

COMPLETION EXERCISES

1. That the powers of government are separated vertically into the national government and state government is called dual _____.

2. That federal law invalidates conflicting state law is due to the _____.

3. The primary power of the federal government to regulate business comes from the _____, which is found in Article I, Section 8 of the Constitution.

4. The way that the taxes of an interstate business are allocated among various states is called _____.

5. Freedom of the press prohibits _____ on publications.

6. To prove libel against a public figure or official, a plaintiff must prove _____.

7. The state (government) cannot constitutionally act arbitrarily or fundamentally unfairly because of the _____ clause.

8. The so-called "incorporation clause" is the _____ clause of the _____ Amendment.

9. For the state (government) to classify people according to race will be evaluated by a court under the _____ test.

10. Under the equal protection clause, state discrimination against a business is evaluated by a court according to the _____ test.

TRUE-FALSE SELECTIONS

1. _____ The Supremacy Clause prohibits the states from "impairing the obligation of contract."

2. _____ Business activities that merely affect interstate commerce substantially can be regulated by Congress.

3. _____ For the state of Michigan to regulate the width of railroad tracks would likely be unconstitutional because such regulation requires national uniformity.

4. _____ A state government cannot tax retail goods if they have foreign origin.

5. _____ A state government that taxes interstate business but not intrastate business is acting unconstitutionally.

6. _____ Only the federal government can regulate gambling on Native American reservations.

7. _____ Basic constitutional rights are absolute.

8. _____ It denies you your First Amendment rights when your private employer fires you for speaking out in support of U.S. foreign policy.

9. _____ Constitutional due process applies to prevent the state (government) from acting arbitrarily, without notice, or fundamentally unfairly.

10. _____ Government discrimination based on gender is evaluated by courts according to the quasi-strict scrutiny test.

MULTIPLE CHOICE PROBLEMS

1. If a federal law clearly and expressly states that only federal law regulates a certain area of business activity, the federal law is said to do what to state law that regulates in the same area?

    a. Pre-empt it.
    b. Apportion it.
    c. Separate it.
    d. Apply the nexus.

2. The Civil Rights Act of 1964 was passed by Congress under the specified power of what clause?

    a. Due process clause.
    b. Equal protection clause.
    c. Privileges and immunity clause.
    d. Commerce clause.

3. Select the most *incorrect* statement concerning freedom of speech:

    a. Freedom of speech covers symbolic speech, such as burning the American flag.
    b. Freedom of speech is also called freedom of expression.
    c. Commercial speech is protected equally with political speech.
    d. Freedom of speech is constitutionally protected only from governmental action.

4.   Select the most *incorrect* statement:

   a.   The minimum rationality approach to equal protection usually results in the challenged classification being found unconstitutional.
   b.   The ethical idea embodied in the equal protection clause is that the law should not treat people differently without a satisfactory reason.
   c.   For a regulatory agency to fail to give notice before adopting a new rule denies due process.
   d.   Due process is likely an issue in more litigation than any other constitutional phrase.

5.   The doctrine concerning where it is appropriate to tax land is most appropriately called the doctrine of:

   a.   Apportionment.
   b.   Nexus.
   c.   Taxable situs.
   d.   Primary taxation.

DISCUSSION ANALYSIS

Hotdog vendor X is granted a city license to sell hotdogs on certain city sidewalks. Hotdog vendor Y is denied such a license. On what constitutional basis can Y challenge the denial? What test will be used to determine the constitutionality of the denial? What arguments by the city could justify the denial of the license?

Chapter
7

The Property System

The concept of *property* can be used as a focal point for understanding the subjects of this book. **Property** is the legal right to exclude others from resources. Resources are anything someone may need or want. Property can also be described as a bundle of rights, but the single right of exclusion includes all of the other rights. In order to be meaningful, property law must be adequately enforced. Business and the private market rest on the foundation of a property system of law.

A key question for any society is how it orders the relationships among people as they compete for limited and valued resources.

I.   The Problem of Limited Resources

    A.   Western political theory states that government is created in order to deal with the problem of limited resources. Law is the state's framework for handling issues related to resources. There are at least two basic legal frameworks.

        1.   The state assumes ownership and controls production and distribution of resources, for example in communism.
        2.   The state recognizes and enforces the individual's rights to acquire, possess, use, and transfer resources. This is the system of law we call private property, or property.

    B.   Societies tend to adopt a mixture of the two frameworks for resource allocation.

    C.   The property system is superior to the state-run framework if the goal is to maximize production for the society. It is also more conducive to individual freedoms.

    D.   In order to function properly, the property system must be applied generally and equally to all members of society, i.e., property must be applied under *the rule of law*.

THE THREE FACES OF PROPERTY

Private property protects private persons. It allows them to exclude others, even usually the state, from their lawfully acquired resources. This is the most important type of property for the purposes of business studies.

Public property represents the state's (government's) right to exclude people from public resources.

Common property has two meanings. It can be the right, shared by all, to common natural resources. It can also be private ownership, shared by two or more people, of a specific resource, such as a piece of land. Common owners exclude others from harming common resources.

II.　　Property and Prosperity

　　　A.　　Property, as a system of law, is central to the legal environment of business and to the achievement of prosperity within a society.

　　　B.　　Property promotes incentive. People are willing to produce more when their efforts are protected by the system of property law.

　　　C.　　Property establishes conditions favorable to capital formation. Capital formation concerns the production of new or different resources. Examples are the use of a house as collateral for a loan and the sale of stock shares by a corporation. But such loans and sales are not possible unless the law recognizes property in houses and corporate stock.

　　　D.　　Property allows resources to be easily divisible, so that owners can dispose of any part of their resources while maintaining interest in the remainder.

III.　　Two Basic Divisions of Property: Real Property and Personal Property

　　　A.　　The two basic legal divisions of property are: real property and personal property.

　　　B.　　**Real property** consists of land and interests in land, for example, mining rights and leases. Land ownership is also known as *real estate* or *realty*.

　　　　　1.　　Real property rules are very formal, due to the historical importance of land. Transfer of ownership should be written.
　　　　　2.　　A **fixture** is an object of personal property that has become part of a real property either by physical attachment to the real property (for example, carpeting) or by a use that is closely associated with the property's use (for example, manufacturing equipment at a manufacturing plant). Without a

specific agreement to the contrary, fixtures are considered part of a real property when it is sold.

C. **Personal property** applies to moveable resources. There are two types of personal property:

1. *Tangible property* applies to physical, touchable things, such as cars and computers. These are also known as goods.
2. Intangible resources are non-goods, such as corporate stock.

ACQUIRING RESOURCES IN A PROPERTY SYSTEM

There are only five legal ways to become an owner of something in a property system. In such a system **ownership** means the same thing as property, that is the right to make resources exclusive.

IV. Acquiring Resources through Exchange

A. *Exchange* of resources is the most common way to acquire a property in resources. Buying a car is exchanging money for the car. At a job, you exchange your services for a paycheck.

B. **Contract** rules govern the exchange of resources in a property system. They make agreements to exchange resources legally binding and enforceable, including agreements to exchange resources in the future. Contract rules allow lawsuits for breach of such agreements. They are key to the right of property, foundation of the modern private market.

V. Acquiring Resources Through Possession

A. The first person to reduce previously unowned things to possession usually becomes their owner.

B. Ownership of abandoned resources is acquired by reducing them to possession. An example is a ship abandoned at sea, which can be possessed and controlled by a new owner.

C. Lost items can also be acquired through possession, after the finder observes a statutory procedure designed to find the previous owner.

D. Land can be acquired through **adverse possession**, if certain conditions are met:

1. Open and notorious occupation of the land.
2. Occupation must be actual and exclusive. Building a fence or a structure on the land, for example, would constitute actual occupation.
3. Possession must be continuous, that is not interrupted.
4. The possessor must not have the owner's permission to be on the land; the possession must be wrongful.
5. After a prescribed period of time, often 10 to 20 years, the possessor becomes the new owner.

E. Governments may encourage ownership of land through possession.

1. The **Homestead Act** of 1862 granted land to settlers who possessed their homestead for five years and made certain improvements to it.
2. In poor nations one of the best ways to distribute land is for the government to grant ownership of land to squatters on the land (those who occupy land without owning it or having permission to be there). It prevents the violence that can accompany unauthorized squatting. U.S. history reveals many instances of squatting that led to ownership.

VI. Acquiring Resources Through Confusion

A. Ownership through **confusion** arises when *fungible* (identical) goods are mixed together by different owners. A common example is bushels of grain in a silo.

B. Careful records must be maintained when fungible goods are mixed. Lacking evidence, a court will assume all parties claiming the mixed mass own equal shares. If there is evidence of intentionally wrongful confusion, however, the court will grant ownership of the entire confused mass to the innocent party.

C. The doctrine of confusion illustrates the importance of *boundaries* to the concept of property, and it explains one determination of ownership when resource boundaries are not certain.

VII. Acquiring Resources Through Accession

A. The doctrine of **accession** refers to something added. The doctrine assumes ownership of an original thing to which something else of value was added.

B. When you apply effort and/or ingenuity to transform raw materials into finished products, you also own the finished products. Generally, because you own your efforts, you own what they produce, be it a paycheck, a work of art, or another object.

VIII. Acquiring Resources Through Gift

   A.   In the making of a **gift**, no mutual exchange of resources occurs. A *donor* gives something to a *donee*, who becomes the new owner. There are two rules specifying when a gift has taken place:

   1.   The donor *intends* to make the gift.
   2.   The donor *delivers* the gift to the donee by physical transfer. *Constructive delivery*, for example turning over car keys or a deed to land, is adequate delivery in some instances.

   B.   A *testamentary gift* is one made through a will. Ownership passes upon the death of the donor and the proving of a valid will specifying the gift.

IX. Types of Ownership

   A.   The bundle of rights and powers of land ownership are called an **estate**. **Fee simple** represents the maximum estate allowed under law. The fee simple *absolute* estate has no limitations or conditions attached. The fee simple *defeasible* estate may have a condition attached to its conveyance (transfer).

   B.   A **life estate** grants an ownership in land for the lifetime of a specified person. Upon the grantee's death, the land reverts to the original grantor, who is said to keep a *reversion* interest in the land. If the land goes to someone other than the grantor upon the grantee's death, that person has a *remainder* interest. Reversion and remainder property interests are also called *future* interests as opposed to the life estate, which is a *present* interest. Subject to any attached conditions, all of these estates can be capitalized or transferred.

   C.   A **leasehold estate** is the property right granted to tenants by a landlord.

   1.   Tenants have a qualified possession, use, and transfer of the land, qualified in that they cannot *waste* the land, which means do something that substantially reduces the value of the land.
   2.   Unless prohibited by the lease (which it often is), the resources owned by tenants can be capitalized by transfer to someone else. For example, the tenant can sell the balance of time remaining on the lease at a profit.
   3.   A landlord may lease land for a *definite duration* of time, or for an *indefinite duration* with rent payable at periodic intervals, or simply *at will*, for as long as both shall agree.

D. Both personal and real property interests can have concurrent owners, that is, more than one person can own the same thing. The ownership is *undivided*, meaning that no concurrent owner owns a specific piece of the resources.

　1. *Concurrent ownership*, such as *shareholding* in a corporation, greatly facilitates almost all forms of modern private enterprise.
　2. **Joint tenancy** and the **tenancy in common** are also forms of concurrent ownership. In these forms, the property interest is undivided, but the tenants in common can own different shares of the resources, whereas the joint tenants must have equal ownership shares. Joint tenants, but not tenants in common, can have *right of survivorship*, meaning that if one joint tenant dies, the remaining tenant becomes the sole owner of the entire resource.

X. Ownership is frequently indicated by the term **title**. Someone who owns something has title to it. To pass title is to transfer ownership.

A. A **deed** is the document of title that transfers ownership of land. It contains a precise legal description of the land, describing exact location and boundaries. This precise identification of land minimizes buyer and lender risk, and thus provides the basis for much capital formation.

　1. A *warranty deed*, given by a seller to a buyer, promises that the seller has good ownership and the full power to convey it. The buyer can sue the seller if someone else claims the land.
　2. A *special warranty deed* specifies that certain legal claims against the land, like mortgages, exist but guarantees no other claims exist.
　3. A *quit claim deed* makes no guarantees other than that the grantor (seller) surrenders all claim against the land.

B. Buyers and lenders are also protected by registration statutes. Buyers register their deeds to land and lenders register their mortgage claims against land, and then they are legally and publicly identified.

XI. **Eminent domain** is recognized by the Fifth Amendment of the U.S. Constitution. It is the power of the government to take private property for "public use" upon the payment of "just compensation." The government uses eminent domain to force private owners, generally of land, to exchange their resources for money so that the state can build roads or for other public uses.

A. The exact interpretation of the eminent domain clause is controversial. If the government merely regulates the land, is it a "taking"? The Supreme Court has ruled that whether a regulation is a "taking" depends on the nature and extent of the regulation, which must be evaluated on a case-by-case basis.

B. In *Lucas v. South Carolina Coastal Council* the U.S. Supreme Court ruled that a zoning regulation that prohibited all forms of land development (such as building a house) on certain coastal lands was a "taking" and thus required just compensation.

XII. Since, in law, property is not a *thing*, but rather an owner's *right* to exclude others from resources, one of the most important resources is the *use* owners can make of other resources. The legal protection to use resources in many ways helps make the marketplace dynamic and responsive to needs and wants.

A. Owners have a property in using their efforts, just as owners of land can make many uses of the land. One can also exclude others from the further resources one acquires with one's efforts. This property is closely related to concepts like "freedom" and "liberty."

B. Generally speaking, owners are prohibited from using their resources in ways that harm or injure the resources of other owners. Two limits on land use that protect the equal right of all land owners are relevant to this point:

1. The doctrine of **nuisance** limits certain uses of one's land. In most jurisdictions the common law cases regarding nuisance have been put in statutory form. There are two types of nuisance:

    a. A **public nuisance** is one arising from some use of land that causes inconvenience or damage to the public. Public nuisance claims may be brought only by a public official, unless a private individual has suffered some special damage to their property as a result of the public nuisance.

    b. A **private nuisance** is any *unreasonable* use of one's property so as to cause substantial interference with the enjoyment or use of another's land. When a private nuisance suit is brought, the unreasonableness of the interference is measured by a balancing process in which the character, extent, and duration of harm to the plaintiff is weighed against the social utility of the defendant's activity and its appropriateness to its location. The court may award damages if the plaintiff has suffered economic loss. The court may also order the defendant to correct the problem or cease the nuisance-creating activity.

2. **Zoning ordinances** are generally laws that divide counties or municipalities into use districts designated residential, commercial, or industrial. They may also specify the height, size, number, and location of buildings that can be built on land or impose aesthetic requirements. Zoning boards or commissions, which are generally agencies of local governments, enforce the zoning ordinances. An owner can request a *variance* to allow use of land in a way not permitted. Zoning ordinances allow uses of land that existed prior to passage of the ordinances. Such uses are called "nonconforming." Zoning regulations are intended to protect the use value of other land owners.

71

INTELLECTUAL PROPERTY

Intellectual property applies to allow owners to exclude others from (1) intangible resources like certain secrets that businesses have, (2) the copying of various creative expressions, and (3) the reproducing of inventions and marks that identify the producers of goods and services.

Intellectual property laws arose out of the common law, but they also reflect constitutional and statutory adoption. Intellectual property laws, such as those applying to copyrights and patents, give incentive to the common good; they add "the fuel of interest to the fire of genius."

XIII.   A **trade secret** is a property in any form of information (1) that the owner has taken reasonable measures to keep secret and (2) which has economic value from not being known to the public. The taking of trade secrets, often called *misappropriation*, is a crime under the Economic Espionage Act of 1996; but misappropriation is widespread and costs U.S. businesses tens of billions of dollars a year.

XIV.   A **patent** is a property granted by federal law in inventions.

    A.   To obtain a patent, an inventor files an application with the PTO explaining why the invention is different from *prior art*, that is, from all the previous and related inventions or state of knowledge. A *patent examiner* considers the application; and, in communication with the applicant, determines what aspects of the invention (what *claims*) deserve the patent. However, only a court can finally determine patent validity.

    B.   After a patent is issued, the patent owner may have to defend its property against infringers, those who make, use, or sell the invention without a license from the owner. When the patent owner files a lawsuit, it is common for the alleged infringer to respond by attacking the validity of the patent, often by attacking its subject matter. The subject matter for a potential patent is quite broad. The Patent Statute of 1952 and its amendments identify patentable subject matter as:

        1.   Processes
        2.   Machines
        3.   Compositions of matter
        4.   Improvements to processes, machines, or compositions of matter
        5.   Nonfunctional designs of a manufactured article
        6.   Certain plaints

    C.   In *J.E.M. Ag Supply, Inc. v. Pioneer Hi-Brid International, Inc.*, the U.S. Supreme Court ruled that hybrid corn and other newly developed plant breeds are patentable subject matter under § 101 of the Patent Act.

D. To be patentable, not only must the subject matter of an invention be appropriate, it must be *nonobvious*, *novel*, and *useful*.

    1. The character of *nonobviousness* refers to the ability of an invention to produce surprising or unexpected results, that is results not anticipated by *prior art* (the previous state of knowledge in the field). The nonobvious standard is measured in relation to someone who has at least an ordinary understanding in the prior art. This standard is often the subject of dispute.

    2. The characteristic of *novelty* indicates that something is new and different from the prior art. The test is met when no single prior element of art meets all of the invention's claims. If the invention has been previously described in a publication or put to public use more than one year before a patent application on it is filed, it fails the *one-year rule* of the novelty test.

    3. To be valid, inventions other than designs or plants must be useful, that is must do something. *Usefulness* is also defined as *utility*, and patents that are not plant or design patents are called utility patents.

E. As the U.S. Constitution specifies, the property represented by patents runs for limited duration. Statute limits utility patents to 20 years, plant patents to 17 years, and design patents to 14 years. For the duration of a patent, the owner can sue those who infringe on it. When a patent expires, the invention is in the *public domain*, and others may use it without limitation. The explicit purpose of patent law is to make inventions public following the limited period of legal property right.

XV. **Trademarks** constitute a second general form of intellectual property. They may be registered with the PTO and are some of the most valuable properties that businesses own. They are an information property, exclusively distinguishing the reputation and goodwill of a particular business from that of all other businesses. The function of trademarks is recognizability or *distinctiveness*. They protect both businesses and consumers from confusion regarding who makes or provides what. Misappropriation of trademarks is a major business problem.

A. The Lanham Act of 1946 protects the following marks used to represent a product, service, or organization:

    1. Trademark – any mark, word, picture, or design that attaches to goods to indicate their source,

    2. Service mark – a mark associated with a service,

    3. Certification mark – a mark used by someone other than the owner to certify the quality, point of origin, or other characteristics of goods or services,

    4. Collective mark – a mark representing membership in a certain organization or association, and

    5. *Tradedress*, which is not a mark, but a colored design or shape associated with a product or service or a distinctive store decorating motif or package shapes and colors.

B. Under the Lanham Act, a person must qualify a trademark for registration with the PTO by using it in interstate commerce. Posting it on an Internet website qualifies, or an intent-to-use application may be filed, followed by an amended application when actual use begins. The trademark must be distinctive within the context of its use. The PTO will deny registration if:

1. The mark is the same or similar to a mark currently used on similar related goods,
2. The mark contains certain prohibited or reserved names or designs,
3. The mark merely describes a product or service, or
4. The mark is *generic* and represents a product or service.

C. The PTO places a proposed mark in the *Official Gazette*, which gives existing mark owners the opportunity to object to a proposed mark that is similar to their own. If existing mark owners object to the proposed mark's registration, the PTO holds a hearing to resolve the objection and, possibly, to deny registration.

D. A trademark enjoys a potentially unlimited protection period, but after six years the trademark owner must notify the PTO that the trademark is still in use. Every 10 years the owner must renew the trademark.

E. In order for a person's name or descriptive term to achieve full trademark status and protect, it must be listed on the PTO's *Supplemental Register* for five years *and* acquire a *secondary meaning*, that is a public meaning that makes it distinctive and different from its meaning as a name or descriptive term. Thus "Ford" becomes a trademark for a car and "Levi" a trademark for jeans.

F. Trademark law protects the trademark's owner from having the mark used in an unauthorized way. The law establishes both civil and criminal trademark violation.

1. Civil violation of a trademark or patent is termed **infringement**.
2. Trademark owner must be vigilant in protecting their marks; because if a trademark becomes **generic**, it loses its distinctiveness and its status as a protected trademark. A trademark becomes generic if:

   a. An owner does not defend against unauthorized use and
   b. The public becomes confused as to whether a term refers to a *particular* product/service or refers to a *general class* of product/services

3. Criminal trademark penalties apply to those who manufacture or traffic in *counterfeit* trademarked products. What makes counterfeiting criminal is the deliberate intent to pass off fake products as real by attaching an unauthorized trademark.

G. To win a trademark infringement lawsuit, a defendant will usually present one of three basic defenses:

    1. The mark is not distinctive. It is generic, and the PTO should not have protected it in the first instance; or the mark has become generic and now stands for a class of items.

    2. There is little chance of the public's being confused by use of a term trademarked by someone else. This is called the confusion defense.

    3. The use is a *fair use*. Fair use of a registered trademark is allowed in the context of a discussion, criticism, or parody of the trademark, the product, or its owner. The use of a rival's trademark in comparative advertising is also a fair use.

H. Cyber technology produces a combination of old and new trademark issues. Two issues raise interesting trademark questions:

    1. What is the relationship between a website domain name registered with the Internet Corporation for Assigned Names and Numbers and a trademark registered with the PTO? There have been many attempts to register domain names containing well-known trademarks belonging to others. That is generally a violation of trademark law. The Anticybersquatting Consumer Protection Act of 1999 provides a remedy of statutory damages and transfer of a *famous* trademark domain name to the trademark owner if it was registered in "bad faith."

    2. Does use of someone else's trademark in a metatag constitute illegal infringement? A metatag is a key word embedded in a website's programming that is designed to guide an Internet search to the website. Initial court decisions suggest that using the trademarks of others as metatags is infringement.

I. The Federal Trademark Dilution Act of 1995 prohibits you from using a mark the same as or similar to another's "famous" trademark so as to dilute its significance, reputation, and goodwill.

    1. Even if the use of a similar mark by another (the "junior" mark) does not confuse the public, the owner of the "senior", famous trademark can still get an injunction prohibiting further use of the junior mark based on **trademark dilution**. If the infringer "willfully intended to trade on the owner's reputation or to cause dilution of the famous mark," the court also may award the owner actual damages, the infringer's profits, and attorney's fees.

    2. In *Mosely v. Secret Catalogue, Inc.*, the U.S. Supreme Court ruled that the mere fact that a witness thought of the trademark "Victoria's Secret" when he saw the name "Victor's Secret" (a name that was changed to "Victor's Little Secret") on a lingerie store was not enough to establish trademark dilution. The Court observed that the evidence did not show that the capacity of the famous mark to identify and distinguish goods and services had been lessened.

XVI. **Copyright** gives a property a certain creative work that keeps others from reproducing it without the owner's permission. The copyright attaches not to an idea or to facts but to the original *expression* of an idea or facts.

    A.   *Three criteria are necessary for copyright protection to occur:*

        1.   A work must be *original*. It must be created, not copied.
        2.   The work must be *fixed in a tangible medium* of expression like a book, canvas, compact disc, tape, or computer disk.
        3.   The work must show *some creativity*.

    B.   Copyright law protects authors rather than inventors. The works of authors are of a literary, dramatic, musical, graphic, choreographic, audio, or visual nature; and they receive automatic federal protection under the Copyright Act of 1976 from the moment the author creates them. The copyright allows the holder to control the reproduction, display, distribution and performance of a protected work. The copyright runs for the author's lifetime, plus 70 additional years, for all works published after 1977.

    C.   An action for copyright infringement cannot be begun unless the author has properly filed copies of the protected work with the Copyright Office. One who infringes on a copyright cannot be held liable for actual or statutory damages unless a copyright symbol or notice accompanies the protected work. When the author has observed the proper formalities, she or he may recover actual or statutory damage, attorney's fees, and any profits the infringer has made. Illegally reproduced copies may also be seized, and willful copyright violations are criminal offenses.

    D.   **Fair use** of copyrighted materials is not an infringement of the owner's property. Fair use includes copying for "criticism, comment, news reporting, teaching, scholarship, or research." In determining fair use, a court will consider:

        1.   The purpose and character of the use, including whether such use is for commercial or nonprofit educational purposes
        2.   The nature of the copyrighted work
        3.   The amount and substantiality of the portion used in relation to the copyrighted work as a whole
        4.   The effect of the use upon the potential market for the copyrighted work

    E.   In *Campbell v. Acuff-Rose Music, Inc.*, the U.S. Supreme Court ruled that 2 Live Crew's parody of "Oh, Pretty Woman" by Roy Orbison was a fair use of copyrighted material.

    F.   Criminal prosecutions and civil lawsuits for "file sharing" copyrighted material over the Internet are growing. Both the film industry and the music industry have become more active in pressing civil lawsuits as well as criminal prosecutions for illegal file sharing.

1. A district court has ruled that the *manufacturers* of file-sharing programs did not illegally contribute to the violation of copyright law since the programs could be used for file sharing of non-copyrighted materials.

2. The users of file-sharing programs who send or download copyrighted songs and videos are violating copyright law. The market resource of a copyrighted product is diminished for the copyright owner when file sharers misappropriate music.

3. Congress passed the *Digital Millennium Copyright Act* in 1998, making it illegal to try to get around devices used by copyright owners to keep their works from being infringed. The act will be used particularly to prevent the production, marketing, or sales of a product or service designed to get around technological protections of computer software, videos, and compact disks.

XVII. As this chapter has explained, property law founds the marketplace in the modern nation. It is key to the greatest production of limited resources and is a prime determinant of wealth in the world today. It is important that business students appreciate the fundamental role of law in business and the necessity for a strong legal system, even when they oppose the wisdom of specific rules or regulations. The major issues of poverty and prosperity involve the understanding of property law's effects on society.

Property law also permits the accumulation of unequal exclusive resources. A property system functions best when there is a large middle class with adequate resources and a well-educated populace that understands the benefits of property. Otherwise, in a democracy the temptation is great to redistribute resources through taxation, and at some point the motivation to produce additional limited resources diminishes.

COMPLETION EXERCISES

1. The most important type of property for the purposes of business study is _____.

2. The two basic divisions of property cover _____ and _____.

3. An object of personal property that becomes protected by real property law is called a _____.

4. _____ rules govern the exchange of resources in a property system.

5. One can become an owner of land through occupation alone according to the law of _____.

6.   Ownership of fungible goods that are mixed together is determined according to the law of _____.

7.   The property right granted to a tenant by a landlord is called a _____.

8.   The constitutional power to take private property for a public use is called _____.

9.   The document of title used to transfer land is called a(an) _____.

10.   An owner's unreasonable use of her land so as to interfere with the enjoyment of another's land is called a(an) _____.

TRUE-FALSE SELECTIONS

1.   _____   The illegal taking of trade secrets is called "misappropriation."

2.   _____   The violation of a trademark is called "infringement."

3.   _____   A statutory property right in a new invention is termed a "patent."

4.   _____   Violation of patent, trademark, and copyright law can be a crime as well as a tort.

5.   _____   The duration of a copyright runs for an author's lifetime.

6.   _____   File sharing of copyrighted materials over the Internet is a fair use.

7.   _____   The Digital Millennium Copyright Act makes it illegal to sell a device to get around technological copyright protections.

8.   _____   The domain name registration of another's trademark is a fair use of that mark.

9.   _____   A mark that becomes generic is protected under trademark law.

10.   _____   A person's name can achieve trademark protection when it has secondary meaning.

MULTIPLE CHOICE PROBLEMS

1. Select the most *incorrect* statement:

   a. Plant patents grant property protection for 17 years.
   b. Utility patents grant property protection for 20 years.
   c. Design patents grant property protection for 14 years.
   d. Public domain patents grant property protection for 25 years.

2. Select the most *incorrect* statement. To be patentable, the subject matter must be:

   a. Nonobvious.
   b. Novel.
   c. Physical.
   d. Useful.

3. A poultry processing plant which is located near a public park gives off odors that make the park unusable. The plant may have committed a:

   a. Private nuisance.
   b. Public nuisance.
   c. Nonconforming use.
   d. Constructive taking.

4. Which type of deed offers the greatest protection to a new landowner?

   a. Warranty deed.
   b. Special warranty deed.
   c. Quit claim deed.
   d. Concurrent deed.

5. Select the most *incorrect* statement:

   a. Fee simple represents the maximum estate allowed under law.
   b. Unless prohibited by lease, a tenant can sell what is protected by his or her exclusionary right.
   c. Under the law of accession because you own your efforts, you own what they produce.
   d. A testamentary gift is made during the lifetime of the donor.

Chapter 7

DISCUSSION ANALYSIS

Why is property as a system of law central to understanding the success of the private market?

Chapter
8

Principles of Contract Law

A **contract** is a legally enforceable **promise** or an exchange of promises. The enforcement of contracts is essential in the operation of our property-oriented private-enterprise system. It is the way we exchange resources in this system.

Every day millions of contracts are created and performed. Real-life contract problems usually involve business-related and people-related considerations as well as legal rules. There are legal issues about:

1. When the "deal" becomes a contract
2. Whether the verbal "deal" must be in writing to be enforceable
3. Whether an error in the price excuses your company from having to sell its products at that price.

There are also nonlegal business considerations in every contract. If your company tries to get out of the deal the customer believes exists, you risk losing that customer's future business.

I. The rules of contract law underlie the private enterprise system at every turn. Most people contract daily for a great variety of goods and services that they purchase or lease.

   A. *A contract need not be a formal written document*, and those who make a contract do not have to use the word "contract" or recognize that they have made a legally enforceable promise.

   B. Contract law enables people to make private agreements legally enforceable. It gives people the certainty they need to rely on promises contained in agreements. It helps make buyers and sellers willing to do business together.

   C. Contract law also provides enormous flexibility and precision in business dealings.

      1. It provides flexibility in that you can agree (or require agreement) to literally anything that is not illegal or against public policy.
      2. It gives precision in that with careful thinking you can make another agree to exactly the requirements that accomplish even a very complex business purpose.

II.   There are two sources of contract law:

    A.   Most contract law in this chapter is common law. Common law comes from judges' decisions. The courts have developed principles controlling contract formation, performance, breach, and remedies in countless cases.

    B.   Another source of contract law is legislation, such as Article 2 of the **Uniform Commercial Code** (UCC), which covers the sale of **goods**. Goods are tangible (touchable, i.e., physical), movable items of personal property. Every state has adopted this portion of the UCC, making state contract law uniform in the area of contracts involving goods.

III.   Contractual terminology helps classify different types of contracts.

    A.   Bilateral and unilateral contracts, which involve either an exchange of promises by the parties or a promise conditioned on the performance of an act.

        1.   A **bilateral contract** is an agreement containing mutual promises. It involves two promises, two rights, and two duties. Most business contracts take the bilateral form. Courts presume a bilateral nature of an agreement whenever there is doubt about the form.

        2.   A **unilateral contract** is an agreement with only one promise, one duty and one right.

    B.   **Express contracts** arise from discussions in which parties actually discuss the promised terms of their agreement. **Implied-in-fact contracts** arise from the conduct of the parties rather than from words.

        1.   Parties should be cautious to rely on implied-in-fact contracts. A rule of thumb is that expressing one's contractual commitment is better than leaving things unstated.

        2.   In *Bennett v. Emerson Electric Co.*, the federal 10th Circuit court of appeals ruled that preemployment statements made by the defendant employer's president and vice-president provided a basis for the jury to find an implied contract for three years even though the employer's letter confirming an offer of employment was silent as to a length of time for employment and the employer had terminated the employment after several months.

    C.   A contract **implied in law**, often called a **quasi-contract**, is arises in a situation when one party is unjustly enriched at the expense of another, as for example, when a debtor overpays a creditor. The law may imply a duty on the creditor to return the overpayment under quasi-contract. Courts apply quasi-contract in a fairly limited number of cases based on unjust enrichment.

IV. Five terms related to the enforceability of agreements in contract law are:

   A. An **enforceable contract** is an agreement which courts will order parties to perform or to pay consequences for the failure of performance. That is the ultimate purpose of a contract.

   B. An **unenforceable contract** is a contract in which a defense exists that denies the legal enforcement of an agreement, in which a nonperforming party has a justifiable reason for noncompliance with a promise.

   C. Courts refer to a **valid contract** when an agreement is enforceable because all the essential requirements are present.

   D. A **void contract** is one that appears to be an agreement but lacks an essential requirement for validity and enforceability, as when an apparent agreement has an illegal purpose.

   E. A **voidable contract** is an agreement when one party has the right to withdraw from the promise made without incurring any legal liability. These agreements are enforceable in court until a party with the legal right to do so decides to void the contract, thereby making the agreement unenforceable. This middleground situation arises when a party to the contract lacks capacity or is disadvantaged by specific situations.

V. That parties perform their commitments is vital to contract law. In a complicated business transaction, the performance by one party becomes very important in determining the rights and duties under the contracts. The key terms related to performance are *executed* and *executory*.

   A. An **executed contract** is one in which the parties have performed their promises.

   B. An **executory contract** is one in which the parties have not yet performed their agreement. Since most business contracts are bilateral in nature, involving an exchange of promises by the parties, most contracts are executory at some time.

VI. A party who does not live up to the obligation of contractual performance is said to **breach** the contract.

   A. There are several remedies or solutions available for a breach of contract. They include:

       1. Negotiated settlement – the parties resolve a breach of contract through a voluntary negotiated settlement

2. Arbitration – the parties agree to abide by the decision of a neutral third party or parties

3. Various damage awards following a lawsuit – *compensatory damages* (put the plaintiff in the same position as if the contract had been performed); *consequential damages* (arise from unusual losses which the parties knew would result from breach of the contract); *liquidated damages* (where real damages are likely to be uncertain, parties may specify in the contract what the damages should be); *nominal damages* (a small amount warded to the plaintiff for a breach of contract which causes no financial injury to the plaintiff)

4. **Specific performance** – the remedy ordered by a court when subject matter of the contract is unique, it is an order that the breaching party specifically perform the contractual promise made

5. **Recission** or **restitution** – the requirement imposed by a court that each party return the consideration given the other; often used in fraud, misrepresentation, or repudiation cases. In *Mobil Oil v. United States*, the U.S. Supreme Court ruled that when the government repudiated (rejected, or refused to perform) an oil exploration contract with Mobil Oil that it had to make a restitution to the company of $158 million that the company had given to the government as a "bonus" payment at the beginning of the contract.

B. The various remedies are usually mutually exclusive, although you might get both compensatory and consequential damages for the same breach of contract.

C. The victim of a contract breach must **mitigate** damages when possible, in other words, the victim must take reasonable steps to reduce them.

CONTRACT FORMATION

How a contract is formed is one of the most important issues to understand about contract law. Many agreements are void, and thus unenforceable, because they lack some essential element of contract formation.

There are five essential elements of a valid contract:

1. Offer
2. Acceptance
3. Consideration
4. Capacity of parties to contract
5. A legal purpose

These elements must come together to form contracts. This section discusses the elements and the process of a contract formation.

VII. An **offer** contains a specific promise and a specific demand. An *offeror* (person making the offer) must intend to make the offer by making a commitment to the *offeree* (the person to whom the offer is made). When issues about the offer arise, the court answers the questions by measuring intent from a reasonable person's perspective. This standard is known as the objective, rather than the subjective, intent of the offeror.

   A. Under the common law of contracts, contractual terms must be definite and specific. An offer to purchase at a "reasonable price" cannot be the basis for a contract because of **indefiniteness**. However, under the UCC, contracts for the sale of goods can leave open nonquantity terms to be decided at a future time.

   B. Offers create a legal power in the office to bind the offeror in a contract. However, that legal power does not last forever. When an offer *terminates*, the offeree's legal power to bind the offeror ends. An offer terminates:

      1. By provision in the offer, stating when the offer terminates
      2. By lapse of a reasonable period of time if the offer fails to specify a time; what is "reasonable" depends on the circumstances
      3. By rejection of the offer. A **counteroffer** is also a rejection
      4. By destruction of the subject matter
      5. By the contractual performance becoming illegal

VIII. **Acceptance** of an offer is necessary to create a valid, enforceable contract. An offer to enter into a *bilateral* contract is accepted by the offeree's making the required promise. *Unilateral* contracts are accepted by performing a requested act, not by making a promise. The language of the offer determines whether acceptance should be a promise resulting in a bilateral contract or an act resulting in a unilateral contract. The rights and duties of the contracting party can turn on the form of the acceptance.

   A. In *Sharp Electronics Corp. v. Deutsche Financial Services Corp.*, the federal 4th Circuit court of appeals examined a financing arrangement between Sharp and Deutsche regarding the former's wholesale customers. Determining the arrangement to constitute offers to enter into unilateral contracts, the court held that Deutsche could change the terms under which it would finance Sharp's customers, and Sharp's continued applications for customer financing were subject to the changed terms. Thus, Deutsche was not liable for a $1.3 million default in payment by Montgomery Ward, one of Sharp's wholesale customers.

   B. For an acceptance to create a binding contract, standard contract law requires that the acceptance must "mirror" the offer, that is must match it exactly. This is the **mirror image rule**.

      1. If the acceptance does not mirror the offer and changes the terms of the offer or adds new terms, it is not really an acceptance. It is a *counteroffer*.

2. The UCC has changed the mirror image rule with regard to merchants contracting for the sale of goods. An acceptance between merchants creates a binding contract even though it proposes new or different terms. The new or different terms become part of the contract unless one of the following takes place:

    a. The offer expressly limits acceptance to the original terms
    b. The proposed terms materially alter the contract
    c. The offeror rejects the proposed terms

C. In general, an offeree's failure to reject an offer does not imply acceptance. *Silence is not acceptance*, even if the offer states that the offeror will treat silence as acceptance.

1. There are exceptions to this rule, such as a contract that specifies that future shipments of goods be made automatically unless the offeree expressly rejects them.
2. A related doctrine looks at the parties' prior *course of dealing* – the way they have done business in the past. Silence may well imply acceptance if the parties have previously dealt with each other in this way.
3. The UCC also says that a contract may arise from the *conduct* of a buyer and seller of goods. Emphasis is placed on how the parties act rather than on a formal offer and acceptance of terms.

D. An acceptance usually becomes binding on the parties *when the offeree dispatches it*, unless the offeror specifies a particular time. Since the offeree frequently mails the acceptance the acceptance becomes binding when it is "deposited" with the postal service – hence the **deposited acceptance rule**, also called the **mailbox rule**.

1. The importance of the deposited acceptance rule is that the offeror cannot revoke the offer once the offeree has accepted it.
2. It is also significant that an offeror's revocation is not effective until the offeree actually receives it. Thus, a deposited acceptance creates a binding contract even though a revocation is also in the mail.
3. In *University Emergency Medicine Foundation v. Rapier Investments, Inc.*, the federal 1st Circuit court of appeals decided that a billing and accounts receivable services company had given a required 4-month notice to University Emergency Medicine in order to prevent their contract from renewing for an additional one-year term. The court ruled that the termination notice was effective when sent within the 4-month requirement, according to the terms of the contract.

IX. Courts will not generally enforce contractual promises unless they are supported by **consideration**. *Consideration is the receipt of a legal benefit or the suffering of a legal detriment*. There must be some incentive or inducement for a person's promise or it is not binding, and hence not enforceable through legal action. In a bilateral contract, each party promises something to the other; the binding promises are the consideration. In a unilateral contract, the consideration of one party is a promise; the consideration of the other party is performance of an act.

A. An important part of consideration is that it must be *bargained for*. A promise to make a gift is not binding, because no bargained-for consideration supports the · promise. Similarly, *prior consideration* is not consideration; a gift promised for consideration performed in the past is unenforceable.

B. When reasonable grounds for a lawsuit exist, an agreement not to sue is consideration to support a promise. Likewise, when a dispute is resolved, as by a compromise over an amount owed, the agreed upon **accord and satisfaction** is consideration.

C. A party to an agreement does not give consideration by promising to do something that *he or she is already obligated to do* called the *preexisting obligation rule*.

D. *The preexisting obligation rule does not apply to a sale-of-goods contract*. The UCC states that parties to a sale-of-goods contract may make binding modifications to it without both parties giving new consideration.

   1. The rules of consideration also do not apply to a **firm offer**. A firm offer exists under the UCC when a merchant offering goods promises in writing that the offer will not be revoked for a period not to exceed three months. The promise binds the merchant, although the offeree buyer gives no consideration to support it.
   2. With offers *not* involving sales of goods by a merchant, a promise not to revoke an offer must be supported by the offeree's consideration to be binding. Such an arrangement is called an **option**.
   3. The doctrine of **promissory estoppel** arises in general contract law when a promisee justifiably relies on a promisor's promise to his or her economic injury. The promisor must know that the promisee is likely to rely on the promise. This exception to the rule requiring consideration to support a promise is increasingly used when the facts of a business relationship do not amount to an express or implied contract.

X. **Capacity** refers to a person's ability to be bound by a contract. Courts have traditionally held three classes of persons to lack capacity to be bound by contractual promises in various circumstances: minors, those judged mentally incompetent, and the intoxicated.

A. *Minors* (in most states, anyone under 18) cannot usually be legally bound to contractual promises unless those promises involve *necessaries of life* such as food, clothing, shelter, medical care, and – in some states – education, or *unless the minor has misrepresented his or her age*.

1.   A minor can *disaffirm* a contract into which he or she has entered, thereby voiding the contract, and can legally recover any consideration that has been given to an adult, even if the minor cannot return the adult's consideration. The adult is bound by the contract unless the minor elects to disaffirm it.

2.   The minor may disaffirm a contract anytime before reaching the age of majority and for a reasonable time thereafter. If the minor fails to disaffirm within a reasonable time after reaching majority, the minor is said to *ratify* the contract and loses the right to disaffirm.

B.   Adults do not lose capacity to contract simply because of intoxication or mental impairment. Courts usually measure adult capacity to contract by whether the adult was *capable of understanding the nature and purpose of the contract.* The more complex the contract, the more likely the court to rule the person lacks capacity to contract. The contract is then voidable by one who was intoxicated or mentally impaired when the contract was agreed to.

C.   A contract entered into by one who is legally incompetent is voidable. **Voidable** means that the incompetent party (but *not* the competent one) can choose to terminate the agreement and recover what has been transferred to the competent party.

D.   There are several other important situations in which contracts are voidable:

1.   Contracts based on **fraud** are voidable. Fraud involves an intentional misstatement of a material (important) fact that induces one to rely justifiably to his or her injury.

2.   **Misrepresentation** is a misstatement without intent to mislead. Contracts based on misrepresentation are voidable by the innocent party.

3.   Contracts induced by **duress** are voidable. Duress means force or threat of force. The force may be physical, or in some instances, economic.

4.   **Undue influence** occurs when one is taken advantage of unfairly by a party who misuses a position of relationship or legal confidence. Often the party is a family member of someone weakened by age or illness. Contracts entered into under such influence are voidable.

5.   When there is a **mutual mistake** as to a material fact inducing a contract, rescission is appropriate. If the parties would not have contracted had they been award of the mistake, the mistaken fact is considered to be material, and there has not been "voluntary" consent to the contract.

6.   If only one of the parties to a contract is wrong about a material fact, that is a **unilateral mistake**, and a contract results despite the mistake.

7.   **Mutual assent** is a doctrine similar to mutual mistake. It requires that the "minds" of contracting parties must "meet" before a contract exists. Even though two parties may sign a piece of paper called a "contract," there is no mutual assent if each believes the contract involves something different, and there is no real contract.

XI.   A basic requirement of a valid contract is *legality of purpose*. Contracts that require commission of a crime or tort or violate accepted standards of behavior (*public policy*) are void. When a contract is **void**, no party to it can take legal action on it.

   A.   If a contract has both legal and illegal provisions to it, courts will often enforce the legal provisions and refuse to enforce the illegal ones. Also, courts will often allow an innocent party to recover payment made to a party who knows, or should know, that a contract is illegal. Courts may allow a person to recover compensation under quasi-contract for services performed on an illegal contract.

   B.   Contracts that restrain trade are often illegal and void. They include contracts to monopolize, to fix prices between competitors, and to divide up markets.

   C.   **Covenants not to compete**, however, are important in protecting employers from having the employees they train leave them and compete against them. They also protect the buyer of a business from having the seller set up a competing business. Even though these contracts restrain trade, they are legal as long as they have a valid business purpose and are "reasonable as to time and space" limitation.

XII.   *In most instances contracts do not have to be in writing to be valid and enforceable.* However, certain contracts do have to be in writing, or at least evidenced by writing, to be enforceable. The law requiring that certain contracts be in writing is the **statute of frauds**. Certain common contracts must be evidenced by some form of written agreement.

   A.   Sales of interest in land are common contracts covered by the statute of frauds. The term "sales of interest in land" covers other kinds of interests in land that just contracts to sell the land itself. The doctrine of **part performance** creates an exception to the requirement that sales of interests in land must be in writing. The courts will enforce an oral agreement involving land title if the part performance clearly establishes the intent of the parties as buyer and seller.

   B.   If a person promises to repay a loan of another if that person does not make payments, that person is making a **collateral** promise. Such a secondary or conditional promise, if made at a time different from the original obligation, must be in writing to be enforceable. If the person makes an original promise to repay the loan, at the time of the loan's initiation, it is not a conditional promise, and no written agreement is required.

   C.   An oral contract that the parties *cannot perform within one year* is not enforceable. The period of performance may actually last longer than one year, but it must be possible to complete the performance of the contract within one year for an oral contract to be enforceable. For instance, a contract "to build the Great Wall of

China" *can* under its terms be performed within one year even if in fact it takes much longer to do so.

D.   Under the UCC, the statute of frauds covers the sales of goods of $500 or more, except for certain exceptions, such as when the seller is to specially manufacture the goods for the buyer and has begun to do so.

E.   Most states require insurance policies to be written; some states require written estimates in contracts for automobile repair.

F.   The **parol evidence rule** states that parties to a complete and final written contract cannot introduce oral evidence in court that changes the intended meaning of the written terms unless oral modifications were made *after* the parties made the written contract.

OTHER CONTRACT ISSUES

Other important contract issues to understand include interpretation of contracts, assignment of contracts, performance of contracts, and discharge of contracts.

XIII.   When disagreement about contractual performance exists, interpretation of the terms often becomes necessary.

A.   Common words are given their usual meaning. If a word has a particular *trade usage* (common usage in business), courts will give it that meaning.

B.   Courts will give legal terms their legal meaning. Because many terms have both common and legal meanings, it is important to have an attorney examine contracts drawn up by others. For example "delivery to the buyer" *does not make the seller responsible for shipping goods to the buyer*. **Delivery** is a legal term referring to the transfer of possession from the seller to the buyer. Unless the contract states otherwise, the place of delivery is the seller's place of business.

C.   In the case of printed contracts that are amended by typewritten or handwritten terms, courts interpret *handwritten terms to control typed ones*, and *typed terms to control printed ones*. Writing is interpreted to be the best evidence of the parties' true intentions.

D.   When only one of the parties drafts (writes) a contract, courts will interpret vague or ambiguous terms against the party that drafted them.

XIV.   In addition to the offerer and the offeree, contracts may involve many original parties and sometimes third parties who are not a part of the negotiation resulting in the original contract.

A. The law of **assignment** allows transfer (generally a sale) of rights under a contract. The party that sells the rights is the *assignor*. The party to which the rights are sold is the *assignee*. The party that is obligated to pay, or otherwise fulfill the contract, is the *obligor*.

B. Certain contracts cannot be assigned. An assignment that increases the burden of performance to the obligor cannot be assigned, nor can a *requirements contract* to supply a retail buyer with all the radios needed because it depends upon the buyer's personal situation. Most states regulate the assignment of wages to protect wage earners and their families.

C. Duties, as well as rights can often be assigned, except when performance depends on the character, skill, or training of the party performing the duties.

XV. **Third-party beneficiaries** are parties benefiting by the performing of a contract. A third-party beneficiary has rights to sue to enforce a contract only if the contract *intended* to benefit that party, such as a *creditor beneficiary*.

A. A *donee beneficiary*, whose benefits from a contract were intended as a gift can sue the party who owes them a performance under a breached contract, but they cannot sue the party who contracted to make them a gift.

B. An *incidental beneficiary* is a third party who unintentionally benefits from a contract. This party has no rights under the contract.

XVI. At the time parties reach agreement under a contract the **duty of performance** becomes binding. Failure by either party to perform the consideration promised the other breaches the contract.

A. Parties often put conditions into a contract that affect its performance. If something *must take place in the future before a party has a duty to perform*, it is called a **condition precedent**.

1. A **condition subsequent** *excuses* contractual performance if some future event takes place.
2. Under **concurrent conditions** each party's contractual performance is triggered by the other party's tending (offering) performance. A party must offer to perform before legally holding the other party for nonperformance.
3. **Express conditions** are those set forth in the contract. **Implied conditions** do not appear in the contract but are implied by law.

B.   A party to a contract may not always perfectly perform duties under it. Resolution of issues related to performance of contractual obligations often requires analysis of principles relating to formation as well as performance of contracts.   Courts generally recognize three levels of specific performance:

1.   *Complete performance* recognizes that a contracting party has fulfilled every duty required by the contract and is entitled to complete performance by the other party.
2.   *Substantial performance* represents a less-than-complete performance. A contracting party has honestly attempted to perform but has fallen short. One who substantially performs is entitled to the price promised by the other less that party's damages.
3.   *Material breach* is a level of performance below what is reasonably acceptable. A party that has materially breached a contract cannot sue the other party for performance and is liable for damages arising from the breach.
4.   In *Venture Media Ltd. V. Colt Plastics Co.*, the federal 4th Circuit court of appeals determined that a contract was made when Colt sent a Proposal Form (offer) to Venture and Venture sent a purchase order for $339,996.36 to Colt. Thus, Venture owed Colt for plastic goods delivered but not paid for and for goods specially manufactured for Venture even though undelivered. The court referred to the parties' prior course of dealing and did not find significant Venture's concerns about changes in terms.

XVII. A party to a contract is **discharged** when the party is released from all further obligation of performance. Events that discharge a party to a contract include:

A.   Occurrence of a condition subsequent

B.   Nonoccurrence of a condition precedent

C.   Material breach by the other party

D.   Legal surrender of the right to enforce performance (**waiver**)

E.   Mutual agreement to rescind

F.   Expiration of the statute of limitations for enforceability

G.   The substitution by agreement of one part for another on a contract (**novation**)

H.   Impossibility of performance

I.   Commercial impracticality

J. If the subject matter of the contract is destroyed, a party is discharged because of **impossibility of performance**. Likewise, when the party promising services becomes ill or dies, the party receives discharge from performances. Mere increased difficulty or reduced profitability, however, does not constitute impossibility of performance.

K. Under the UCC a party to a sale-of-goods contract receives discharge from performance because of **commercial impracticability**. The *impracticability* standard is not as difficult to meet as the *impossibility* standard. What constitutes impracticability depends on the circumstances of the situation.

XVIII. Legal enforceability of contractual agreements provides an important framework for promoting certainty and efficiency in commercial dealings. In general, trends in contract law do not affect the basic rules discussed in this chapter, but several trends deserve mention here:

A. As commercial transactions have grown increasingly complex, courts and legislatures have created more and more exceptions to traditional, fairly inflexible requirements of contract formation in an attempt to accommodate law to the actual reality of business dealings.

1. Open-ended contract terms and contract formation by course of dealings are exceptions to traditional rules. Courts' greater willingness to grant damages based on one party's reasonable reliance on another's promises rather than expectations under a formal contract is another example.

2. At the same time, the number of court cases focusing on information and performance of contracts has increased significantly over the last 20 years.

3. During the same period, more and more contracting parties do not litigate to enforce breached agreements, but use arbitration, mediation and negotiation when problems arise under contracts.

B. Although most large corporations have employment contracts for top management, lower-level workers do not have express contracts with their employees. However, courts in growing numbers have been willing to take statements made by employers in personnel manuals and other documents and use them as a basis for implying contract rights for employees.

C. A major trend in contract law has been the passage of many statutes affecting contracts between businesses and consumers. Government at the federal and state levels has stepped in to protect consumers as they make contracts with businesses. One such development has been enactment of "plain English" statutes in several states. These statutes require contracts to be written in a clearly understandable way. Insurance contracts have been a particular subject of such statutes.

XIX. In general, ethical concerns are increasingly reflected in how courts decide contractual disputes. While the traditional rules of contract law are still very important, they cannot always be used to predict what courts will do when one party acts in *bad faith* or violates the *expectations* that another party brings to a business arrangement.

COMPLETION EXERCISES

1. In a property-based legal system, contract is the way we exchange _____.

2. Article 2 of the Uniform Commercial Code (UCC) covers contracts for the sale of _____.

3. A contract can be express, implied in fact, or implied in _____, which is called _____-contract.

4. A(An) _____ contract is one in which the parties have not yet performed their agreement or promises to each other.

5. If the usual remedy for breach of contract is compensatory damages, the remedy when the contract subject matter is unique, like a piece of land, is _____.

6. The 5 essential elements required of a valid contract are offer, acceptance, consideration, capacity, and _____.

7. With regard to merchants, the _____ changes the mirror image rule.

8. _____ is receipt of a legal benefit or the suffering of a legal detriment.

9. _____ refers to a person's ability to be bound by a contract.

10. An agreement that requires a party to commit a crime or a tort is not a valid contract because it has no _____.

TRUE-FALSE SELECTIONS

1. _____ All contracts must be in written form to be valid.

2. _____ A voidable contract is one where one party can legally withdraw his/her promise without liability.

3. _____ Recission is a contract remedy under which each party must return the consideration given the other.

4. _____ In general contract law an offer must contain a specific promise and a specific demand.

5. _____ Under the U.C.C. a contract offer must not be indefinite.

6. _____ Unless the offer states otherwise, an acceptance legally binds the offeror when it is sent (or deposited).

7. _____ Prior consideration is no consideration.

8. _____ Promissory estoppel is an exception to the rule of consideration.

9. _____ A contract that arises because of undue influence is void.

10. _____ A duty of performance under a contract is discharged because of commercial impracticability and impossibility of performance.

MULTIPLE CHOICE PROBLEMS

1. Rob rolls back the mileage on a car he sells to Mary and Mary discovers the deception. The contract is:

   a. Valid.
   b. Void.
   c. Voidable.
   d. Unenforceable.

2. Tiffany offers to give John her car. John accepts. This agreement (select the most *correct* statement):

   a. Is legally valid.
   b. Lacks consideration by John to create a binding contract.
   c. Lacks a legal purpose and is thus void.
   d. Contains the five essential elements of a contract.

3. An offer will terminate and end the power of the offeree to bind the offeror in all of the following situations *except*:

   a. A counteroffer.
   b. Destruction of the subject matter of the contract.
   c. A termination provision of the offer.
   d. A firm offer.

4.   A contract is voidable for all of the following *except*:

    a.   Fraud.
    b.   Duress.
    c.   Unilateral mistake.
    d.   Mutual mistake.

5.   Select the most *incorrect* statement:

    a.   An exception to the Statute of Frauds is the part performance doctrine.
    b.   The parol evidence rule states that parties cannot vary the terms of a written contract by oral evidence of agreement before the written contract.
    c.   The law of assignment generally prohibits a sale of contract rights.
    d.   An intended third-party beneficiary under a contract can enforce its terms.

DISCUSSION ANALYSIS

Arrow Co. contracts with Rayfield Builders to construct a $4 million office building for Arrow. When Rayfield fails to fence the perimeter of the building area as required by contract, Arrow claims that its duties of performance are discharged and the contract terminated. Discuss.

Chapter
9

Torts in the Business Environment

The word **tort** means "wrong." Legally, a tort is a civil wrong other than a breach of contract. Tort involves defining when others injure an owner's resources, including the resources of the person. Tort law sets limits on how people can act and use their resources so they do not violate the right others have to their resources.

Legal wrongs inflicted on the resources of others *may be crimes as well as torts, but the law of tort itself is civil* rather than criminal. The usual remedy in a tort case is dollar damages. Behavior that constitutes a tort is called *tortuous* behavior. One who commits a tort is a *tortfeasor*.

Important to torts are the concepts of duty and causation. One is not liable for another's injury unless he or she has a *duty* toward the person injured. And, of course, there is usually no liability for injury unless one has *caused* the injury.

This chapter divides torts into three main categories: intentional torts, negligence torts, and strict liability torts. It also covers the topics of damages, which concerns the business community because huge damage awards, frequently against businesses, have become common in recent years. Finally, the chapter explores some alternatives to the current tort system, including workers' compensation.

INTENTIONAL TORTS

An important element in the following torts is **intent**, usually defined as the desire to bring about certain results. In some instances the meaning is broadened to include not only desired results but also results that are "substantially likely" to result from an action. The basic types of intentional torts include:

Assault and battery
Intentional infliction of mental distress
Invasion of privacy
False imprisonment and malicious prosecution
Trespass
Conversion
Defamation
Common law business torts

I.   Assault and battery are intentional torts.

       A.   An **assault** is the placing of another in immediate apprehension for his or her physical safety. "Apprehension" includes the expectation that one is about to be physically injured.

       B.   A **battery** is an illegal touching of another. As used here, "illegal" means that the touching is done without justification and without the consent of the person touched. The touching need not cause injury. Intentionally spitting on someone is a battery.

II.   Intentional **infliction of mental distress** is like a battery to the emotions. It arises from intentional, outrageous conduct that carries a strong probability of causing mental distress to the person at whom it is directed. Usually one who sues for infliction of mental distress must prove the defendant's behavior also caused physical symptoms, such as headaches or sleeplessness.

       In *Van Stan v. Fancy Colours & Co.*, the federal 7th Circuit court of appeals ruled that as a matter of law an employer's conduct in telephoning Van Stan at home when he was on vacation and terminating his employment, falsely telling him that the reason was for "low productivity," did not amount to intentional infliction of mental distress, even though the employer knew that Van Stan suffered from bipolar disorder. The court asserted that the employer's conduct "did not rise to the level of extreme and outrageous conduct...."

III.   **Invasion of privacy** is an intentional tort.

       A.   One example of invasion is the use of someone's likeness in advertising without their permission.

       B.   A second invasion of privacy is the defendant's intrusion upon the plaintiff's physical solitude. Illegal searches or invasions of home or possessions, illegal wiretapping, and persistent and unwanted telephoning can provide the basis for this invasion of privacy tort. The invasion of physical solitude must be highly objectionable to a reasonable person.

       C.   The third invasion of personal interest that gives rise to the invasion of privacy tort is the defendant's public disclosure of highly objectionable, private information about the plaintiff. A showing of such facts can be the basis for a cause of action, even if the information is true. Often, though not always, the disclosure of information must be made to the public. The news media are protected under the First Amendment when they publish information about public officials and other public figures.

IV. False imprisonment and malicious prosecution are also intentional torts.

    A. Claims of **false imprisonment** stem most frequently in business from instances of shoplifting. This tort is the *intentional, unjustified confinement* of a non-consenting person. Although most states have statutes that permit merchants or their employees to detain customers suspected of shoplifting, this detention must be a reasonable one.

    B. The tort of **malicious prosecution** is often called *false arrest.* Malicious prosecution arises from causing someone to be arrested criminally without proper grounds, as, for instance, when the arrest is accomplished simply to harass someone.

V. To **trespass** is to enter another's land without consent or to remain there after being asked to leave. A variation on the trespass tort arises when something, such as pollution, is placed on another's land without consent. Although the usual civil action for trespass asks for an injunction to restrain the trespasser, the action may also ask for damages. Trespass is often a crime as well as a tort. Intentional wrongdoing is frequently criminal.

VI. **Conversion** is the wrongful and unlawful exercise of dominion (power) and control over the personal property resources of another. Conversion deprives the proper owner of lawful rights in the resources. The deprivation may be either temporary or permanent, but it must constitute a serious invasion of the owner's rights. Even innocently performed conversion is a tort, as may be the case in certain instances of receiving something stolen.

VII. **Defamation** is the publication of untrue statements about another that hold up that individual's character or reputation to contempt and ridicule. *"Publication" means that the untruth must be made known to third parties.* If defamation is oral, it is called **slander**. Written defamation or defamation published over radio or television is termed **libel**. Punitive damages, as well as actual damages, may be assessed in defamation cases.

    A. False accusations of dishonesty or inability to pay debts frequently bring on defamation suits in business relationships. Employees often sue employers for defamation when employees are fired and employers have told others of the employees' dishonesty or incompetence.

    B. A corporation can also sue for defamation if untrue remarks discredit the way the corporation conducts its business or if they imply the company's entire management is dishonest or incompetent.

C. Because of the First Amendment, special rules regarding defamation apply to the news media. These media are not liable for the defamatory untruths they print about *public officials and public figures unless plaintiffs can prove the untruths were published with "malice" or with "reckless disregard for the truth."* Plaintiffs' verdicts in media defamation cases are often overturned by trial or appellate judges because of the constitutional protection given to speech and the media.

D. There are two basic defenses to a claim of defamation:

1. *Truth* is an absolute defense.
2. The second defense is that the statements arose from *privileged communications*. For example, statements made by legislators, judges, attorneys, and those involved in lawsuits are privileged under many circumstances.

E. Nearly one-third of all defamation suits are brought by employees against present and former employers. Because may of these suits arise when employers give unfavorable job references, many employers will now not give job references.

VIII. The tort of **fraud** is *an intentional misrepresentation of a material fact that is justifiably relied upon by someone to his or her injury.* An intentional misrepresentation is a lie, and it must be of a material fact, that is, an important one. The victim of the fraud must justifiably rely on the misrepresentation and must suffer some injury, usually a loss of money or other resource one owns.

A. Business frauds often involve the intentional misrepresentation of property or financial status.

B. Failing to disclose a material hidden fact is also fraud. There is fraud for failure to disclose as well as fraud in the concealment. In *Wells Fargo Bank v. Arizona Laborers, Teamsters, and Cement Masons*, the Supreme Court of Arizona ruled that a bank's liability was based on fraudulent concealment, i.e., that the bank had taken active steps to prevent the plaintiff from learning of the bank's client's poor financial situation. By actively *concealing* this material information, the bank becomes liable to the plaintiff even though the bank had no relationship to the plaintiff that would have imposed on the bank an obligation to actively *disclose* this information to the plaintiff.

C. Fraud can be committed in the hiring process when employers misrepresent to employees about conditions at a business that later affect employment. Other instances of business fraud can involve misrepresentation about products. Fraud is also the most common cyber-related tort.

D. Anti-fraud laws are a major weapon in the enforcement of good corporate governance. Much corporate misgovernance, especially by managers, arises because of misrepresentations of fact about corporate assets or liabilities. Many specific laws create civil and criminal liability for the fraud of corporate managers and other corporate agents.

E. Fraud violates the principles of property. Fraud does not respect the equal property rights of others.

IX. The label *business torts* embraces different kinds of torts that involve intentional interference with business relations.

A. **Injurious falsehood**, sometimes called *trade disparagement*, consists of the publication of untrue statements that disparage the owner's business or business product or its quality. It is similar to defamation of character, but in disparagement cases the plaintiff must establish the falsity of the defendant's statements as well as show actual damages arising from the untrue statements.

B. A second type of business tort is **intentional interference with contractual relations**. Probably the most common example of this tort involves one company raiding another for employees who are under contract to the second company. One of the most famous tort cases in history involved interference with a contract of merger.

NEGLIGENCE

The second major area of tort liability involves unreasonable behavior that causes injury. This area of tort is called **negligence**. In the United States *more lawsuits allege negligence than any other single cause of action*, mostly because of negligence in automobile accidents.

There are five separate elements that make up negligence. All must be present for the tort of negligence to exist.

1. Existence of a duty of care owed by the defendant to the plaintiff
2. Unreasonable behavior by the defendant that breaches the duty
3. Causation in fact
4. Proximate causation
5. An actual injury

X. A critical element of the negligence tort is **duty**. Without a duty to another person, one does not owe that person reasonable care.

A. *Duty usually arises out a person's conduct or activity.* A person doing something has a duty to use reasonable care and skill around others to avoid injuring them.

B. Usually, a person has no duty to avoid injuring others through *nonconduct.* There may be a moral responsibility, as to warn someone of danger, but no legal duty exists.

C. A person in a *special relationship* to another may have a duty to avoid unreasonable nonconduct. In recent years, negligence cases against businesses for nonconduct have grown dramatically. Many of these cases have involved failure to protect customers from crimes. The extent of a business's duty to protect customers is still evolving.

D. In *Iannelli v. Burger King Corp.*, the Supreme Court of New Hampshire decided that unruly behavior in a restaurant "could reasonably have been anticipated to escalate into acts that would expose patrons to an unreasonable risk of injury." Thus, the restaurant was liable to a patron for failing to deter unruly behavior that led to an assault and battery against the patron.

E. The duty to act reasonably also applies to professional providers. In most negligence cases, the standard of reasonableness is that of a *reasonable person.* In negligence cases involving professionals, however, the negligence standard applied is that of the *reasonable professional.* The negligence of professionals is called **malpractice**.

XI. At the core of negligence is the *unreasonable behavior* that breaches the duty of care that the defendant owes to the plaintiff.

A. The standard of reasonable care continues to evolve, however, and negligence is a mixed question of law and fact. Failure to exercise reasonable care can cost a company substantial sums.

B. A special type of aggravated negligence is **willful and wanton negligence**. This kind of negligence shows an extreme lack of due care, such as in negligent injuries cased by drunk drivers. The significance of this type of negligence is that the injured plaintiff can recover punitive damages as well as actual damages.

XII. In a negligence suit the plaintiff must prove that the defendant actually caused the injury. The courts term this **cause in fact**.

A. Often there are many ways to attribute causation. Courts leave questions of cause in fact almost entirely to juries as long as the evidence reveals that a defendant's alleged carelessness could have been a substantial, material factor in bringing about an injury.

B. A particular problem of causation arises where the carelessness of two or more tortfeasors contributes to cause the plaintiff's injury. Tort law handles such cases by making each tortfeasor *jointly* and *severally* liable for the entire judgment. The plaintiff can recover only the amount of the judgment, but she or he may recover it wholly from either of the tortfeasors or get a portion of the judgment from each.

XIII. In addition to proving that a defendant caused an injury in fact, a plaintiff must also establish **proximate cause**, or, more accurately, *legal cause*.

A. Those engaged in activity are legally liable only for the *foreseeable* risk that they cause. The plaintiff must have been one whom the defendant could reasonably expect to be injured by a negligent act.

B. Proximate cause also requires the injury to be caused *directly* by the defendant's negligence. Causes of injury that intervene between the defendant's negligence and the plaintiff's injury can destroy the necessary proximate causation.

XIV. There are two principle defenses to an allegation of negligence. The defendant must specifically raise these defenses to take advantage of them; in other words, they are *affirmative defenses*. These defenses are valid even though the defendant has actually been negligent.

A. As originally applied, the **contributory negligence** defense absolutely barred the plaintiff from recovery if the plaintiff's own fault contributed to the injury "in any degree, however slight." The trend today, however, is to offset the harsh rule of contributory negligence with the doctrine of **comparative responsibility** (also called *comparative negligence* and *comparative fault*). Under comparative principles, the plaintiff's contributory negligence compares the plaintiff's fault with the defendant's and reduces the damage award proportionally. Adoption of the comparative negligence principle seems to lead to more frequent and larger awards for plaintiffs.

B. If contributory negligence involves failure to use proper care for one's own safety, the **assumption-of-the-risk** defense arises from the plaintiff's knowing and willing undertaking of an activity made dangerous by the negligence of another.

1. Assumption of the risk defense may be implied from the circumstances, or it can arise from an express agreement. Some of these contractual agreements are legally enforceable, but many will be struck down by the courts as being against public policy, especially where a business possesses a vastly more powerful bargaining position than does its employer or customer.

2. It is important to a successful assumption-of-the-risk defense that the assumption was voluntary.

STRICT LIABILITY IN TORT

Strict liability is a catchall phrase for the legal responsibility for injury-causing behavior that is neither intentional nor negligent. Some strict liability torts are more "strict" than others. What ties them together is that they all impose legal liability, regardless of the intent or fault of the defendant.

XV. A major type of strict tort liability is **strict products liability,** for the commercial sale of defective products. In most states *any retail, wholesale, or manufacturing seller who sells an unreasonably dangerous defective product that causes injury to a user of the product is strictly liable.*

A. Strict products liability applies only to "commercial" sellers, those who normally sell products like the one causing injury and who place them in the stream of commerce.

B. An important concept in strict products liability is that of "defect." Strict liability only applies to the sale of unreasonably dangerous *defective* products. There are two kinds of defects:

1. **Production defects** arise when products are not manufactured to a manufacturer's own standards.
2. **Design defects** occur when a product is manufactured according to the manufacturer's standards, but the product injures a user due to its unsafe design. Lack of adequate warnings concerning inherently dangerous products can also be considered a design defect. Lawsuits based on design defects are common but often very controversial.

C. Strict products liability is useful in protecting those who suffer personal injury or property damage. It does not protect businesses that have economic losses due to defective products.

D. Under strict products liability, contributory negligence is not a defense but assumption of the risk is. Misuse is another defense that defendants commonly raise in product liability cases. Defendants have also argued that if a product meets some federally required standard, it cannot be considered defective; but most courts have ruled that federal standards set only a minimum requirement for safe design and that meeting them does not automatically keep a manufacturer from being sued for strict products liability.

XVI. Any time an employee is liable for tortuous acts in the *scope of employment*, the employer is also liable. This is because of the tort doctrine of **respondeat superior** ("let the master reply"). The reason for respondeat superior is that the employee is advancing the interests of the employer when the tortious act occurs. The employer has set the employee in motion and is responsible for the employee's acts.

    A.   Most respondeat superior cases involve employee negligence. Once the employee's fault is established, the employer is strictly liable, even if the employer warned the employee against the tortuous behavior. Some respondeat superior cases involve an employee's intentional tort.

    B.   Usually, the only defense the employer has to the strict liability of respondeat superior is that the employee was *outside* the scope of employment. Sometimes this defense is made using the language **frolic and detour**. An employee who is on a frolic or detour is no longer acting for the employer, such as when a delivery employee leaves his delivery route to go visit a friend and is involved in an accident.

    C.   An employer who must pay for an employee's tort under respondeat superior may legally sue the employee for reimbursement. In practice, this seldom happens, because the employer carries insurance, though the insurer that has paid a claim may then sue the employee who caused the claim.

XVII. In most states, the courts impose strict liability in tort for types of activities they call *ultrahazardous*. Transporting and using explosives and poisons fall under this category, as does keeping dangerous wild animals. Artificially storing large quantities of liquid in storage tanks or behind dams is also an ultrahazardous activity.

XVIII. There are other types of strict liability torts:

    A.   Many states impose strict liability upon tavern owners for injuries to third parties caused by their intoxicated patrons. The acts imposing this liability are called **dram shop acts**.

    B.   Common carriers, transportation companies licensed to serve the public, are also strictly liable for damage to goods being transported by them. They can, however limit their liability in certain instances through contractual agreement, and they are not liable for:

        1.   Acts of God, such as natural catastrophes
        2.   Action of an alien enemy
        3.   Order of public authority
        4.   The inherent nature of the goods, such as perishables
        5.   Misconduct of the shipper, such as improper packaging

DAMAGES

The crucial controversy in personal injury torts today may be in the area of damages. The average personal injury award has been increasing at nearly double the rate of inflation. The size of the damage award is largely determined by juries, but judges also play a role in damages, especially in damage instructions to the jury and in deciding whether to approve substantial damage awards.

XIX. The purpose of damages awarded in tort cases is to make the plaintiff whole again, at least financially.

    A. **Compensatory damages** are awarded for three major types of loss that potentially follow tort injury:

        1. Past and future medical expenses
        2. Past and future economic loss
        3. Past and future pain and suffering

    B. Calculation of damage awards creates significant problems, and compensatory damage awards for pain and suffering are particularly controversial. These awards measure jury sympathy as much as they calculate compensation for any financial loss. Due to the recent dramatic increases in the size of awards, many individuals and businesses may be underinsured for major tort liability.

XX. **Punitive damages** punish defendants for committing intentional torts and for negligent behavior considered "gross" or "willful and wanton."

    A. The key to the award of punitive damages is the defendant's motive. Usually it must be judged "malicious," "fraudulent," or "evil." Increasingly, punitive damages are also awarded for dangerously negligent conduct. These damages are also intended to deter future wrongdoing. Because they make an example out of the defendant, punitive damages are sometimes called *exemplary damages*.

    B. There is much controversy about how appropriate it is to award punitive damages against corporations for their economic activities. There are several main reasons for the controversy:

        1. Instead of punishing guilty management for wrongdoing, punitive damages may end up punishing innocent shareholders by reducing their dividends.
        2. Punitive damages are a windfall to the injured plaintiff, who has already received compensatory damages.

3.   Instead of punishing guilty companies, punitive damages may punish other companies, which have to pay increased insurance premiums, and may punish consumers, who ultimately pay higher prices.

4.   An award of punitive damages greatly resembles a criminal fine, yet the defendant who is subject to these criminal-type damages lacks the right to be indicted by a grand jury and cannot assert the right against self-incrimination. Also, the defendant is subject to a lower standard of proof than in a criminal case. Defendants in tort suits have challenged awards of punitive damages on a constitutional basis. Currently, the Supreme Court has ruled that punitive damages which exceed approximately 10 times the compensatory damages are unconstitutional.

ALTERNATIVES TO THE TORT SYSTEM

Of common law origin, the tort system has developed slowly over several centuries. The tort system has come under much criticism because of aspects of its development. The **contingency fee**, which permits a plaintiff to sue without first having to pay an attorney, encourages litigation. Even if a plaintiff loses a tort action, the plaintiff does not have to reimburse the defendant's often substantial legal expenses. Also, the easy availability of punitive damages and general concern over the role of the civil jury in handing down large damage awards contribute to the criticisms of the tort system.

Perhaps the most important problem of the tort system is that it is rarely a cost-effective way of compensating those who are injured by others. Litigation expenses, including legal fees, consume all but 40 to 60 percent of the insurance dollars paid out due to tort litigation.

There are many alternatives to tort litigation. Arbitration and no-fault insurance are two alternatives. Workers' compensation acts are a third alternative, which are important to the business community.

XXI.   About one hundred years ago, the tort system was largely replaced in the workplace by a series of workers' compensation acts. **Workers' compensation** laws are state statutes designed to protect employees and their families from the risks of accidental injury, death, or disease resulting from their employment. They impose a type of strict liability on employers for accidental workplace injuries suffered by their employees.

   A.   A common law that existed *prior to passage of the workers' compensation laws* did not give adequate protection to employees from the hazards of their work. It provided the employer with the means of escaping tort liability in most cases through three defenses:

      1.   *Assumption of the risk*, if the injured employee had been award of the dangers that existed

      2.   *Contributory negligence*, if the employee had in any way contributed to the injury through negligence

3. *The fellow servant rule*, if the negligence of another employee was at fault in the injury.

B. All states now have workers' compensation legislation, modeled on an 1897 act of the British Parliament. The laws vary a great deal from state to state, but certain general observations can be made about them:

1. The death, illness, or injury covered must arise *out of and in the course of the employment*. The negligence or fault of the employer in causing an on-the-job injury is not an issue.
2. Cash payments are awarded for loss of income. The payments are subject to a stated maximum and are calculated by using a percentage of the wages of the employee. Medical benefits are also provided for in the statutes.
3. In some states employers may elect to self-insure their workers' compensation risk. In other states all employers pay into a state fund used to compensate workers. The amounts of the employers' payments are based on the size of the payroll and the experience of the employer in having claims filed against the system by its employees.
4. Workers' compensation laws are usually administered exclusively by an administrative agency called the industrial commission or board, which has quasi-judicial powers. The agency's rulings are subject to review by the courts.

C. The test for determining whether an employer must pay workers' compensation to an employee are simply:

1. *Was the injury accidental?*
2. *Did the injury arise out of and in the course of employment?*

D. In *Pee v. AUM, Inc.*, the Supreme Court of South Carolina ruled that an employee's unexpected development of carpal tunnel syndrome was an "injury by accident" and thus covered by Worker's Compensation even though this "repetitive trauma has no definite time of occurrence."

E. The **exclusive remedy rule**, which is written into all compensation statutes, states that an employee's sole remedy against an employer for workplace injury or illness shall be workers' compensation.

1. In the past few years, courts in a few important jurisdictions have created exceptions to this rule, recognizing, in part, that workers' compensation laws do not adequately compensate badly injured workers.
2. The exclusive remedy rule does not protect employers who intentionally injure workers. That raises the question of how "intentional" an injury has to be.

F. Many problems confront the state workers' compensation system.

1. There are fifty separate nonuniform acts that make up the system. States that have broadened coverage have boosted the cost of doing business within their borders and so discourage business from locating or remaining there.
2. Workers' compensation payments have tripled in the last decade.
3. The nature of injuries suffered under workers' compensation programs is changing due to the movement of our national economy from a manufacturing to a service emphasis. In particular, the number of mental stress claims has risen.
4. Slowly developing occupational diseases present a major problem, making it difficult for affected workers or their families to recover workers' compensation years after the cause of the injury.

    G. One remedy for these problems would be federal reform. Congress, however, has not adopted a uniform federal act.

COMPLETION EXERCISES

1. A civil wrong other than a breach of contract is called a _____.

2. The desire to bring about certain results is called _____.

3. Three main categories of tort are _____, _____, and _____.

4. Punching someone, or even spitting on them intentionally, offensively, and without consent, constitutes the tort of _____.

5. Intentional wrongdoing frequently can constitute both a tort *and* a(an) _____.

6. Publishing untrue statements about another person that holds up that person to contempt or ridicule is called _____.

7. _____ is an intentional misrepresentation of a material fact that is justifiably relied on to the injury of someone.

8. More lawsuits allege _____ than any other single cause of action.

9. Professional negligence is called _____.

10. Someone who causes injury while using explosives or poisons can be held strictly liable for _____.

TRUE-FALSE SELECTIONS

1. _____ The doctrine that holds employers liable for the torts (usually negligence) of their employees within the scope of employment is called respondeat superior.

2. _____ Past and future pain and suffering is not a part of compensatory damages for tort.

3. _____ Punitive damages that exceed 10 times compensatory damages have been held unconstitutional.

4. _____ Worker's compensation laws apply the fellow servant rule.

5. _____ For an injured employee to recover worker's compensation the injury must be accidental.

6. _____ Under the exclusive remedy rule, an injured employee can sue the employer for negligence.

7. _____ The intentional, unjustified confinement of someone is called malicious prosecution.

8. _____ In making a contract, concealing material facts and failing to disclose hidden material facts can constitute fraud.

9. _____ To be held liable, the plaintiff must have been one whom the defendant could reasonably expect to be injured by the negligent act.

10. _____ Under comparative negligence, the defendant is responsible for the full amount of damages caused to the plaintiff.

MULTIPLE CHOICE PROBLEMS

1. It may be immoral not to help an injured person, but a pedestrian who witnesses an automobile accident does not usually legally have to assist the injured because:

   a. There is no intent present.
   b. There is no duty to assist.
   c. The injuries did not arise in the scope of employment.
   d. The injuries were not foreseeable.

2. Select the most *incorrect* statement about strict products liability:

   a. It applies only to commercial sellers.
   b. Contributory negligence is not a defense to it.
   c. Assumption of the risk is not a defense to it.
   d. It does not protect businesses that have economic losses due to defective products.

3.   Roger, an Acme Co. employee, hates bugs. One day a roach crawls across the ceiling of the office where Roger is working. Roger stands on a chair to kill the roach with his shoe, but while slapping at the insect, falls and breaks his arm. Acme Co.'s best defense against Roger's worker's compensation claim is that Roger's injury:

   a.   Did not arise out of employment.
   b.   Did not arise in the course of employment.
   c.   Was not accidental.
   d.   Was the result of an assumption of the risk.

4.   A store manager grabs the arm of an obnoxious customer and hustles him out of the store. The manager and the store may be liable for:

   a.   Invasion of privacy.
   b.   Intentional infliction of mental distress.
   c.   Assault.
   d.   Battery.

5.   A jury awards a plaintiff $2.4 million against a retailer, a wholesaler, and a foreign manufacturer in a products liability case. Because of joint and several liability, the plaintiff can collect (select the most *correct* statement):

   a.   The entire amount of damages from any one of the defendants.
   b.   No more than $800,000 (1/3 of the amount) from each defendant.
   c.   No more than $1.2 million from each of two defendants if the third is bankrupt.
   d.   No more than $1.2 million from each of two defendants if one of them is not available to the court's jurisdiction.

Chapter 9

DISCUSSION ANALYSIS

Does the tort system need reforming? If so, in what ways? Discuss.

Chapter
10

The Criminal Law and Business

This chapter discusses the criminal law as it is related to business. A crime is a wrong against society. Some crimes, such as murder or rape, are said to be *malum in se* or inherently wrongful. Conduct which is not inherently wrongful may become a crime because a legislative body decides that it is in the interest of society to prohibit certain conduct, such as price-fixing by competitors.

Employees of a business are more likely to commit nonviolent crimes than violent ones. These crimes often have a significant negative impact on a business as well as on the economy and society itself. **White-collar crimes** are those committed by business entities and their officers, accountant, lawyers, and other employees who work at a desk rather than on the factory floor. They are almost always nonviolent crimes such as accounting fraud and other types of fraud, bribery, false statements, money laundering, racketeering, forgery, and income tax evasion.

A corporation can be punished with a fine; or it can be ordered out of business, a type of death sentence. Individuals guilty of a crime can be fined, imprisoned, or banned from certain types of work. White-collar crimes may be committed with the intent to harm the employer (embezzlement, selling trade secrets, or payment of false invoices, for example) or to benefit the employer, with the intent to harm others, such as competitors or customers.

It is estimated that American businesses lose over $100 billion annually as a result of crimes by employees that are intended to harm their employers. Companies must charge customers higher prices to make up for losses due to these white-collar crimes. This chapter will help you understand the consequences of white-collar crime so that you will not be involved in criminal conduct and will be encouraged to prevent it by others.

I. Crimes can be classified as *felonies* or *misdemeanors*, based on the punishment imposed in the event of a conviction.

   A. **Felonies** are punishable by fine or imprisonment in a penitentiary for a period of one year or more. Felony cases begin with **indictment** by a grand jury, which determines that there is sufficient evidence to warrant a trial. A petit jury then determines the guilt or innocence of the accused.

   B. **Misdemeanors** are punishable by a fine or a jail sentence of less than one year. Misdemeanors are usually commenced by the government filing a charge called an **information**.

II. Criminal conduct involves a combination of *act* plus *intent*.

A. Many criminal statutes use the word **willfully** to define criminal intent. Willfully means that the act was committed voluntarily and purposely with the specific intent to disobey or to disregard the law.

B. Some criminal statutes use the word **knowingly** to describe criminal conduct. Knowingly means the criminal act was done voluntarily and was not a mistake or accident. Knowledge can be inferred if the accused deliberately blinded himself or herself to the existence of a fact.

C. A few laws provide that conduct which is reckless is a crime even though the one doing the act does not intend to do harm, as with reckless driving. *Reckless disregard for the truth* is often the basis of white-collar criminal conduct.

CRIMINAL CASES

Criminal cases are brought by public officials such as a United States attorney or a states attorney (also called "district attorney") on behalf of the people. The defendant in criminal cases has three possible pleas to enter to an indictment charging violation:

1. Guilty
2. Not guilty
3. **Nolo contendere**, Latin for "no contest." This plea allows sentencing just as if the defendant had pleaded or been found guilty. The defendant avoids the cost of trial as well as the effect of a guilty plea, such as creating a strong basis for a subsequent civil damage suit.

III. The Fifth Amendment to the U.S. Constitution provides that before anyone can be tried for a capital or otherwise infamous crime, there must be a presentment or an indictment by a grand jury. This protection prevents political trials and justified prosecutions by placing a group of citizens between prosecutors and persons accused of major crimes.

A. A **grand jury** normally consists of 23 citizens, at least 16 of who must be present for the grand jury to hear evidence and vote on cases. For an indictment to be returned, a majority of the grand jury must find that a crime has been committed and that the evidence warrants the accused's standing trial. This determination is **probable cause**.

B. Since probable cause is the standard for grand jury action, it is not difficult to obtain an indictment. Even an indicted person, however, is entitled to the **presumption of innocence** – to be presumed innocent until found guilty by a petit jury.

C.   Grand juries also serve as an investigative body and occupy a unique role in our criminal justice system.

1.   Persons who are the targets or subjects of investigations may be called before grand juries and may be questioned under oath about possible illegal conduct. They are entitled to invoke their Fifth Amendment privilege against self-incrimination and may refuse to answer questions. They may consult with counsel and benefit from legal advice at any time; however, *defense counsel is not allowed to accompany a witness into the grand jury room.*

2.   Grand jurors may also subpoena business records. Witnesses may be called and questioned about documents and records delivered in response to a subpoena.

D.   Proper functioning of the grand jury system depends upon the secrecy of the proceedings. This secrecy protects the innocent accused from disclosure of the accusations made against him or her before the grand jury. In judicial proceedings, however, transcripts of grand jury proceedings may be obtained if necessary to avoid possible injustice.

IV.   A **conspiracy** is an agreement or a "kind of partnership" for criminal purposes in which each member becomes the agent or partner of every other member. Conspiracy to commit a criminal offense is itself a criminal offense. No formal agreement is required, nor do members of the conspiracy need to plan all the details of the scheme.

A.   The essence of a conspiracy offense is *the making of the agreement itself followed by the commission of any overt act.* An **overt act** is any transaction or event knowingly committed by a conspirator in an effort to accomplish some object of the conspiracy, even an act that is innocent on its own. Planning to rob a bank is not itself a crime. However, buying masks to further the plan is an overt act that makes the planners criminally responsible for conspiracy.

B.   To convict a person of conspiracy, it is not necessary for the government to prove the conspirators actually succeeded in accomplishing their intended crime. The evidence must show the four elements of a conspiracy beyond a reasonable doubt:

1.   Two or more persons, in some way or manner, came to a mutual understanding to try to accomplish a common and unlawful plan.

2.   The defendant willfully became a member of such conspiracy.

3.   During the existence of the conspiracy, one of the conspirators knowingly committed at least one of the overt acts described in the indictment.

4.   Such overt act was knowingly committed in an effort to carry out or accomplish some object of the conspiracy.

C. A person may be convicted of conspiracy even if he or she did not know all the details of the unlawful scheme.

    1. If a defendant has an understanding of the unlawful nature of a plan and knowingly and willfully joins in that plan on one occasion, that is sufficient evidence for conviction.

    2. A person may become a coconspirator through participation in routine business meetings if the meetings are followed by illegal conduct.

    3. If illegal plans or conduct are in the planning process, it is imperative that persons not wishing to participate in the conspiracy *disassociate themselves from the process immediately upon discovery of the illegal scheme.*

    4. Conspiracy charges or their threat are often used to get those who know about a crime to testify against others who are more involved.

D. Circumstantial evidence may prove a conspiracy.

    1. A person can be charged with conspiracy even if the individual becomes involved after the conspiracy is stopped and the criminal conduct does not occur.

    2. The fact that law enforcement discovers a plot to commit a crime and thwarts it does not prevent prosecution for a conspiracy. The threat of a conspiracy is a public danger beyond the commission of the crime because it is likely that the conspirators will commit more crimes.

E. A party may be guilty even though one of the coconspirators is acquitted by a jury. In *United States v. Hughes Aircraft Co.*, the federal Ninth Circuit court of appeals ruled that a corporation (Hughes) could be held liable for the conspiracy of its managerial employees and could be held liable in spite of the fact that the employee who criminally defrauded and made false statements to the government regarding a defense contract was acquitted (found not guilty).

V. If a person acts under the direction of someone accused of criminal activities, this person might be held responsible for **aiding and abetting** in the commission of the crime. The charge of aiding and abetting is similar to the allegation of participating in a conspiracy. The individual accused of aiding and abetting did not necessarily commit the same criminal acts of others.

A. Allegations of aiding and abetting, like those of conspiracy, are used to indict persons only minimally involved with the actual substantive crime. To avoid going to trial, many accused of these crimes will agree to testify against those more directly involved in return for lesser punishment or even immunity from prosecution.

B. At the state level, a charge similar to the federal charge of aiding and abetting is that a person is an **accessory** to a crime.

1. An *accessory before the crime* assists in preparation for the crime and may be punished the same as the person who committed the crime.
2. An *accessory after the fact* is accused of being involved after the crime is committed and is subject to specific penalties as provided for in laws declaring assistance of criminals to be unlawful.

CONSTITUTIONAL ISSUES

The Bill of Rights contains protections for persons accused of crimes. These first ten amendments to the Constitution were adopted to overcome the concern that the Constitution granted power to a central government at the expense of the individual citizen. These rights protect not only persons accused of crimes but also businesses from improper regulation.

VI. The Fourth Amendment protects individuals and corporations from unreasonable searches and seizures. It primarily protects persons from unwarranted intrusions on their privacy by *requiring the police to obtain a court order called a search warrant.*

A. Generally, the search warrant must be obtained by police prior to a search of a person, any premises, or other property, such as the trunk of an automobile. Before a court will issue a search warrant, *the police must offer evidence that a crime has been committed, and there is cause to believe the intended search will assist in its investigation.*

B. To protect police officers, courts have held that *officers making an arrest do not need a search warrant to search that person and the immediate area around that person for weapons.*

1. Officers are given far more latitude in searching an automobile than in searching a person, a home, or a building.
2. The right to search for evidence extends to the premises of persons not suspected of criminal conduct, such as attorneys and newspaper offices.
3. Electronic surveillance has been held not to violate the Fourth Amendment is used pursuant to a court-authorized order.

C. Fourth Amendment protection extends to certain civil matters, such as the inspections of buildings for code violations, if the owner objects.

D. *In pervasively regulated industries,* the privacy interests of the business are weakened by the government's interest in enforcing regulations. Generally, in these businesses a warrantless inspection of premises may well be reasonable within the meaning of the Fourth Amendment, while a warrantless inspection of a private residence is unconstitutional.

1. Random surveys for compliance with federal standards (for example, safety and health standards) should be expected by businesses required to conform to the standards.
2. Employees of some businesses, such as airline pilots who are alcohol and drug tested, do not have Fourth Amendment protection because of public policy.
3. Presenting oneself at an airport checkpoint or border crossing is also an irrevocable consent to a warrantless search.

VII. The Fifth Amendment is best known for its protection against compulsory self-incrimination. When a person giving testimony pleads "the Fifth," he or she is exercising the right to this protection against being compelled to testify against himself or herself.

A. The Fifth Amendment does not protect the accused from being compelled to produce real or physical evidence, such as fingerprints and bodily fluids.

B. In order to be testimonial and protected, an accused's communication must itself, explicitly or implicitly, relate to a factual assertion or disclosure information.

C. In issues concerning the Fifth Amendment and business proceedings, a businessperson may not be required to testify against himself or herself in any governmental hearing. However, the protection against compulsory self-incrimination does not protect a *corporation* from having to produce records prepared in the ordinary course of business. The Fifth Amendment does not prevent the use of written evidence, such as business records, even if they are incriminating.

D. The only business records protected by the Fifth Amendment privilege against compulsory self-incrimination are those belonging to a sole proprietorship.

E. In determining which documents belong to a corporation, and are thus subject to subpoena, and which documents belong to an individual, and thus *may be* protected under the Fifth Amendment, the courts use a balancing approach.

VIII. The **Double Jeopardy** Clause of the Fifth Amendment provides that "no person [shall] be subject for the same offense to be twice put in jeopardy of life or limb." Individuals cannot be tried twice by the same governmental entity for the same crime based on the same factual situation.

A. If an illegal activity violates both federal and state laws, double jeopardy does not prohibit two trials, one in federal court and the other in the state court system.

B. In *Hudson v. United States*, the U.S. Supreme Court ruled that a "Civil Money Penalty" accused by the Comptroller of the Currency against bankers who had violated federal banking statutes was not criminal in nature and did not prohibit subsequent prosecution and conviction of the bankers under the double jeopardy prohibition.

IX. The Sixth Amendment provides multiple protection in *criminal* cases. Essentially, its protections give you the right:

A. To a speedy and public trial

B. To a trial by jury – The jury, drawn from a fair cross section of the community, guards against the exercise of arbitrary power by using the commonsense judgment of the community against the overzealous or mistaken prosecutor. The jury's perspective on facts is used in preference to the professional or, perhaps, biased response of a judge.

C. To be informed of the charge against you

D. To confront your accuser

E. To subpoena witnesses in your favor

F. To have the assistance of an attorney – The right to an attorney exists in any cases where incarceration is a possible punishment. It exists at every stage of the proceeding, commencing with an investigation that centers on a person as the accused. This provision is complicated with reference to corporations, where an attorney who represents the corporation may not also be acting in the best interests of the individual employees of the corporation.

SPECIFIC CRIMES

The following federal crimes are relevant to the conduct of business. Many of these crimes result in civil suits against a business for dollar damages as well as criminal prosecutions.

X. A major recent rend in the criminal law is for states to charge corporate officials with crimes such as assault and battery, reckless **endangerment of workers**, and a form of accidental homicide when a worker is injured or killed on the job if adequate safety precautions are not in place. Some states require employers to warn employees of life-threatening hazards in the workplace, and it is likely more will do so in the near future.

XI. Laws that make it a crime to interfere with government investigations use the term **obstruction of justice** in a comprehensive manner to encompass all steps and stages from the inception of an investigation to the conclusion of a trial. Any act made with the intent to obstruct either the legislative investigations or law enforcement may be a crime.

Otherwise lawful actions can become obstruction of justice if done with corrupt intent. Destruction of business documents in anticipation of a criminal investigation is a good example of obstruction of justice.

XII. It is a federal crime for anyone *willfully to make a false statement to a federally insured financial institution.* To prove the crime of a false statement to a bank, the prosecutor must prove beyond a reasonable doubt that the false statement or report was made with the intent to influence the action of the insured financial institution upon an application, advance, commitment, loan, or any change or extension thereof.

    A. An *insured bank* is one whose deposits are insured by the Federal Deposit Insurance Corporation. An insured credit union is one whose deposits are insured by the National Credit Union Administration.

    B. A statement or report is *willfully false* when made if it relates to a material fact and is untrue and is then known to be untrue by the person making it. A fact is *material* if it is important to the decision to be made by the officers or employees of the institution involved and has the capacity of influencing them in making that decision. It is not necessary to prove that the institution was, in fact, influenced or misled.

XIII. The U.S. Code makes it a federal crime for anyone willfully and knowingly to make a false or fraudulent statement to a department or agency of the United States.

    A. The false statement must be related to a material matter, and the defendant must have acted willfully and with knowledge of the falsity. It is not necessary to show that the government agency was in fact deceived or misled. *Businesses must take care to avoid puffery or exaggerations regarding any matter that is reported to a federal agency.*

XIV. *Larceny,* commonly referred to as theft or stealing, *is the unlawful taking of personal property with the intent to deprive the rightful owner of it permanently.*

    A. Larceny by violence or threat such as with a gun is *robbery.*

    B. *Burglary* is breaking into a building with the intent to commit a felony.

    C. Embezzlement, committed when an employee appropriates funds of his employer to his or her own use, is a common white-collar crime. Padding expense accounts and use of company property without permission are other forms of employee larceny.

    D. Larceny at the top management level of corporations usually has the appearance of being legal. If the business purchases equipment, ostensibly for the business, but in fact used only by an officer, or if it loans large sums to an officer with no expectation of repayment, larceny has occurred. In these cases, what belongs to the shareholders is being stolen.

XV. The U.S. Code contains several provisions making it criminal to carry out a scheme to defraud. (See Chapter 8 for the classic definition and elements of fraud.)

    A.   In addition to mail and wire fraud, covered in section XVI, there are provisions making it a crime for anyone to transport someone or induce someone to travel in interstate commerce for the purpose of executing a scheme to defraud that person of money or property having a value of $5,000 or more.

    B.   Federal law also outlaws fraud by use of counterfeit access devices. An *unauthorized access device* is any access device (bank cards, account numbers, plate, codes, etc.) that is lost, stolen, expired, revoked, cancelled, or obtained with intent to defraud.

    C.   The Securities Exchange Act of 1934 and Rule 10(b)5 of the Securities and Exchange Commission cover fraud in the purchase or sale of a security like stocks or bonds (see Chapter 16). Many prosecutions of violations of securities fraud are the result of accounting fraud based upon false financial statements.

    D.   The Department of Justice has specialized investigative units concentrating on healthcare fraud. Criminal law enforcement against businesses in this area usually involves false claims under the False Claims Act submitted for payments under government programs. Healthcare fraud investigations are aided by information revealed in "whistle-blower" suits brought by former corporate insiders under the federal False Claims Act. This act allows a citizen "relater" who successfully brings a lawsuit that recovers fraudulently obtained federal funds to keep a portion of the recovery as a bounty.

XVI. Various provisions of the U.S. Code make it illegal to use either the Postal Service or electronic means of interstate communication to carry out a scheme to defraud. These provisions provide significant criminal penalties for **mail or wire fraud**. Each use of mail or wire communications constitutes a separate violation, so fines and imprisonment sanctions can be enormous.

    A.   Courts have held that the use of mail or wire communication (including radio, television, telephone, or Internet) can be proven by circumstantial evidence. The accused person does not have to actually place a letter in the mail or send an e-mail message. Others may do so. In *Schmuck v. United States*, the U.S. Supreme Court ruled that the mailing of customers' title-application forms by automobile dealers was adequate use of the mail to apply the federal mail fraud statute against someone who rolled back odometers on cars and then sold them to unwitting dealers who resold them to customers. The Court noted that final registration of title (ownership) "was essential to the perpetuation of Schmuck's scheme."

B. Mail and wire fraud covers a wide range of wrongful activities, however the prosecutor must establish the presence of a **scheme to defraud**. This phrase includes a plan or program designed to take from a person the intangible right of honest services, in other words, a course of action that deceives others.

C. *A statement or representation is false or fraudulent if it is known to be untrue or is made with reckless indifference as to its truth or falsity.* It may also be false or fraudulent if it constitutes a half-truth or effectively conceals a material fact with intent to defraud.

D. **Intent to defraud** means to act knowingly and with the specific intent to deceive someone, ordinarily for the purpose of causing some financial loss to another or bringing about some financial gain to oneself. The government must establish beyond a reasonable doubt that the defendant acted with specific intent to defraud. There is no need to prove actual damage.

E. **Good faith** is the defense often asserted against the allegations of an intent to defraud indictment. If the defendant simply made a mistake in judgment or an error in management, there was no intent to defraud.

XVII. **Bankruptcy crimes** are those committed in the course of bankruptcy proceedings, which are conducted in federal courts. It is a crime for the bankruptcy debtor to falsify the information filed in the proceedings. It is also a crime for anyone to present a false claim in any bankruptcy proceeding.

A. The felony offense of **concealment** is committed by anyone who conceals resources belonging to the estate of a debtor in bankruptcy. It must be fraudulently done, with intent to deceive or cheat any creditor, trustee, or bankruptcy judge. The acts of concealment may have begun *before* as well as be committed *after* the bankruptcy proceeding began.

B. It is no defense that the concealment may have proved unsuccessful, nor is it a defense that there was no demand by any officer of the court or creditor for the property alleged to have been concealed.

XVIII. The most controversial of the federal criminal laws relating to business is the Racketeer Influenced and Corrupt Organizations Act, commonly known as **RICO**. This law imposes criminal and civil liability upon those businesspersons who engage in certain *prohibited activities* and who engage in interstate commerce.

A. Each prohibited activity is defined to include, as one necessary element, proof of either of a *pattern of racketeering activity* or of *collection of unlawful debt*.

B. **Racketeering** is defined in RICO to mean "any act or threat involving" specified state law crimes, and "act" indictable under various specified federal statutes, and certain federal "offenses." *Pattern* is not defined other than to say that it *"requires at least two acts of racketeering activity"* within a ten-year period. RICO liability can extend to any person who:

   1. Uses or invests income from prohibited activities to acquire an interest in or to operate an enterprise.
   2. Acquires or maintains an interest in or control of an enterprise.
   3. Conducts or participates in the conduct of an enterprise while being employed by or associated with it.
   4. In *H.J. Inc. v. Northwestern Bell* the U.S. Supreme Court determined that under RICO a telephone company could be found to be engaging in a pattern of racketeering by giving over a six-year period numerous bribes to members of the public utilities commission, such as paying for parties, meals, sports tickets, and airline tickets.

C. The RICO statute also makes it unlawful for any person employed by or associated with any enterprise to conduct or participate in a violation. When a person incorporates and that person is the president and sole shareholder of the corporation, courts have ruled that there are two separate entities and both may have RICO liability.

D. RICO suits have been filed against accounting firms, brokerage houses, banks, and other businesses. RICO cases constitute almost 10 percent of the caseload in federal courts, and more than 75 percent of these lawsuits involve allegations of fraud.

E. RICO provides drastic remedies. Conviction for a violation of RICO carries severe criminal penalties and forfeitures of illegal proceeds, *triple damages*, cost, and attorneys' fees.

XIX. One of the most significant trends in the criminal law is the result of the rapid increase in use of the Internet. Billions of dollars are flowing through cyberspace, and criminals are taking advantage of the system. Electronic theft is not limited to money.

A. Cybercrime is more difficult to detect than crimes that preceded the Internet. Proof based on digital evidence about anonymous persons seldom leads to convictions.

B. Electronic crimes are most often committed by employees. They have been caught issuing corporate stock to themselves, stealing and selling company plans to competitors, as well as committing other crimes. Typically, investors have little or

123

no knowledge of losses resulting from cybercrime, as such losses are usually hidden in cost of goods sold or in bad debt write-offs. To prevent electronic crimes, access to confidential information should be limited and carefully controlled.

XX. In an effort to make the criminal justice system more just and help ensure that similar crimes receive similar sentences, in the late 1980s a federal sentencing commission developed **sentencing guidelines** for federal crimes. The commission used a mathematical approach, assigning a number to each type of crime and to all attending circumstances. Punishment and deterrence are goals of the guidelines.

A. The law authorizes judges to depart from the guidelines when they encounter factors not considered by the commission. If a judge intends to impose a sentence in excess of the guidelines, the defendant must be informed in advance of this fact and of the reasons for the departure. In most cases, judges determine the sentence by relying on a probation officer's report.

B. Guidelines for sentencing corporations and other organizations emphasize monetary penalties, because corporations cannot be jailed. In most criminal cases involving organizations, however, corporate officers can also be charged. The guidelines are designed to provide adequate deterrence and incentives for organizations to maintain internal mechanisms for preventing detecting and reporting criminal conduct.

C. In *United States v. Steven Nesenblatt*, the federal 9th Circuit court of appeals upheld the district court's enhancement of a criminal sentence in a $260 million bank fraud scheme involving the defendant's various business enterprises. The case illustrates how the Federal Sentencing Guidelines apply to enhance or reduce someone's criminal sentence.

XXI. The corporate governance scandals in the last few years have resulted in changes and new developments in society's approach to white collar crime.

A. *One of the important trends is to use income tax evasion as the theory to be used against white-collar criminals.* Income tax evasion is much easier to prove than crimes such as obstruction of justice.

B. A second important trend is the government's practice of starting an investigation of lower middle level managers, charging them with conspiracy if wrongful conduct is found, and then *plea bargaining* with them, agreeing to drop or reduce the charges in exchange for testimony against persons higher in the organizational chart. Prosecutors are able in this way to work their way up to the real target of the investigation – top management. Investigations may also proceed horizontally to catch friends and associates who assist in illegal conduct.

C. White-collar criminals may be treated as street thugs, being handcuffed and led to jail with TV cameras running. Prosecutors often insist on high sums for bail, and they may object to the source of the bail funds, if they were illegally obtained. Prosecutors may also insist on some prison time for defendants who plea bargain. Criminal punishment often includes seizure of assets as well.

COMPLETION EXERCISES

1. It is estimated that American businesses lose more than _____ annually to employee crime.

2. Crimes punishable by one year or more imprisonment are called _____, by less than one year imprisonment are called _____.

3. Nolo contendere is Latin that means _____.

4. Persons charged with felony crimes have a constitutional right to be indicted by a _____.

5. The making of a criminal plan followed by an overt act toward committing the crime is itself a crime called _____.

6. At the state level, aiding and abetting a crime is called being a(an) _____ to the crime.

7. The constitutional requirement of a search warrant is found in the _____ Amendment.

8. The constitutional prohibition against self-incrimination is found in the _____ Amendment.

9. The constitutional right to the assistance of an attorney is found in the _____ Amendment.

10. Destruction of business documents in anticipation of a particular criminal investigation is an example of the crime of _____.

TRUE-FALSE SELECTIONS

1. _____ It is a federal crime negligently to make a false statement to a federally-insured bank in order to obtain a loan.

2. _____ For an employee to misappropriate the employer's funds is a crime called embezzlement.

3. _____ Many federal acts prohibit fraud that has a substantial impact on interstate commerce.

4. _____ A common defense to the crime of fraud is that the defendant acted with "good faith."

5. _____ A violation of RICO requires there to be "at least four acts of racketeering activity" within an eight year period.

6. _____ RICO cases constitute almost 10 percent of the entire caseload of the federal courts.

7. _____ In most instances when corporations are charged with crime, corporate officers can also be criminally charged.

8. _____ A prosecutor agreeing to reduce or drop charges against an employee, perhaps due to an agreement to testify against someone higher up in a business, is an example of plea bargaining.

9. _____ The U.S. Code prohibits mail and wire fraud.

10. _____ The Fifth Amendment constitutionally guarantees someone accused of crime the right to trial by jury.

MULTIPLE CHOICE PROBLEMS

1. Select the most *incorrect* statement about the Fifth Amendment right against self incrimination:

   a. The right does not protect an accused from being compelled to produce real or physical evidence.
   b. The right does not protect a corporation from having to produce records prepared in the ordinary course of business.
   c. The right protects corporate CEOs from having to testify against themselves in an administrative hearing.
   d. The right protects an accused from being compelled to produce bodily fluids.

2. Select the most *incorrect* statement about grand jury proceedings:

   a. Defense counsel (attorney) may accompany a witness into the grand jury room.
   b. Grand jurors may subpoena business records.
   c. Grand jury proceedings are considered "secret."
   d. A grand jury indictment is based on the standard of "probable cause."

3.   The defendant in a criminal case may plead any one of the following except:

    a.   Guilty.
    b.   Not guilty.
    c.   Res judicata.
    d.   Nolo contendere.

4.   Cassandra is arrested and prosecuted by the state of Kentucky for hiding in her house a Louisville business owner wanted for criminal fraud. She is most likely to be prosecuted for which of the following crimes?

    a.   Aiding and abetting.
    b.   Accessory before the fact.
    c.   Accessory after the fact.
    d.   Conspiracy.

5.   RICO offenses, mail and wire crimes, Securities Exchange Act violations, and various Medicare-related health care crimes are usually based on:

    a.   Conspiracy.
    b.   Aiding and abetting.
    c.   Fraud.
    d.   Larceny of various types.

Chapter 10

DISCUSSION ANALYSIS

Discuss how the authorities use criminal charges like conspiracy and aiding and abetting to further corporate governance.

Chapter
11

Corporate Governance and Business Organizations

The phrase *corporate governance* has at least two meanings. This chapter discusses both of these meanings.

First, corporate governance relates to how business organizations are operated, led, or governed. The word *corporate* in the phrase *corporate governance* relates to the combination of people rather than being limited to only the business organization known as a corporation.

The second meaning of corporate governance concerns how the law provides regulation of business organization. For the most part, state laws govern the legal entities available to businesspeople through which business is conducted.

This chapter addresses both statutory and common law governing business organizations and how these organizations do business. It also focuses on factors used to select the best organizational form, the various choices of organizations, and agency principles related to the performance of business transactions.

I. The number of owners of a business organization is an important factor in its organizational form. There are three possible basic forms and several hybrid forms, which will be discussed in sections 7-12 of this chapter. There are two important terms relating to the number of owners of a business organization:

   A. **Closely held** organizations are owned by only a few persons. Family-owned and operated businesses are common examples of closely held organizations. These businesses are usually the ones facing the decision of selecting an appropriate organizational form.

   B. **Publicly held** organizations may be owned by hundreds, if not thousands, of persons, as in the case with those whose stock is traded on a public exchange. The form of organization of these businesses is usually a corporation.

Chapter 11

FACTORS TO CONSIDER WHEN SELECTING A BUSINESS' ORGANIZATIONAL FORM

1. The cost of creating the organization
2. The continuity or stability of the organization
3. The control of decisions
4. The personal liability of the owners
5. The taxation of the organization's earnings and its distribution of profits to the owners

II. The word *creation* refers to the legal steps necessary to form a particular business organization.

   A. Cost of creation is usually not a major factor in considering which form of business organization a person will choose to operate a business.

   B. The most significant creation-related issues are how long it will take to create a particular organization and how much paperwork is involved.

III. The *continuity* of an organization is associated with its stability or durability.

   A. When selecting the best organizational form for a business activity, the crucial issue with respect to continuity is the method by which a business organization can be dissolved. A **dissolution** is any change in the ownership of an organization that changes the legal existence of the organization.

   B. The questions to ask about dissolution are:

      1. Is the organization easily dissolved?
      2. What impact does a dissolution of the organizational form have on the business activity of that organization?

IV. An issue of vital importance to business owners is the factor of managerial *control*: who is managing the organization?

   A. When businesspeople have equal voices in management, difficulties can arise when they disagree, unless there are methods in place to resolve potential deadlocks.

   B. If business activities are not to suffer, or the organization even to fail, consideration of potential dispute resolution mechanisms is essential when selecting a form for a business venture.

V.   The *liability* factor in business organizations concerns to what degree is the owner of a business personally liable for the debts of the organization? This is a very important factor to consider with regard to each of the organizational forms presented in this chapter.

    A.   Generally, businesspeople want to limit their personal liability.

    B.   Organizations that appear to limit personal liability for the owners may not, in fact, accomplish that goal when actually conducting business transactions.

VI.   *Taxation* is often viewed as *the most critical factor* when selecting the form of business organization.

    A.   To make decisions about taxation and business organization, you must answer questions such as:

      1.   How is the income earned by the business taxed?
      2.   How is the money distributed to the business owners taxed?
      3.   Is it possible that owners may have to pay taxes on money that is attributed to them as income but which they have not actually received?

    B.   The double taxation of corporate income has both advantages and disadvantages, which will be discussed later.

SELECTING THE BEST ORGANIZATIONAL FORM

The following six sections apply the various factors to consider when deciding which organizational form is best for a particular business activity. Forms of business organizations include sole proprietorships, general partnerships, corporations, limited partnerships, subchapter S corporations, and hybrid organizations like the limited liability company and the limited liability partnership.

VII.   The **sole proprietorship** is the easiest and least expensive business organization to create. In essence, the proprietor obtains whatever business licenses are necessary and begins operations. Legally, no formal documentation is needed. Thus, there are advantages to this form of organization; but as the business becomes successful, there are also disadvantages in the areas of continuity, liability, and flexible tax planning.

    A.   Ownership of a sole proprietorship cannot be transferred (although its assets can be sold). A proprietorship's continuity is tied directly to the will of the proprietor. In essence, the proprietor may dissolve his or her organization at any time by simply changing the organization or terminating the business activity.

131

B.   The sole proprietor is in total control of his or her business's goals and operations. The owners of all other organizational forms usually share control to some degree. As long as this control issue is carefully thought out, there can be real value in heaving more than one voice in control of managing a business enterprise.

C.   Legally speaking, a sole proprietor personally has unlimited liability for the debt of the proprietorship. The desire to avoid the potentially high risk of personal liability is an important reason why other organizational forms might be viewed as preferable to the proprietorship.

D.   All the sole proprietorship's income subject to taxation is attributed to the proprietor. The proprietor must then pay the applicable personal tax rate on the income earned by the business, whether the proprietor actually receives any of the income from the organization or not. *If profits are retained for business expansion purposes, the owner still must pay taxes on the income.*

VIII.   In general, a **partnership** is an agreement between two or more persons to share a common interest in a commercial endeavor and to share profits and losses. The word *persons*, in this context, should be interpreted to allow business organizations, as well as individuals, to form a partnership.

A.   A partnership is easily created. The cost of creation is relatively minimal, and a partnership does not need to get permission from each state in which it does business.

1.   If the parties to a business conduct their affairs as a partnership, a partnership exists, whether the persons involved call themselves partners or not. The defining elements of a partnership are:

a.   *Two or more persons*
b.   *A common interest in business*
c.   *Sharing profits and losses*

2.   Even though existence of a partnership can be implied from the conduct or actions of the parties, partners should never rely on implied agreements. They should draft a formal document called the **articles of partnership**.

3.   The right of partners to select a name for their partnership is limited in many states in two ways:

a.   A partnership may not use any word in the name, such as "company," that would imply the existence of a corporation.
b.   If the name is other than that of the partners, the partners must give notice as to their actual identity under the state's **assumed name statute**. Failure to comply with this disclosure requirement may result in the partnership's being denied access to courts, or it may result in

criminal action being brought against those operating under the assumed name.

B.   It is generally said that a partnership organization is easily dissolved. This presents special considerations with regard to continuity.

    1.   *A general partnership is dissolved any time there is a change in the partners,* for example, if a partner dies, retires, or otherwise withdraws from the organization. If a person is added as a new partner, there is a technical dissolution of the organization.

    2.   Even if the partnership agreement provides that the partnership will continue for a stated number of years, any *partner still retains the power to dissolve the organization.* Liability may be imposed on the former partner for wrongful dissolution, but the partnership is nevertheless dissolved.

    3.   A dissolution does not necessarily destroy the business of a partnership. The winding up of liquidating of a business is termination of the business; dissolution simply means the legal form of organization no longer exists.

    4.   To prevent problems that may arise when a partner dies or withdraws from a partnership, the articles of partnership should include a **buy and sell agreement**. This agreement provides for the amount and manner of compensation for the interest of the deceased or withdrawing partner. Buy and sell agreements often use formulas to compute the value of the withdrawing partner's interest and provide for the time and method of payment.

C.   The decision of who has what voice in management – i.e., who controls the partnership – is of crucial importance to the business's success and to the welfare of the partners' relationship with each other.

    1.   In a general partnership, *unless the agreement provides to the contrary, each partner has an equal voice in the firm's affairs.* The possibility of a deadlock among partners is very real, especially when there are only a few partners and an even number of them.

    2.   *Partners may agree to divide control* in such a way as to make controlling partners and minority partners. A written partnership agreement should provide specific language governing issues of managerial control.

D.   *All partners in a general partnership are jointly and severally liable for the partnership's obligations.* The partners' personal assets, which are not associated with the partnership, may be claimed by the partnership's creditors. This personal liability of each partner extends to the organization's entire debt, not just to a pro rata share. Among the partners, anyone who has to pay the creditor more than her or his pro rata share of the liability usually can seek contribution from the remaining partners.

E. Like proprietorships, *partnerships are not a taxable entity*. The partnership's owners are taxed as individuals.

1. *A partnership files an information return* that allocates to each partner his or her proportionate share of profits or losses from operations, dividend income, capital gains or losses, and other items that would affect the income tax owed by a partner.

2. Partners then report their share of such items on their individual tax returns, irrespective of whether they have actually received the items.

3. If a partnership suffers a *net loss*, the pro rata share of this loss is allocated to each partner, and it can be used by the partners to reduce their personal taxable income.

4. *If the partnership retains any profits for the purpose of expansion, the partners are still taxed individually on these profits*, even though they actually received nothing.

IX. A corporation is an artificial, intangible "person" created under the authority of a state's law. A corporation is known as a **domestic corporation** in the state in which it is incorporated; in all other states, this corporation is called a **foreign corporation**. As a creature of state legislative bodies, it is much more complex to create and to operate than other forms of business.

A. A corporation is created by a state issuing a **charter** upon the application of individuals known as **incorporators**. They are more costly than partnerships to form. Among the costs of incorporation are filing fees, license fees, franchise taxes, and various other expenses.

B. In contrast to a partnership, a corporation usually has "perpetual existence." That means in terms of continuity, the corporation can go on forever.

C. There are three groups that can exert some *managerial control* within the corporation: The **shareholders** own the corporation and elect the members of the board of directors. These **directors** set the objectives or goals of the corporation and appoint its officers. These **officers**, such as the president and vice president, are charged with managing the daily operations of the corporation. Who, among these groups, actually controls the corporation depends on the size of the ownership base.

1. In very large corporations, *management* (a combination of the directors and officers) exerts control by using corporate records and funds to solicit **proxies** from the shareholders who do not attend the meetings at which the directors of the company are elected. Technically, a proxy is an agent appointed by a shareholder for the purpose of voting the shares. Management then votes the stock of these shareholders, and thus usually can maintain control with only a small minority of actual stock ownership.

2. In *closely held corporations*, one shareholder, or a small group of shareholders, can own an actual majority of the issued shares and can control the election of a board of directors, often electing themselves. In a very real sense, those who own a majority of a closely held corporation can rule with near absolute authority.

    a. Although minority shareholders, the "minority interest," in a closely held corporation are subject to the decisions of the majority, the directors and officers stand in a *fiduciary relation* to the corporation. This relation imposes a duty on directors to act for the best interests of the corporation rather than for themselves individually.

    b. If the majority is acting illegally or oppresses the rights of the minority shareholders, a lawsuit known as a **derivative suit** may be brought by a minority shareholder on behalf of the corporation. Such suits may seek to enjoin the unlawful activity or to collect damages for the corporation.

    c. If a shareholder desires to dispose of a minority interest in a closely held corporation, there is no ready market for the stock unless there is a valid buy and sell agreement. As with partnerships, buy and sell agreements are absolutely essential in closely held corporations.

D. Corporate shareholders are said to have **limited personal liability**. Because of the separation of shareholders from management, the owners are liable for the debts of the corporation only to the extent of their investment in the cost of the stock.

1. It is too broad a generalization to say without qualification that the investors in a corporation have limited liability but those in a partnership have unlimited liability.

    a. For example, if the company is a small, closely held corporation with limited assets and capital, shareholders will usually be required to add their own individual liability as security when obtaining credit for the company.

    b. Shareholders in closely held corporations do have limited liability for contract like obligations that are imposed as a matter of law, such as taxes. Liability is also limited when the corporate obligation results from torts committed by company employees while doing company business.

2. When courts find that the corporate organization is being *misused*, the corporate entity can be disregarded, resulting in unlimited liability to the shareholders. This has been called **piercing the corporate veil**. This **alter-ego theory** may also be used to impose personal liability upon corporate officers, directors, and stockholders. If there is such a unity of ownership and interest that separateness of the corporation has ceased to exist (for example, when the corporation's and a shareholder's bank accounts are the same), the alter-ego theory will be followed and the corporate veil will be pierced. If the

owner has respect for the existence of the organization, however, wrongful activity in itself will not result in a piercing of the corporate veil.

    a.   In *Meyer v. Holley* the U.S. Supreme Court ruled that the owner/president of a real estate sales company could not be held personally liable under the Fair Housing Act for illegal racial housing discrimination by one of the company's salespersons. Note that the salesperson and the company – a corporation – could be held liable.

E.   With regard to taxation, there are certain advantages and disadvantages to the corporate organization. Corporations must pay income taxes on their earnings.

    1.   The separate corporate income tax may work as an advantage if the corporation makes a profit that is to be retained by the corporation to support growth. In that case, no income is allocated to the shareholders and their personal taxable income is not increased. The corporate rate of taxation may be lower than the individual rates.

    2.   There are also tax disadvantages to the corporate form of organization. When the corporation suffers a loss for the year, the loss cannot be distributed to shareholders to reduce their personal tax liability, although it can be used to offset corporate income earned in other years. When a profit is made by the corporation and it pays a dividend to its shareholders, that profit will be taxed twice: once at the corporate level, and again as part of the shareholder's personal incomes. This situation has been called the **double tax** on corporate income. *There are, however, a number of techniques for avoiding double taxation.*

        a.   Reasonable salaries paid to corporate officials may be deducted in computing the taxable income of the business. In a closely held corporation in which all or most shareholders are officers or employees, this technique may avoid double taxation of substantial portions of income. The Internal Revenue Code, however, disallows deductions for excessive or unreasonable compensation and treats such payments as dividends.

        b.   Corporations provide expense accounts for many employees, including shareholder employees. These expenses for travel, meals and entertainment may be deducted only when directly related to business; and there are numerous technical rules and limitations.

        c.   The capital structure of the corporation may include both common stock and interest-bearing loans from shareholders. Interest paid by the corporation to the shareholders is deductible as an expense of the company and thus subject only to tax as interest income to the owners. If the corporation is found to be undercapitalized, however, the Internal Revenue Code has a counteracting rule that will cause the interest to be taxed.

d. Corporations can also avoid double taxation by not paying dividends, instead accumulating the earnings. When a corporation retains earnings in excess of $250,000, the Internal Revenue Service requires it to demonstrate the business purpose for which it needs the retained earnings. If it cannot show the need to retain the earnings, for example for growth, an additional tax is imposed.

e. *If a corporation files under Subchapter S of the Internal Revenue Code, the corporate tax is eliminated.* (See Section XI of this chapter.)

X. A limited partnership basically has all the attributes of a partnership except that one or more of the partners are designated as **limited partners**. This type of partner is not personally responsible for the debts of the business organization. However, they are not permitted to be involved in the control of operations of the limited partnership. The management is left in the hands of one or more **general partners** who remain personally liable for the organization's debts. This can be an attractive form of business organization.

A. Like a general partnership, a limited partnership is created by agreement. As in the case of a corporation, however, state law requires the contents of a certificate to be recorded in a public office. The limited partnership certificate must be recorded in the county where the partnership has its principal place of business, and a copy must be filed in every community where the partnership conducts business. If an accurate certificate is not on record, the limited partners become liable as general partners.

B. The principles guiding partnerships also apply to limited partnerships if there is a change in the general partners. A limited partner may assign his or her interest to another without dissolving the limited partnership.

C. In a limited partnership, the general partners are in control. Limited partners have no right to participate in management. *A limited partner who participates in the organization's management becomes liable as a general partner if a third party had knowledge of the limited partner's activities.* Permitted activities include, but are not limited to:

1. Acting as an agent or employee of the partnership
2. Consulting with or advising a general partner
3. Acting as a guarantor of the partnership's obligations
4. Receiving a share of the profits
5. Voting on matters of fundamental importance such as dissolution, sale of assets, or change of the partnership's name

D. The true hybrid of the limited partnership is revealed in the area of owners' liability. The general partners have unlimited liability but *the limited partners are not*

137

personally liable for the partnership's debts. The limited partners' liability typically will not exceed the amount of their investments.

    1.   Under the Revised Uniform Limited Partnership Act (RULPA), a limited partner's surname may not be used in the partnership's name unless there is a general partner with the same name.

    2.   As discussed above, limited partners become liable as general partners if they participate in the organization's management.

XI.   Subchapter S of the Internal Revenue Code makes it possible for shareholders of certain corporations to unanimously elect to have their organization treated like a partnership for income tax purposes. Organizations subject to this election often are referred to as **S corporations**.

    A.   *S corporations have all the legal characteristics of corporations except that shareholders in the S corporations are responsible for accounting on their individual income tax returns for their respective shares of the organization's profits or losses. Not tax is assessed on the corporate income itself, although it must file an information return with the IRS.*

    B.   In *Bufferd v. Commissioner* the U.S. Supreme Court ruled that "the limitations period within which the IRS must assess the income tax return of an S corporation shareholder runs from the date on which the shareholder's return is filed" rather than when the corporate return is filed.

    C.   S corporations cannot have more than seventy-five shareholders, each of whom must elect under subchapter S. Only individuals can elect under subchapter S; therefore, partnerships, limited partnerships, or corporations cannot be shareholders in an S corporation.

    D.   There are many technical rules of tax law involved in S corporations. The rule of thumb, however, is that this method of organization has advantages for a business operating at a loss and for businesses capable of paying out net profits as earned. Losses can be deducted on the returns of the shareholders, and corporate tax is avoided on the net profits. If net profits must be retained in the business, income tax is paid on earnings not received, making subchapter S tax treatment disadvantageous. There is also, then, a danger of double taxation to the individual upon the death of a shareholder.

XII.   The **limited liability company** (LLC) is a relatively new organizational alternative. The **limited liability partnership** is a variation of the LLC *often used by professionals*, such as doctors, lawyers, and accountants. *LLCs and LLPs are treated by the IRS as nontaxable entities, much like partnerships.* The owners have more flexibility than with the S corporation, while not having to struggle with the complexities of a limited partnership. LLCs and LLPs have characteristics of both a partnership and a corporation.

A.   An LLC is created through filings much like those used when creating a corporation. **Articles of organization** are filed with a state official. Instead of "incorporators" the term **organizers** is used. The name of the LLC must acknowledge the special nature of this organizational form by including a version of the phrase "limited liability company," or an appropriate abbreviation in the company name. An LLC created in a state other than the one in which it is conducting business is called a foreign LLC. It must apply to the state to legally transact business, and it must file annual reports with the states in which it operates.

B.   The owners of LLCs are called **members** rather than shareholders or partners. Membership is not limited to individuals, unlike in the S corporation. The transferability of a member's interest in the company is restricted in the fashion of a partner; and anytime a member dies or withdraws from the LLC, there is a dissolution of the business organization. The business of the LLC may be continued rather than wound up, however.

C.   Unless the articles of organization provide for one or more **managers**, the managerial control of an LLC is vested in its members.

    1.   Regardless of whether members or managers control the LLC, a majority of these decision makers decide the direction of the organization. Under state law, in a few situations unanimous consent of the members is required for a binding decision.

    2.   Similarly to partners, members of LLCs make contributions of capital and share in the LLC's profits and losses.

D.   For liability purposes, members do act as agents of their LLC. However, *they are not personally liable to third parties*.

E.   State laws and the IRS recognize LLCs as nontaxable entities. As always, careful analysis is needed in every situation to determine whether this type of tax treatment is in the members' best interests.

XIII.   There is no organizational form that is the "right" one. The preceding sections have presented background material for consideration when this important decision is made. The criteria used to select a form of organization should be reviewed periodically in consultation with attorneys, accountants, bankers, and insurers. Each form will always have its advantages and disadvantages that must be weighed.

Chapter 11

AGENCY PRINCIPLES

Organizations cannot accomplish anything without the help of individuals, who are referred to as agents. Practically all business transactions involve agents. The following sections concern the general principles of the law of agency.

XIV. The application of agency law involves the interaction among three parties. Individuals usually are these parties, but agency relationship can also involve business organizations.

A. A **principal** interacts with someone (or some organization) for the purpose of obtaining that second party's assistance.

B. The second party is the **agent**. The agent acts on behalf of the principal with a **third party**. The usual legal purpose of the agent is to create a binding relationship (contract) between the principal and the party, with the understanding that any liability involves the principal-third party relationship. To accomplish this substitution of liability, the agent must comply with certain duties owed to the principal:

1. A duty of loyalty to act for the principal's advantage and not to act to benefit the agent at the principal's expense
2. A duty to keep the principal fully informed
3. A duty to obey instructions
4. A duty to account to the principal for monies handled

C. In the law of agency, the employer/business organization is the principal. The employee is the agent. *Whether employee conduct creates liability for the employer is the usual agency issue facing businesses.* Such issues may involve either contracts or torts.

XV. For an employee to bind the employer to a contract that the employee negotiates with a third party, the employer must have *authorized* the employee's actions. Contractual authority can take one of four forms. Only when one of these types of authority is present will the principal and the third party become contractually bound.

A. **Actual authority** and **expressed authority** express the wishes of the employer that the agent act on behalf of the employer. This authority may be in writing or in the form of an oral statement. "Act as store manager in my absence" is an example of express authority.

B. **Implied authority** is shown by means of an agent's position with the company as well as by a history of express authority situations. Store managers usually have the implied authority to purchase inventory on credit.

C. **Apparent authority** may exist in the case of recent termination without notification to third parties. While the employer may be liable for the terminated agent's actions, the employer will then have a claim against the terminated agent for breaching the duty of loyalty owed to the employer.

D. The basic concepts of agency law apply to the operation of business organizations, although sometimes the law provides technical rules. One of these states that a partner in a **trading partnership**, that is, one engaged in the business of buying and selling commodities, has the implied authority to borrow money in the usual course of business and to pledge the credit of the firm. A partner in a **nontrading partnership**, such as an accounting or other service firm, has no implied power to borrow money; and such authority must be actual before the firm will be bound.

XVI. As discussed in Chapter 9, a tort is a breach of duty that causes injury. An agent (as with any employee) who causes harm to a third party may create legal liability for the principal to that third party, depending on whether the agent was acting within the scope of employment when the tort occurred.

A. Partners are liable for all transactions entered into by any partner in the scope of the partnership business and are similarly liable for any partner's torts committed while she or he is acting in the course of the firm's business. Each partner is in effect both an agent of the partnership and a principal.

B. Generally, shareholders of corporations and members of LLCs are protected from tort liability that exceeds the amount of their investment. In cases involving one corporation's potential liability for the acts of another business organization, there may be a *piercing of the corporate veil*, as discussed in Section IX of this chapter.

C. In *United States v. Bestfoods*, the U.S. Supreme Court examined whether a "parent" corporation was liable for a subsidiary corporation's responsibility for environmental cleanup under CERCLA. The Court ruled that the parent might be liable but only if it exercised "operational control" over the subsidiary. The case was sent back to the district court to determine whether such control existed.

COMPLETION EXERCISES

1. Regulation of the relationship between the owners and managers of a corporation is referred to as _____.

2. Regulation of the relationship between a corporation and society is referred to as _____.

3. A business organization owned by only a few people is said to be _____.

4. When the ownership of a business organization is widely spread and often traded over a stock exchange, the business is said to be _____.

5. The most critical factor when selecting the form of business organization is usually _____.

6. The easiest and least expensive business organization to form is the _____.

7. When two or more people intend to carry on a business together for profit, their business is termed a(an) _____.

8. Corporate boards of directors are elected by the _____.

9. The word describing the obligation of corporate officers and board members to act with loyalty and good faith in the best interest of the corporation is _____.

10. The corporate income tax is eliminated if a corporation qualifies under _____ of the Internal Revenue Code.

TRUE-FALSE SELECTIONS

1. _____ A limited partnership has no general partners.

2. _____ Members of an LLC are not personally liable to third parties for the acts of the business.

3. _____ A person who acts on behalf of a principal with a third party is known as an "agent."

4. _____ Under the doctrine of apparent authority, a principal can be liable for the actions of a terminated employee.

5. _____ A partner in a nontrading partnership has the implied authority to borrow money for the business.

6. _____ A dissolution is any change in the ownership of an organization that changes the legal existence of the organization.

7. _____ In Michigan a corporation from New York is known as a foreign corporation.

8. _____ Derivative suits help the managers of very large corporations to maintain control of the corporations.

9. _____ Corporate shareholders have limited personal liability for corporate debts.

10. _____ Corporate earnings are subject to double taxation.

MULTIPLE CHOICE PROBLEMS

1. To prevent many of the problems that arise when a partner dies or withdraws from a business, partners should include what in their articles of partnership?

   a. A derivative charter agreement
   b. A limited personal liability agreement
   c. A buy and sell agreement
   d. An alter ego agreement

2. Which of the following is an advantage of the partnership over the corporate form of business organization?

   a. In a partnership the owners have joint and several liability.
   b. Partners do not have to be concerned about fiduciary duties.
   c. Partnerships are taxable entities.
   d. Partners can deduct net business losses from their personal income taxes.

3. Brown is a shareholder in a corporation. When he discovers that the CEO of the company has defrauded the shareholders he demands that the board of directors fire the CEO and sue her. When the board takes no action against the CEO, Brown

   a. Files a derivative suit.
   b. Pierces the corporate veil.
   c. Personally sues the CEO.
   d. Applies the assumed name statute.

4. Double taxation of corporate income can be reduced by all of the following methods, *except*

   a. Payment of reasonably large salaries to shareholders who work for the corporation.
   b. Deduction of corporate interest payments to shareholders who loan money to the corporation.
   c. Payment of cash dividends.
   d. Filing for Subchapter S status.

5.   The owners of LLCs are called

   a.   Shareholders.
   b.   Members.
   c.   Partners.
   d.   Principals.

DISCUSSION ANALYSIS

John and Mary wish to set up a business to manufacture exercise equipment. Start-up costs are estimated to be $200,000. John plans to contribute $50,000 and is willing to help promote the business, but wishes not to participate in the day-to-day running of the business since he holds another job. Mary has no money to contribute, but she intends to help promote the business and to participate in the management of the business. The business will likely lose money for the first three years of its existence. Discuss what kind of business organization might best suit this new enterprise.

Chapter
12

Corporate Governance and the Regulatory Process

This chapter concerns administrative law – the legal principles relating to regulatory agencies, boards, bureaus, and commissions. Through administrative agencies, the policies of governments, at all levels, result in the regulatory process. Because of the significant impact these agencies can have on businesses and businesspeople, this chapter covers the following topics:

Why our governments have come to rely on the regulatory process
The basic functions of administrative agencies
The organization of these agencies
When courts will review the actions of agencies

ADMINISTRATIVE AGENCIES

The term **administrative agency** is used to describe all the boards, bureaus, commissions, agencies, and organizations that make up the bureaucracy. The process of regulating business through agencies is described as *administrative law*.

The administrative process occurs at all levels of government, and the activities of the government agencies can have a significant impact on the everyday operations of a business. The direct day-to-day legal impact on business of the rules and regulations adopted and enforced by these agencies is probably greater than the impact of the courts or other branches of government.

I. Almost every governmental agency exists because of a recognized problem in society and the expectation that the agency may be able to help solve the problem. Reasons that agencies are the essential part of the regulatory process are:

   A. Agencies provide *specificity*. Legislative branches often cannot legislate in sufficient detail to cover all aspects of many problems, nor can courts handle all disputes and controversies that may arise.

   B. Agencies provide *expertise*. Many agencies are created to refer a problem or area to experts for solution and management. The development of sound policies and proper decisions in many areas requires expertise.

C. Agencies provide *protection*. Many governmental agencies exist to protect the public, especially from the business community. Business often fails to regulate itself, and the lack of self-regulation is contrary to the public interest.

D. Agencies provide *regulation*, often replacing competition with regulation. When a firm is given monopoly power, it loses its freedom of contract, and a governmental body is given the power to determine the provisions of its contracts. This power exists because of the difference of bargaining power between the business and individuals.

E. Agencies provide *services*. The mere existence of most government programs, such as mail delivery and Social Security, automatically creates a new agency or expands the functions of an existing one.

F. In *Chao v. Mallard Bay Drilling, Inc.*, the U.S. Supreme Court examined how both the Occupational Safety and Health Administration and the U.S. Coast Guard protect the health and safety of sailors on various seagoing vessels. The Court concluded that both OSHA and the Coast Guard had jurisdiction (power of law to regulate) certain types of vessels.

II. Most agencies possess and perform functions of the other three branches of government, including rule making, adjudicating (judging), advising, and investigating.

A. Agencies exercise their **quasi-legislative**, or rule-making, power by issuing rules and regulations that have the force and effect of law.

1. Due to the vast volume of new rules and regulations, keeping current challenges many businesses. Rules and regulations may apply to all businesses, irrespective of the industry involved, or they may apply only to an industry.
2. Guidelines are also issued by agencies to supplement rules. Guidelines are administrative interpretations of the statutes that an agency is responsible for enforcing. While guidelines can be helpful in understanding an agency's policy, these guidelines do not have the same force of law as rules and regulations do.

B. The **quasi-judicial**, or adjudicating, function involves both fact-finding and applying law to the facts. This function is similar to what courts do.

1. If violations of the law are found, sanctions, such as a fine or other penalty, may be imposed. In addition, an agency may issue a *cease and desist order*, an order that a violator stop the objectionable activity and refrain from any further similar violations. Violations of a cease and desist order are punishable by fines, which can be quite substantial.

2. Just as most lawsuits are settled, many cases before agencies are settled by agreement between the agency and the business involved, which is called a **consent order**. There is no admission that the business has been guilty of a violation of the law, but there is an agreement not to engage in the business activities that were the subject of the complaint. A consent order saves considerable expense and has the same legal effect as a final cease and desist order.

C. The advisory function of an administrative agency may be accomplished by making reports to the president or to Congress. Many agencies also report information to the general public that should be known in the public interest, and they publish advisory opinions. For example, a commission may give advice as to whether a firm's proposed course of action might violate any of the laws that commission administers. Advisory opinions give a business an indication of the view an agency would take if the practice in question were challenged formally.

D. One of the major functions of all agencies is to investigate activities and practices that may be illegal.

1. Because of the investigative power, agencies can gather and compile information concerning the organization and business practices of any business engaged in commerce to determine whether there has been a violation of law. Investigation is often followed by adjudication.
2. Information furnished to an agency must be truthful. It is a crime to make any false or fraudulent statement in any matter within the jurisdiction of a federal agency.

III. Administrative agencies usually consist of five to seven members, one of whom is appointed as chair. *Usually, no more than a simple majority may belong to the same political party.* Appointments at the federal level require Senate confirmation, and appointees are not permitted to engage in any other business or employment during their terms. Regulatory agencies have large staffs to carry out their duties.

A. Agencies are usually organized as follows:

1. The *chairperson* is designated by the President and presides at agency meetings. The chairperson has higher visibility than the other agency members and, while an equal in voting, also has the power to appoint staff.
2. The *secretary* is responsible for the minutes of agency meetings and is legal custodian of its records. The secretary usually signs orders and official correspondence and is responsible for publication of all actions in the *Federal Register*.
3. The office of *general counsel* is so important in many agencies that the appointment usually requires Senate approval. The general counsel is the

chief law officer and legal adviser, represents the agency in court, and often makes the decision to file suit or pursue other remedies.

4. The *executive director* is the chief operating official of an agency and supervises usual administrative functions, as well as research and planning. Since agencies spend a great deal of time lobbying with Congress, most of them have a legislative liaison, reporting to the executive director for administration.

5. The duties and suborganization of the *director of operations* vary greatly from agency to agency.

6. *Regional offices* investigate alleged violations of the law. Many regional offices have their own administrative law judges and special legal counsel.

B. **Administrative law judges** determine both the law and the facts of specific administrative cases. Like other types of judges, they are protected from liability for damages based on their decisions. This protection is called **immunity**.

1. These administrative law judges hear cases of alleged law violations and apply the law to the facts. The members of the agency board or commission hear only appeals from the decisions of the administrative law judges. The judges are organizationally separate from the rest of the agency.

2. Historically, administrative law judges and all other personnel involved in a quasi-judicial hearing have been employees of the administrative agency bringing the complaint; and they have been accused of being biased in favor of their employer, the agency.

IV. The best way for a business to influence a quasi-legislative decision of an administrative agency is to participate in the *adoption* process. Agencies are required to give public notice of proposed rules or regulations as well as an opportunity for interested parties to express their views on them. There are several means of participating:

A. Agencies hold public hearings on proposed rules. At the hearings, interested parties are allowed to present evidence in support of, or in opposition to, the proposed rule or regulation.

B. Agencies are not politically elected, but they often react to the force of public opinion. Writing letters to agencies may be effective in obtaining action or changing policy.

C. Congressional investigations into agencies' actions may result in budget cutbacks; often the threat of such a proceeding is enough to cause a review of administrative policy. Therefore, writing letters to members of Congress, who in turn ask the agency for an official response or explanation, may be more effective than writing directly to the agency.

JUDICIAL REVIEW OF AGENCY DECISIONS

To clearly understand the role of administrative agencies in our system, it is necessary to understand the answers to such questions as:

* What alternatives are available to a person, business, or industry unhappy with either rules and regulations that have been adopted or with the quasi-judicial decisions?
* What are the powers of courts in reviewing decisions of administrative agencies?
* What chance does a party upset with an agency's decision have in obtaining a reversal of the decision?
* How much deference is given to an agency's decisions?

V.   Any party seeking the judicial review (review by a regular court) of any administrative agency's decision must be able to prove *standing to sue*. To establish standing, the challenging party must address two issues.

   A.   First, the action or decision of the agency must be subject to judicial review; not all administrative decisions are reviewable. The Federal Administrative Procedure Act provides for judicial review except when:

      1.   Statutes prohibit judicial review, or
      2.   Agency action is committed to agency discretion by law

   B.   Second, the plaintiff must be "an aggrieved party." *Generally, the plaintiff must have been harmed by an administrative action or decision to have standing to sue.* It is clear that persons who may suffer economic loss due to an agency's action have standing. Recent decisions have expanded the group of persons with standing to sue to include those who have noneconomic interests, such as First Amendment rights and environmental enjoyments.

VI.   The rule-making function in the administrative process is essentially legislative. Legislatures usually create an administrative agency, which must propose rules and regulations within the confines of its grant of power, or a court will find the proposal void. Once courts decide an agency rule is authorized, they will not inquire into its wisdom or effectiveness; it may only be corrected by the legislature that gave the agency the power to make the rule. There are two basic issues in litigation challenging the validity of a rule made by an administrative agency:

   A.   *Is the delegation valid?* It is important to remember that the delegation of discretion is to the agency, not to the judiciary. Therefore, courts cannot interfere with the discretion given to the agency and cannot substitute their judgment for that of the agency. In essence, there is a policy of deference by the judges to the decision of the administrators. Delegation of quasi-legislative authority to administrative agencies is subject to two constitutional limitations:

149

1. *Delegation of authority must be definite or it will violate due process.* That means it must be set forth with sufficient clarity so that all concerned, and especially, reviewing courts, will be able to determine the extent of the agency's authority. Broad language has been held sufficiently definite to meet this test.

2. The delegation of authority must also be *limited.* It must provide that the agency's powers to act is limited to areas that are certain, even if these areas are not specifically defined. For example regulation of the "securities industry in the public interest" is considered limited and certain.

B. In *U.S. Postal Service v. Gregory*, the U.S. Supreme Court ruled that the dismissal of a postal employee was neither arbitrary nor abusing discretion. It upheld the decision of the Civil Service Systems Protection Board, advising the lower court that it could not substitute its judgment for the Board's.

C. *Has the agency exceeded its authority?* Courts will hold that an agency exceeds its authority if an analysis of legislative intent confirms the view that the agency has gone beyond that intent.

D. In *FDA v. Brown & Williamson Tobacco Corp.*, the U.S. Supreme Court examined the Food, Drug, and Cosmetic Act and other statutes and determined that Congress had not granted authority to the FDA to regulate tobacco products.

VII. Judicial review of what agencies decide in their administrative law courts is quite limited. Administrative agencies are frequently called upon to interpret the statute governing an agency, and because of the expertise and knowledge within the agencies, the agencies' constructions are generally persuasive to the courts.

A. In reviewing the procedures of administrative agencies, courts lack the authority to substitute their judgment or their own procedures for those of the agency. Judicial responsibility is limited to ensuring consistency with statutes and compliance with the due process clause of the Constitution for a fair hearing. Two doctrines guide courts in the judicial review of agency adjudications:

1. The doctrine of **exhaustion of remedies** is a court-created rule that limits when courts can review administrative decisions. Courts refuse to review administrative actions until a complaining party has exhausted all of the administrative remedies and procedures available to him or her for redress. With few exceptions, judicial review is available only for *final actions* by an agency; *preliminary orders*, such as a decision to file a complaint, are not reviewable. The reasons for exhaustion of remedies are:

   a. To allow the administrative system to make a factual record, to exercise its discretion, and to apply its expertise in its decision making

       b.   To allow an agency to discover and correct its own errors, and thus dispense with any reason for judicial review

       c.   To avoid the premature interruption of the administrative process

   2.   **Primary jurisdiction** applies when a claim is *originally filed in the courts*. It comes into play whenever enforcement of the claim requires the resolution of issues that, under a regulatory scheme, have been placed within the special competence of an administrative body. In such a case, the judicial process is suspended pending referral of such issues to the administrative body for its views. Primary jurisdiction ensures uniformity and consistency in dealing with matters entrusted to an administrative body. It is invoked when referral to the agency is preferable because of its specialized knowledge or expertise in dealing with the matter in controversy.

VIII.   When a court reviews the findings of fact made by an administrative body, it presumes them to be correct. It examines the evidence by analyzing the record of the agency's proceedings. It upholds the agency's findings and conclusions on questions of fact if they are supported by *substantial evidence in the record*.

   A.   If substantial evidence in support of the decision is present, the court will not disturb the agency's findings, even though the court itself might have reached a different conclusion on the basis of other conflicting evidence also in the record. Thus, a business's chance of winning a judicial reversal of an agency decision is slight unless the agency's decision is arbitrary and capricious, denying the business *due process* of law.

   B.   In *Holly Farms Corp. v. Nat'l Labor Relations Board* (NLRB), the U.S. Supreme Court decided that the NLRB's ruling that the collection of broiling chickens was a separate "processing operation" rather than a "farming operation" was a "reasonable" interpretation of the relevant statute that must be followed. The case involved whether certain employees were covered by the National Labor Relations Act for unionizing purposes.

IX.   The Equal Access to Justice Act (EAJA) requires the federal government to pay the reasonable attorneys' fees of small businesses, nonprofit groups, and most individuals who can show they were unjustly treated by the federal government. Prior to enactment of this law, small companies and individuals were reluctant to take on the U.S. government because of litigation costs.

   A.   Congress limited eligibility to collect attorneys' fees to small organizations and individuals with net worth of less than $1 million.

   B.   The law grants legal fees only to parties that overcome the government's position in court, administrative proceedings, or a settlement. Even then, the government agency is not required to pay if it can show that its original position was *substantially justified*. The word "substantially" means to be justified in substance or in the main, not justified to a high degree.

C. Under the EAJA, the amount of fees awarded must "be based upon prevailing market rates for the kind of quality of the services furnished," but in general not to exceed $75 per hour.

CRITICISM OF ADMINISTRATIVE AGENCIES

The independent regulatory agencies and the administrative process face many problems and are subjected to a great deal of criticism. Agencies are often charged with being too vast to be efficient and effective. One of the major criticisms of the fourth branch of government is its high cost.

X. Regulation is a form of taxation. It increases the cost of government, both directly and indirectly. Regulation significantly increases the cost of doing business, and these costs are passed on to the tax-paying, consuming public. The consumer, for whose protection many regulations are adopted, pays both the direct cost (in taxes) and the indirect cost (when purchasing goods and services).

A. The existence of a governmental agency usually forces a business subject to the agency's jurisdiction to create a similar bureaucracy within its own organization to deal with the agency.

B. Other costs the public must absorb result from agency regulations that inhibit competition and innovation. Regulation may protect existing companies by creating a barrier to entry into a market. It protects "cozy competition" to such an extent that often the parties objecting most to deregulation are the businesses being regulated.

C. A major cost of doing business is the cost of the burdensome paperwork involved in filing applications, returns, reports, and forms.

D. Historically, there has been little or no cost-benefit analysis when new rules and regulations were proposed. The primary focus of policymaking by way of social regulation has been on such benefits as a cleaner environment, safer products, healthier working conditions, and so on. The public, and especially consumers, has frequently been forced to pay for many things it did not want or need in the sense that the cost far exceeded the benefits.

E. Cost-benefit analysis, however, becomes ethically awkward when there is an attempt to place a dollar value on things not usually bought and sold, such as life, health, or mobility. On closer examination, it is obvious that in many cases it is not possible to weigh the costs against the benefits of regulation.

COMPLETION EXERCISES

1. The term _____ is used to describe the Environmental Protection Agency, the Federal Trade Commission, and other parts of the bureaucracy.

2. The rules and regulations issued by the Nuclear Regulatory Commission are part of its _____ power.

3. The _____ requires the federal government under certain circumstances to pay the reasonable attorney fees of those who litigate against the federal government.

4. An administrative order that requires a rule violator to stop what it is doing is called a _____.

5. _____ determine both the law and the facts of administrative cases.

6. The best way for a business to influence a proposed rule of the FCC is to participate in the _____.

7. Any party seeking the judicial review of a decision by the FAA must initially be able to show _____.

8. Delegation of authority by the legislature must be definite or it will violate _____.

9. A business cannot obtain judicial review of a decision by an FTC administrative law judge until the business has _____ at the FTC.

10. A case challenging a rule of the SEC that is originally filed in a federal court will likely be transferred for consideration by the SEC because of the doctrine of _____.

TRUE-FALSE SELECTIONS

1. _____ The Equal Access to Justice Act benefits small businesses and large corporations equally.

2. _____ Agencies help provide specificity of business regulation.

3. _____ Agencies are not permitted to perform functions similar to those of the three regular branches of government.

4. _____ The President usually appoints administrative agency members who are all from the same political party.

5. _____ The general counsel of the SEC is appointed by the chair of the SEC.

6. _____ Administrative law judges are protected from liability for damages based on their decisions.

7. _____ Judicial review of preliminary orders of the EPA is often available to a party that has standing to sue.

8. _____ The factual conclusions of the EEOC are likely to be overruled by a court if they are not supported by the preponderance of evidence on the record.

9. _____ The cost of administrative regulation is ultimately borne by consumers.

10. _____ An agency decision is likely to be reversed by a court if the decision denies due process of law.

MULTIPLE CHOICE PROBLEMS

1. All of the following are functions of administrative agencies *except*:

   a. Prosecuting alleged violators.
   b. Adjudicating alleged violations of law.
   c. Deciding the constitutionality of the actions of alleged violators.
   d. Advising businesspersons of the legality of their contemplated actions.

2. The Acme Corporation seeks to have the federal courts review the fact-finding of the FTC, which has found the comany in violation of the FTC Act. Select the most *incorrect* statement:

   a. The reviewing court will not reweigh the FTC's evidence.
   b. The reviewing court will not hear new evidence which the Acme Corporation wishes to introduce.
   c. The reviewing court will not substitute its view of the evidence for that of the FTC.
   d. The reviewing court will not require substantial evidence on the record.

3. What is the power of an administrative agency to try cases?

   a. Quasi-legislative power.
   b. Quasi-executive power.
   c. Quasi-investigatory power.
   d. Quasi-judicial power.

4.   The chair of the Federal Trade Commission is designated by the

a.   President.
b.   Election of the commissioners.
c.   Department of Commerce.
d.   Attorney General.

5.   Regkill is a private organization that opposes "wasteful and unnecessary" government regulations. Regkill files suit against the Federal Trade Commission challenging the FTC's new merger guidelines. Select the most *correct* statement.

a.   Regkill has a right to obtain judicial review of the guidelines.
b.   Regkill cannot obtain judicial review unless it can prove that the guidelines are "wasteful and unnecessary."
c.   Regkill cannot obtain judicial review unless it can prove that the costs of the guidelines exceed their benefits.
d.   Regkill cannot obtain judicial review unless it can prove that it is an aggrieved party.

DISCUSSION ANALYSIS

The CEO of your company is preparing to testify before the Senate Commerce Committee and asks you to prepare a memorandum of general criticisms of regulatory agencies. What do you write?

Chapter 13

Antitrust Laws – Regulating Competition

Questions of antitrust laws apply equally to small businesses and huge multinational corporations. Six of the ten largest criminal fines throughout the 1990s resulted from domestic and international enforcement of antitrust laws. Job loss, or even a prison sentence, could also await an individual who fails to understand and comply with antitrust laws.

I.   What is the meaning of "trust" and "antitrust"?

    A.   Trusts are a legal arrangement used for centuries for socially desirable purposes. A **trust** is a fiduciary relationship (a relationship requiring highest legal loyalty and good faith) concerning property in which one person, known as the **trustee**, holds legal title (ownership) for the benefit of another, known as the **beneficiary**. The trustee has the duty to manage and preserve the trust resources for the use and enjoyment of the beneficiary.

    B.   In the last part of the nineteenth century, the trust device was used extensively to gain monopolistic control of several industries. Through it, a group of corporations in the same type of business could unite in a trust to eliminate competition among themselves. The effect of these concentrations was to destroy the private market – "to restrain trade," as the Sherman Act would put it.

    C.   By the end of the nineteenth century business and industrial combinations were so powerful that reformers called on government to break these monopolies. The government responded by enacting the **Sherman Act** in 1890. Since the purpose of the Sherman Act and other laws discussed in this chapter was to "bust" the trusts, these laws became known as the *antitrust laws*. The Sherman Act still provides the basic framework for the regulation of business and industry. It seeks to preserve competition by prohibiting two types of anticompetitive business behavior:

        1.   Contracts, combinations, and conspiracies in restraint of trade or commerce
        2.   Monopolies and attempts to monopolize

    D.   The Sherman Act was general and often ambiguous. In 1914 Congress, recognizing that the Sherman Act needed to be more specific, enacted the **Clayton Act** as an amendment to the Sherman Act. The Clayton Act was amended in 1936 and 1950 to clarify its provisions.

E. In 1914 Congress also passed the **Federal Trade Commission Act**. This act created the Federal Trade Commission (FTC), an independent administrative agency charged with keeping competition free and fair.

F. The antitrust laws are enforced by the federal and state governments. Private parties also may bring civil suits seeking monetary damages or injunction as a means of enforcing the antitrust laws.

THE SHERMAN ACT

This section presents the basic provisions and analysis of the Sherman Act, so that you may appreciate the importance of the act in our legal and regulatory environment of business.

II. Section 1 of the Sherman Act prohibits contracts, combinations, and conspiracies in **restraint of trade** or commerce.

A. *Contracts* in restraint of trade usually result from verbal or written agreements. An express agreement is not required to create a contract in restraint of trade. Such contracts may be implied.

B. *Combinations* usually result from conduct.

C. *Conspiracies* are usually established by agreement and followed up by some act carrying out the plan of the conspiracy. The acceptance of an invitation to participate in a plan that is in restraint of interstate commerce is sufficient to establish an unlawful conspiracy. Circumstantial evidence may be used to prove a conspiracy.

D. The most common contract in restraint of trade is an agreement among competitors to charge the same price for their products (**price fixing**). Such agreements among producers to set prices in advance rather than allow prices to be set by the operations of a free market are obviously anticompetitive and in restraint of trade.

E. In Sherman Act cases the facts must show that an allegedly illegal activity was either in interstate commerce or had a substantial effect on interstate commerce.

III. Section 2 of the Sherman Act regulates **monopoly** and the attempts to monopolize any part of interstate or foreign commerce. The law establishes the means to break up existing monopolies and to prevent others from developing. A monopoly is generally 80% or more control of a market.

A. Under Section 2, it is a violation for a firm to monopolize, attempt to monopolize, or conspire to monopolize any part of interstate or foreign commerce.

B. Proof of monopoly power alone is not enough. Some monopolies are lawful. If monopoly power is "thrust upon" a firm or if it exists because of a patent or franchise, there is no violation of Section 2 if the firm does not engage in conduct that has the effect or purpose of protecting, enforcing, or extending the monopoly power.

C. The power must have been either acquired or used in ways that go beyond normal, honest industrial business conduct for a violation to exist. To be illegal, the monopoly must have been *deliberatively* acquired or used. **Predatory conduct** would prove deliberativeness. Predatory conduct is seeking to advance market share by injuring actual or potential competitors by means other than improved performance. Proof of predatory conduct may be found in pricing policies such as:

1. Profit-maximizing pricing
2. Limit pricing, where the price is limited to levels that tend to discourage entry
3. The practice of price discrimination

D. In determining whether monopoly exists a court must decide:

1. What the *relevant product market* is, i.e., what is the product (or service) being monopolized. For instance, is the relevant product market "dog food" or "*dry* dog food"?
2. What the relevant *geographic market is*, i.e., in what part of the country is the monopoly occurring. Is it statewide, regionally, or national.
3. In monopoly cases the plaintiff always argues for narrow definitions of the relevant markets because monopoly is more likely to exist in narrow markets. The defendant argues for broad markets.

IV. Although Section 1 of the Sherman Act declares "*every* contract … in restraint of trade" to be illegal, the Supreme Court has held that Congress did not really mean *every*. The courts follow two principles and a middle ground to guide applicability in antitrust law:

A. The **rule of reason** requires that restraint of trade cases or attempts to monopolize are violations only if they constitute *unreasonable* restraint of trade or attempts to monopolize. The *test of reasonableness* has two parts:

1. The nature of character of the contracts
2. Surrounding circumstances giving rise to the influence or presumption that the contracts were intended to restrain trade and enhance prices.

B. The concept of **per se illegality** simplifies proof in cases in which it is applied. This concept applies to activities that have such a harmful effect on competition that elaborate inquiry as to the precise harm they may cause or business excuse for committing them is not necessary. Proof of the activity is proof of the violation. *Unreasonableness* is presumed.

C. The middle ground between the above two principles is called the **quick look** analysis. The activity does not involve clearly anticompetitive activities, so the per se illegal analysis is not applicable. However, the court believes that the activity tends to be anticompetitive and so a thorough economic analysis is not necessary.

D. In *California Dental Assoc. v. FTC*, the U.S. Supreme Court observed that rule of reason, per se, and quick look illegality blur and that in this case the lower court should have looked more carefully at how the FTC assumed that dental advertising restrictions were per se illegal.

V. The Sherman Act, as amended by the Clayton Act, recognizes four separate legal sanctions:

A. Federal criminal penalties may be imposed. Crimes under the Sherman Act are felonies. *Individuals may be fined up to $350,000 and imprisoned up to three years. Corporations may be fined up to $10 million for each offense.*

B. When the success of a criminal prosecution is doubtful, the court may issue an *injunction* that will prevent and constrain anticompetitive behavior, or even break up a corporation. It takes less proof to enjoin an activity (*preponderance of the evidence*) than it does to convict of a crime (*beyond a reasonable doubt*).

C. Injured private parties may collect **triple damages**, plus court costs and reasonable attorneys' fees. This award both compensates the victims of anticompetitive behavior and punishes the defendants, imposing financial burdens far in excess of any fine that could be imposed, because the liability of defendants is based on tort law and is said to be *joint and several*. If there are ten defendants and nine of them settle out of court, the tenth defendant, if convicted, can be required to pay triple the damages caused by all ten.

D. To avoid the impact of a criminal guilty plea or a conviction on a pending civil antitrust suit, the criminally accused defendant often pleads **nolo contendere** (no contest). Since the plea technically is interpreted as avoiding a conviction, civil plaintiff is left with the burden of proving the antitrust violation.

VI. Certain businesses may be *exempt* from the Sherman Act because of a statute or as the result of a judicial decision. Insurance, shipping, investment companies, labor unions, and activities required by state law are all often exempt. The exemptions are narrowly construed, however, and do not mean that every activity of a firm is necessarily exempted simply because most activities are exempted.

A. For example, in 1943 the Supreme Court created a **state action exemption** to the Sherman Act. This exemption, known as the **Parker v. Brown doctrine**, is based on the reasoning that the Sherman Act *does not apply to state government*. When a state acts in its sovereign capacity, it is immune from federal antitrust scrutiny. The state must *intend* to restrict competition and exercise *oversight* in imposing its restriction on competition.

B. The **Noerr-Pennington doctrine** exempts concerted joint efforts to lobby government officials, regardless of the anticompetitive purposes of the lobbying effort. This exemption is based on the First Amendment right to petition government for a redress of grievances and recognition of the value of the free flow of information.

TYPES OF CASES

The types of Sherman Act cases typically heard in courts can be divided into *price fixing*, *territorial agreements*, and *concerted activities*. Price fixing cases are based on the philosophy that a competitive marketplace requires prices to be set by the operation of private markets. No competitor should have the economic power to set prices. The legal analysis used in price fixing cases is hotly debated regardless of the form of pricing agreements: horizontal, vertical, or indirect.

VII. **Horizontal price fixing** is agreement *between competitors* to fix prices. The term *price fixing* means more than setting a price. The price fixing covered by the Sherman Act is that which threatens free competition.

A. It is no defense that the prices fixed are fair or reasonable. It is no defense that horizontal price fixing is engaged in by small competitors to allow them to compete with large competitors. All price fixing is illegal, i.e., it is *per se* illegal.

B. Price fixing in the service sector has been illegal since the 1970s. It is just as illegal to fix the price of services as it is to fix the price of goods; nor is the establishment of ethical standards by professional groups, in an effort to avoid price fixing charges, legal.

VIII. **Vertical price fixing** or **resale price maintenance** is the attempt *by manufacturers* to control the ultimate *retail price* for their products.

A. Most resale price maintenance schemes run afoul of the Sherman Act; but it is possible for a manufacturer to legally control the resale price of its products by simply announcing its prices and refusing to deal with those who fail to comply. Under the **Colgate doctrine**, the Supreme Court recognizes that such independent action by a manufacturer is legal if there is no coercion or pressure other than the announced policy and its implementation.

B. A vertical restraint imposed by a single manufacturer or wholesaler may stimulate interbrand competition as it reduces intrabrand competition. The Supreme Court has announced that the rule of reason is the correct analysis when determining the legality of vertical price fixing situations.

C. In *State Oil Co. v. Khan*, the U.S. Supreme Court reviewed a number of its prior decisions related to vertical price fixing and determined that "rule of reason analysis will effectively identify those situations in which vertical price fixing amounts to anticompetitive conduct." State Oil Co. had effectively imposed maximum gas prices with its franchisee.

IX. Indirect price fixing is also illegal. Even the exchange among competitors of price information has been found illegal.

X. Territorial agreements restrain trade by allocating geographical areas among competitors. They may be either horizontal or vertical.

A. In a **horizontal territorial agreement**, *competing businesses* agree that each shall have an exclusive territory. Such horizontal agreements are per se illegal.

B. A **vertical territorial agreement** is one *between a manufacturer and a dealer* or distributor which assigns the dealer or distributor an exclusive territory, while the manufacturer agrees not to sell to other dealers or distributors in that territory so long as the dealer does not operate outside the territory. These vertical arrangements *are not per se violations*; they are subject to the rule of reason.

XI. When competitors share some activities or join together in the performance of a function, they engage in **concerted activities**. Concerted activities are often beneficial to society even though they reduce competition. Congress has enacted several laws to permit certain concerted activities in recognition of these benefits. The National Cooperative Production Amendments Act has three basic provisions that govern these activities:

A. *Joint production ventures* (two companies joining together to produce something) *will be subject to the rule of reason analysis* rather than the per se illegality standard.

B. A joint production venture must notify the Justice Department and the FTC of its plans to engage in joint activities.

C. In a private civil antitrust action brought against the joint production venture, the plaintiff can be awarded only *actual damages plus costs*. The joint production venture will *not* be subject to triple damages.

XII. By 1914 it had become apparent that the Sherman Act had not entirely accomplished its purpose, and practices that reduced competition were commonplace. In order to improve the antitrust laws, Congress enacted the Clayton Act and the Federal Trade Commission Act. The Clayton Act outlawed practices that have the effect of *substantially lessening competition or that tend to create a monopoly*. This made it possible to attack and remedy monopolistic practices before they could inflict full harm on the marketplace.

XIII. The Clayton Act, as originally adopted in 1914 made it unlawful for a seller to discriminate in the price that is charged to different purchasers of commodities when the effect may be to lessen competition substantially or to tend to create a monopoly in any line of commerce. Note that "price discrimination" is *not* the same thing as "price fixing."

   A. Discrimination in price on account of differences in the grade, quality, or quantity of the commodity sold was not illegal under the 1914 act. In the 1920s and early 1930s, big retailers used the techniques such as large-volume discounts to obtain more favorable prices than their smaller competitors received. These practices led to the 1936 Robinson-Patman amendment to the Clayton Act, also called *Section 2*.

   1. The **Robinson-Patman amendment** attempts to ensure quality of price to all customers of a seller of commodities for resale, thus eliminating the advantage of the larger buyer's quantity-purchasing ability. Violation of this statute is illegal for both the seller and *for a buyer who knowingly receives a lower price*.

   2. The Robinson-Patman amendment also outlaws **predatory pricing**. Predatory pricing is pricing below marginal cost by a company willing and able to sustain losses for a prolonged period to drive out competition.

   a. Under the Robinson-Patman amendment (Section 2) it is a crime for a seller to sell at lower prices in one geographic area than elsewhere in the United States to eliminate competition or a competitor.

   b. It is also a crime under the Robinson-Patman amendment for a seller to sell at unreasonably low prices to drive out a competitor.

   c. Section 2 is violated civilly anytime a seller sells across a state line to two different buyers at different prices *and* the effect may be substantially to lessen competition or tend to create a monopoly.

   d. In *Texaco v. Hasbrouck*, the U.S. Supreme Court upheld the liability of Texaco under Section 2 upon the finding that gas wholesalers who received a better price from Texaco than retailers did were actually themselves engaging in retail operations encouraged by Texaco. Thus the wholesalers were competitors of the retailers.

B. The Robinson-Patman amendment recognizes certain exceptions or defenses.

    1. Sellers may select their own customers in good-faith transactions and not in restraint of trade. Thus, sellers may choose to sell only to high volume purchasers.

    2. Price changes may be made in response to changing conditions, such as actual or imminent deterioration of perishable goods (changing conditions defense).

    3. Price differentials based on differences in the cost of manufacture, sale, or delivery of commodities are permitted. This is the **cost justification defense**.

    4. A seller in good faith may meet the equally low price of a competitor, the **good-faith meeting-of-competition defense**. This defense is available to both the seller and the buyer.

XIV. *Section 3* of the Clayton Act limits the use of certain types of contractual arrangements involving goods when the impact of these contracts may substantially lessen competition or tends to create a monopoly. Section 3 applies to several practices.

A. A **tying contract** is one in which a product is sold or leased only on the condition that the buyer (or lessee) purchase a different product or service from the seller or lessor. It is considered unfair or harmful to the seller's competitors who could otherwise sell products or services to the buyer. A common type of tying arrangement is known as **full-line forcing**. In full-line forcing, the buyer or lessee is compelled to take a complete product line from the seller.

B. A **reciprocal dealing** arrangement exists when two parties face each other as both buyer and seller. One party agrees to buy the other's goods but only if the second party buys goods from the first party.

C. An **exclusive dealing** contract contains a provision that one party or the other (buyer or seller) will deal only with the other party. Such agreements tend to foreclose a portion of the market from competitors. For example, in a **requirements contract**, a buyer agrees to purchase all of its needs of a given contract from the seller during a certain period of time. In effect, the buyer is agreeing not to purchase any of the products from competitors of the seller.

D. In addition to illegality under Section 3, the courts tend to give per se violation treatment to tying and exclusive contracts under the Sherman Act if they substantially affect commerce.

XV. *Section 7* of the Clayton Act makes certain mergers and acquisitions illegal. **Mergers** occur when companies A and B join together, leaving only a larger company A. However, Section 7 applies also when A buys stock in B or buys the assets of B. For our purposes, the word "merger" covers all these acquisitions too.

A.   A **horizontal merger** usually combines two businesses in the same field or industry. Because the acquired and acquiring companies have competed with each other, the merger reduces the number of competitors and leads to greater concentration in the industry.

    1.   A **market extension merger** describes an acquisition in which the acquiring company extends its markets.

    2.   Market extension mergers may be either in new products (**product extension**) or in new areas (**geographic extension**).

B.   A **vertical extension merger** brings together one company that is the customer of the other in one of the lines of commerce in which the other is a supplier.

C.   A **conglomerate merger** is one in which the businesses involved neither compete nor are related as customer and supplier in any given line of commerce.

D.   In 1950, Congress passed the **Celler-Kefauver amendment**, which plugged the stock-versus-assets loophole of the Clayton Act by also covering the acquisition of assets. This amendment prohibited all acquisitions in which the effect lessened competition substantially in any line of commerce in any section of the country.

E.   In merger cases the plaintiff and defendant must define the relevant markets just as in III (D) above.

THE FEDERAL TRADE COMMISSION ACT – UNFAIR COMPETITION

The Federal Trade Commission (FTC) enforces the Clayton Act, as well as Section 5 of the Federal Trade Commission Act, which made "unfair methods of competition" in commerce unlawful. The **Wheeler-Lea amendment** in 1938 added that "unfair or deceptive acts or practices in commerce" are also unlawful under Section 5.

XVI.   The FTC has broad, sweeping powers and a mandate to determine what methods, acts, or practices in commerce constitute unfair competition. The term *unfair methods of competition* was designed by Congress as a flexible concept, which can apply to a variety of unrelated activities.

    A.   To decide whether challenged business conduct is "unfair" as a method of competition or as a commercial practice, the FTC asks three major questions if there is no deception or antitrust violation involved:

        1.   Does the conduct injure consumers significantly?
        2.   Does the conduct offend an established public policy?
        3.   Is the conduct oppressive, unscrupulous, immoral, or unethical?

B. Answering any one of these three questions affirmatively could lead to a finding of unfairness. Even if anticompetitive acts or practices *fall short* of transgressing the Sherman or Clayton Act, the FTC may find that the business practice is unfair and prohibit it.

C. In *Toys "R" Us, Inc. v. FTC*, the federal 7th Circuit court of appeals upheld the FTC's determination under the FTC Act that Toys "R" Us had applied pressure on its suppliers to boycott (fail to deal with) some of Toys "R" Us's competitors.

XVII. The primary function of the FTC is to *prevent* illegal business practices *rather than punish* violations. It prevents wrongful actions by the use of cease and desist orders. To prevent unfair competition, the FTC issues trade regulation rules that deal with business practices in an industry plus FTC guidelines on particular practices. FTC guidelines are administrative interpretations of the statutes the commission enforces. Private parties cannot sue under the FTC Act.

COMPLETION EXERCISES

1. A fiduciary relationship where one owns resources for the benefit of another is another as a _____.

2. The antitrust law passed by Congress in 1890 is the _____.

3. In 1914 Congress amended antitrust by passing the _____.

4. The administrative agency charged with keeping competition free and fair is the _____.

5. An agreement among competitors to charge the same price for their products is called _____.

6. 80% or more control of a product or service market in a particular geographic area is called _____.

7. When unreasonableness is presumed in a restraint of trade case, the restraint is said to be a _____ violation of Section 1 of the Sherman Act.

8. Injured private parties can collect _____ damages for a Sherman Act violation.

9. When manufacturers attempt to control the retail price of a product sold by a retailer, the practice is known as _____.

10. The Robinson-Patman amendment prohibits _____ when the effect may be to lessen competition substantially or tend to create a monopoly.

TRUE-FALSE SELECTIONS

1. _____ Price discrimination is the same practice as price fixing.

2. _____ Joint ventures are subject to the rule of reason analysis rather than being per se illegal.

3. _____ Pricing below marginal cost to drive out competition is known as predatory pricing.

4. _____ Cost justification is no defense in a price discrimination case.

5. _____ Section 7 of the Clayton Act applies to business acquisitions known generally as mergers.

6. _____ Exclusive dealing contracts are per se illegal.

7. _____ Full line forcing is a type of tying contract.

8. _____ The Wheeler-Lea amendment applies to Section 5 of the FTC Act.

9. _____ The primary function of the FTC is to punish illegal business practices.

10. _____ Private parties have standing to sue under the FTC Act.

MULTIPLE CHOICE PROBLEMS

1. Juan and Mary work for competing sales companies. They agree that Juan's sales reps will sell exclusively in the northern half of the state; Mary's reps will sell exclusively in the southern half of the state. Select the *incorrect* choice:

    a. What Juan and Mary have done constitutes a misdemeanor.
    b. Juan and Mary have subjected their companies to possible triple damages.
    c. Juan's and Mary's conduct constitutes a per se violation of the Sherman Act.
    d. Juan and Mary as well as their companies can be held criminally responsible for what they did.

2.   For company X to determine whether or not it can legally merge with company Y, it must consider all of the following *except*:

    a.   The relevant product (or service) market
    b.   The relevant geographic market
    c.   The potential adverse effect of the merger on competition
    d.   The per se illegality of mergers.

3.   Select the most *correct* statement. For Sherman Act crimes:

    a.   Individuals can be fined up to $350,000.
    b.   Individuals can be imprisoned up to 3 years.
    c.   Corporations can be fined up to $3 million.
    d.   Injunctions restraining anti-competitive practices and monopoly can be issued by a court.

4.   Which of the following restraints are most likely to be per se restraints of the Sherman Act?

    a.   Horizontal restraints.
    b.   Vertical restraints.
    c.   Requirement contracts.
    d.   Joint production ventures.

5.   Which of the following does *not* establish an exemption to the Sherman Act?

    a.   Parker v. Brown doctrine
    b.   Noerr-Pennington doctrine
    c.   Normal labor union activities
    d.   Nolo contendere plea

DISCUSSION ANALYSIS

Arnett Inc., a manufacturer of widgets, sells to different retailers at different prices. Explain the circumstances under which Arnett would *not* be in violation of the Clayton Act, Section 2 (Robinson-Patman amendment).

Chapter
14

Employment and Labor Laws

As a business manager, a working knowledge of laws and regulations related to employment are vital to your success. This chapter discussed one of the most important policy initiatives of the federal government in the employment setting, the union-management relationship.

CURRENT TRENDS AND ISSUES

The following three sections discuss legal issues involving the federal Fair Labor Standards Act, the employment-at-will doctrine, and employees' privacy rights. A fourth section raises some questions concerning how the business manager should handle an employee's complaint prior to taking any action relating to the employee.

I.   The federal government regulates wages and hours through the **Fair Labor Standards act (FLSA)**, which was originally enacted in 1938. Amendments to the FLSA have kept it up to date.

     A.   The FLSA sets minimum wage (currently $5.15 per hour), sets overtime rates (at least 1 ½ times hourly rate over 40 hours weekly).

     B.   In *Christensen v. Harris County*, the U.S. Supreme Court ruled that under the FLSA employers could require employees to take time off from work paid at the employees' regular wage rather than paying them 1 1/2. their regular wage for overtime the employees' worked.

II.   Historically, unless employees contracted for a definite period of employment, employers were able to discharge them without cause at any time. This is called the **employment-at-will** doctrine. Now many federal and state laws limit employers in their right to terminate employees, even at-will employees.

     A.   The Labor-Management Relations Act prohibits employers from firing employees for union activities.

B. Under contract theory, many courts have stated that at-will employment contracts, though not written, contain an implied promise of good faith and fair dealing by the employer. This promise can be broken by unjustified dismissal of employees.

C. Other courts have held employers liable for breach of contract for discharging an employee in violation of statements made in a personnel handbook about discharge procedures.

D. Many cases that limit at-will employment state that the employer has violated *public policy*.

E. Many contract and tort exceptions to employment at will have involved one of three types of employer behavior:

1. Discharge of employee for performance of an important public obligation, such as jury duty
2. Discharge of employee for reporting employer's alleged violations of law (whistle-blowing)
3. Discharge of employee for exercising statutory rights

III. Workers' privacy is an area of concern to both the federal government and the states. There are a number of privacy concerns being addressed by privacy-related statutes and court decisions.

A. Several states guarantee workers access to their job personnel files and restrict disclosure of personal information to third parties.

B. Under the 1988 Employee Polygraph Protection Act, a federal statute, private employers generally are forbidden from using lie detector tests while screening job applicants. Current employees may not be tested randomly but may be tested as a result of a specific incident or activity that causes economic injury or loss to an employer's business.

C. At present there is no uniform law regarding employee drug testing, although some states have placed some limits on a private company's right to test for drugs. Public employees are protected from some drug testing by the Fourth Amendment's prohibition against *unreasonable* searches; however, exactly when drug tests are unreasonable is subject to much debate.

D. The expectation of privacy regarding e-mail is very limited. In *Garrity v. John Hancock Ins. Co.*, a federal district court determined that an employer's investigation of the plaintiff employees' sexually-oriented email sent to co-workers did not violate their privacy, nor did publication to other employees of the termination of plaintiff employees for violating the employer's well-known policy prohibiting sexually-oriented email defame the plaintiff employees.

IV.   Most employers strive to obey the law. They still risk lawsuits, however, including many brought by unsatisfactory employees who have been disciplined, denied promotion, or discharged. Detailed documentation, sometimes called the **paper fortress**, is vital in successfully responding to unjustified employee lawsuits.

A.   Each potential employee should be required to carefully study a well-written job description of the position for which he or she is applying.

B.   Once a new employee is hired, the employer should give the employee a personnel manual, which outlines work rules and job requirements. Clear identification of employer expectations and policies helps provide a defense against employee lawsuits if subsequent discipline or discharge of the employee becomes necessary. The employer should have the employee sign a form indicating receipt and understanding of the manual. This form should go in the employee's personnel file.

C.   Regular written evaluations of employee performance should also be entered into the personnel file. A chronological record of unsatisfactory work performance is a very useful defense against unjustified lawsuits.

D.   Anytime an employee breaks a work rule or performs unsatisfactorily, the employer should issue the employee a written warning and place a duplicate in the personnel file. In addition, employers should either have an employee sign that he or she has received a written warning or else note in the personnel file that the employee has received a copy of it.

E.   In an actual termination conversation, the employer should provide the employee with specific reasons for discharge, taken from the personnel file.

LABOR-MANAGEMENT RELATIONSHIP

The goal of labor law is successful **collective bargaining**, the process by which labor and management negotiate and reach agreements on matters of importance to both – matters such as wages, hours and other terms and conditions of employment. Collective bargaining can be successful only if the bargaining power of the parties is equal.

V.   Prior to 1935, Congress viewed the labor-management relationship as being unbalanced. In a series of laws that are thought of as being prolabor, Congress attempted to correct the perceived inequities.

A.   The first federal statute of any importance to the labor movement is the **Clayton Act** of 1914, which was passed principally to strengthen the antitrust laws.

1. The Clayton Act stated that antitrust laws regulating anticompetitive contracts did not apply to labor unions or their members *in lawfully carrying out their legitimate activities*.
2. Although the Clayton Act exempted employees from the claim that they were restraining trade through unionization, this law did not expressly grant employees the protected right to join a union.

B. Among the first industries to unionize were the railroads. In 1926, Congress enacted the **Railway Labor Act** to encourage collective bargaining in the railroad industry and thereby resolve disputes that might otherwise disrupt transportation and result in violence.

1. The act was later extended to airlines, and today it applies to both air and rail transportation.
2. The act established the three-member **National Mediation Board**, which must designate the bargaining representative for any given bargaining unit of employees in the air and rail industries. If mediation does not resolve disputes, the Board can take further steps to encourage agreement before management lockouts or worker strikes become legal.

C. Prior to 1932, management often made it a condition of employment that employees agree to not join a labor union. These agreements were known as **yellow-dog contracts**. In 1932, the **Norris-LaGuardia Act** made yellow-dog contracts illegal.

D. The Norris-LaGuardia Act listed specific acts of persons and organizations participating in labor disputes that *were not subject to federal court injunctions*. They are:

1. Striking or quitting work
2. Belonging to a labor organization
3. Paying strike or unemployment benefits to participants in a labor dispute
4. Publicizing the existence of a labor dispute or the facts related to it, including picketing
5. Assembling peaceably to promote interests in a labor dispute
6. Agreeing with others or advising or causing them to do any of the above acts without fraud or violence

E. Under the Norris-LaGuardia Act, an injunction may be issued to enjoin an *illegal* strike. Note that the Norris-LaGuardia Act does not limit the jurisdiction of state courts in issuing injunctions in labor disputes.

THE WAGNER ACT

The labor movement received its greatest stimulus for growth with the enactment in 1935 of the National Labor Relations Act, known as the **Wagner Act**. In this act, Congress explicitly affirmed labor's right to organize and to bargain collectively. Key provisions of the act are:

1. Creating the National Relations Board (NLRB) to administer the act.
2. Providing employees the right to select a union to act as their collective bargaining agent, i.e., to represent them in negotiations with management.
3. Outlawing certain conduct by employers that generally has the effect of either preventing the organization of employees or emasculating their unions where they do exist; these forbidden acts are called *unfair labor practices*.
4. Authorizing the NLRB to conduct hearings on unfair labor practice allegations and, if unfair practices are found to exist, to take corrective action including issuing cease and desist orders and awarding dollar damages to unions and employees.

VI. Established by the Wagner Act, the **National Labor Relations Board** operates as an independent administrative agency of the U.S. government.

A. The NLRB consists of five members, appointed by the President with the advice and consent of the Senate. There is also a general counsel of the Board who supervises operations of the NLRB, to help the Board to perform its quasi-judicial function of deciding unfair labor practice cases free of bias.

B. The board determines policy questions, such as what types of employers and groups of employees are covered by the labor law. Courts are bound to defer to the rulings of the NLRB as long as the board members reach a reasonable result.

C. Congress gave the NLRB jurisdiction over any business "affecting commerce." Some employers and employees *are specifically exempt* from NLRB jurisdiction, however:

1. Employees of federal and state governments
2. Employees of political subdivisions of the states
3. Persons subject to the Railway Labor Act
4. Independent contractors
5. Individuals employed as agricultural laborers or domestic servants in a home
6. Individuals employed by their spouse or parent

D. The NLRB has never been able to exercise fully the powers given it because of budget and time constraints. It has limited its own jurisdiction to businesses of certain size. As a result of this policy, federal laws do not cover many small employers, which are subject to applicable state law. Of course, the board may decide to take jurisdiction over *any* business that affects interstate commerce.

E.   Congress has granted the NLRB the authority to conduct the quasi-judicial hearing that are required to investigate and to enforce sanctions if unfair labor practices occur. The NLRB has discretion to order whatever action is necessary to correct the unlawful practice.

VII.   A major purpose of the Wagner Act is to require employers to recognize and negotiate with unions that are appropriately certified as representing the employee unit. Union certification may occur in any one of several ways.

A.   An employer may voluntarily recognize that its workers desire to have a certain labor union represent them. Such voluntary recognition occurs in relatively few situations.

B.   More common is the NLRB's certification of a union as the *bargaining agent* for a group of employees. There are two kinds of certification processes:

1.   Unionization elections are by *secret ballot* and are supervised by the NLRB.

a. The NLRB conducts elections upon receipt of a petition signed by at least *30 percent* of the employees.
b. The Board decides what unit of employees is appropriate for purposes of collective bargaining and therefore which employees are entitled to vote in the election.
c. In *NLRB v. Kentucky River Community Care, Inc.*, the U.S. Supreme Court emphasized that the burden of proving that an employee is a supervisor (and thus a non-voting part of management in a union certification election) is on the party claiming that the employee is a supervisor. In this case the NLRB had incorrectly placed the burden on the employer to prove that certain employees were *not* supervisors.

2.   Cards may substitute for an election.

a. A union seeking to represent employees may solicit cards from them indicating their willingness for the union to represent them.
b. An employer *may then recognize* the union as the bargaining agent for its employees if the cards are signed by a majority of the employees. The employer, however, also has *the right to insist on an election* unless the NLRB issues a bargaining order, which it may do if the cards are unequivocal and clearly indicate that the employees signing the cards are authorizing the union to represent them.

VIII.   The Wagner Act set forth five kinds of *unfair labor practices* that management must not engage in. Conduct may be, and often it, a violation of more than one of these practices. The unfair labor practices are:

A. Interfering with unionization, which has two distinct parts:

1. It is unfair for an employer to *interfere with the efforts of employees to form, join, or assist labor organizations.* This prohibition is intended to prevent "scare" tactics, such as threats to fire union organizers, as well as certain other activities calculated to erode employee support for the union. In *Allentown Mack Sales v. NLRB*, the U.S. Supreme Court decided that an employer's polling of employees to determine whether they continued to support their union was not an unfair labor practice when there was no substantial evidence on the record to show the employer lacked reasonable doubt about the employee's continued union support. In other words, when the employer was genuinely in doubt concerning the employees' support for the union, the poll did not interfere unfairly with unionization.

2. It is unfair for an employer to interfere with "concerted activities for mutual aid or protection." *This violation does not have to involve a union*; the act protects any group of employees acting for their mutual aid and protection. The term **concerted activity** is given a broad interpretation in order to create a climate that encourages unionization and collective bargaining. Even the actions of a sole employee may be protected by the concerted activity language of the Wagner Act if the employee has a grievance that may affect other workers, e.g., an employer may not discipline an employee who complains about safety conditions that affect other employees.

B. It is unfair for employers *to dominate a labor organization by giving it support*, financially or in any other way, such as providing a meeting place. Employers must also remain strictly neutral in the case of a controversy between competing unions.

C. An employer may neither *discharge nor refuse to hire an employee in order to encourage or discourage membership* in any labor organization.

1. The law does not oblige an employer to favor union members in hiring employees, nor does it restrict management in the normal exercise of any employer's right to select or discharge employees. However, the employer may not abuse that right by discriminatory action based on union membership or activities that encourage membership in a labor organization.

2. An employer may not go *partially* out of business because some of its employees have organized, nor may it temporarily close that portion of its business that has unionized. Partial closings to "chill" unionism are unfair labor practices.

D. Employees are protected from being discharged or from other reprisals by their employers because they have sought to enforce their rights under the Wagner Act by *filing charges or giving testimony* in NLRB proceedings. The employer can defend itself by proving to the NLRB that the employee was discharged because of misconduct or for other legitimate reasons.

E.   The fifth unfair labor practice occurs *when management refuses to bargain with the collective bargaining representative of its employees*, i.e., the union. Judicial decisions have added the concept of *good faith* to interpretations of the Wagner Act, meaning that employers must approach the bargaining table with a sincere intent to find a basis of agreement. There is no requirement of either side that they actually reach agreement, only that they bargain in good faith. Employers are not required to bargain on every issue of interest to employees; some bargaining issues are voluntary.

        1.   **Compulsory bargaining issues** are those issues concerned with *wages, hours, and other terms and conditions of employment*. The employer is *required* to bargain on these issues.

        2.   **Voluntary bargaining issues** are matters on which the employer *may or may not* choose to bargain. Such issues include whether to automate and lay off workers and at what price the employer will sell products or services.

THE TAFT-HARTLEY ACT

After passage of the Wagner Act, unions grew rapidly in strength and influence. By 1946, many felt that unions, with their ability to call nationwide, crippling strikes, had the better bargaining position over management. To balance the scale, the Labor-Management Relations Act (the **Taft-Hartley Act**) was passed in 1947.

The purposes of the Taft-Hartley Act are to ensure the free flow of commerce and to provide procedures for avoiding disputes that jeopardize the public health, safety, or interest. It recognizes that each party to collective bargaining needs protection from wrongful interference by the other, and that employees sometimes need protection from the union itself. The Act also authorized the creation of the Federal Mediation and Conciliation Service to assist the parties in settling labor disputes.

Major provisions of the Taft-Hartley Act:

1.   Provide for an *80-day cooling-off period* in strikes that imperil the nation's health or safety
2.   Reinforce the employer's freedom of speech in labor-management relations
3.   Outlaw the *closed-shop* concept but permits *union ships* in the absence of a state *right-to-know* law
4.   Permit suits by union members for breach of contract against unions
5.   Create six unfair labor practices by unions

IX.   The purpose of the *80-day cooling-off period* in the Taft-Hartley Act is to limit the adverse impact of nationwide strikes by steelworkers, mineworkers, autoworkers, and longshoremen that can paralyze the economy.

A.   The President appoints a board to study a threatened or actual strike or lockout. If the board finds the national interest is threatened, that there is a *national emergency*, the President goes to federal court for an injunction ordering the suspension of the strike or lockout for 80 days.

B.   During the 80-day period, the Federal Mediation and Conciliation Service works with the labor-management parties to try to achieve an agreement.

C.   If there is no agreement, there may be a strike. However, experience has shown that most disputes are settled during the 80-day period.

X.   Before 1947, employers had complained that the Wagner Act violated their right of free speech. *Taft-Hartley recognizes that employers have the right to make statements that cannot be construed as threats of reprisal or promises of benefit*; in other words, employers may not make statements that can reasonably be construed as intimidating employees, given the particular circumstances. Mere predictions or prophesies, however, are protected speech.

XI.   After the Wagner Act, unions were able to insist in many bargaining situations that management *hire only union members*. In essence, to apply for a prospective job, a person would have to join the union. These situations became known as **closed shops**. *Taft-Hartley outlawed closed shops.*

A.   Taft-Hartley still permits the **union shop**. In a union shop contract, which also is known as a **union security clause**, *the employer agrees that after an employee has been hired that employee must join the union as a condition of continued employment.*

B.   If a state has adopted a **right-to-work law**, *the union shop is prohibited*. Workers may choose not to join a union and are not required to pay representation fees to the union that represents the employees. Such workers are still subject to the terms of the collective bargaining agreement, and the union must handle their grievances with management.

XII.   The Taft-Hartley Act provides that suits for breach of a contract between an employer and a labor organization can be filed in the federal district courts without regard to the amount in question. A labor organization is responsible for the acts of its agents and may sue or be sued by either employers or union members. Many suits against unions are by members alleging a breach of the duty of fair representation.

A.   The *duty of fair representation* by the union applies not only to the *negotiation* of a collective bargaining agreement but also to the *administration* of the agreement.

B.   Unions must fairly represent employees in disputes with the employer regarding the *interpretation* and *application* of the terms of an existing contract.

C.   Unions must fairly represent an employee in his or her grievance against the employer.

D.   A union member may also sue a local union for failing to enforce the international union's constitution and bylaws.

XIII.   Congress attempted to balance its setting forth in the Wagner Act of unfair labor practices by management by creating *unfair labor practices by unions* in the Taft-Hartley Act. They are:

A.   *Restraining or coercing an employee to join a union* or an employer in selecting representatives to bargain with the union. A common example occurs when unions threaten non-union employees in order to get them to join the union.

1.   A union may not restrain or coerce employees in the exercise of their rights to bargain collectively.
2.   Employees are guaranteed the right to *refrain* from union activities *unless they are required to join the union by a legal union shop agreement*.

B.   *Causing or attempting to cause the employer to discriminate against an employee who is not a union member* unless there is a legal union shop agreement in effect (prevents the use of the union shop as a means of intimidating employees who are at odds with union officials over their policies).

C.   Refusing to bargain with the employer if it is the NLRB-designated representative of the employees (complementary to the fifth unfair labor practice by management).

D.   Striking, picketing, or engaging in secondary boycotts for illegal purposes.

1.   Jurisdictional strikes are prohibited. A **jurisdictional strike** is used to force an employer to assign work to employees in one craft union rather than another. Such disputes are between two unions and must be submitted to the NLRB by the unions.
2.   Unions may not threaten or coerce an employer to recognize or bargain with one union if another one has been certified as the representative of its employees.
3.   Unions may not threaten, coerce, or restrain a third person, not party to a labor dispute, for the purpose of causing that third person to exert pressure on the company involved in the labor dispute (**secondary boycott**). Strikes and picketing must be directed at the employer with which the union actually has a labor dispute.

E.   Charging new members excessive or discriminatory initiation fees when there is a union-shop agreement.

F.   Causing an employer to pay for work not performed (featherbedding) (not of much importance today).

XIV.   In 1959, Congress passed the **Landrum-Griffin Act**, or Labor-Management Reporting and Disclosure Act (LMRDA) to address widespread corruption, violence, and lack of democratic procedures in some labor unions. This act provides for union reform, and its provisions constitute a *"bill of rights"* for union members. It also continues to try to balance the bargaining power between labor and management by adding one unfair labor practice by management and two by unions.

A.   Under the Landrum-Griffin Act, it is also an unfair labor practice for both the employer involved and the union to enter into a **hot-cargo contract**. A hot-cargo contract is one in which an employer voluntarily agrees to handle or work on goods or materials going to or coming from an employer designated by the union as "unfair." The law also forbids an employer and a union to make an agreement under which the employer stops doing business with any other employer.

B.   Picketing to force an employer *to recognize an uncertified union* is an unfair labor practice in the following cases:

1.   When the employer has lawfully recognized another union as the collective bargaining representative of its employees.
2.   When a valid representation election has been conducted by the NLRB within the past 12 months.
3.   When picketing has been conducted for an unreasonable time, in excess of 30 days, without a petition for a representation election being filed with the NLRB.

COMPLETION EXERCISES

1.   The federal government regulates hours through the _____.

2.   Historically, employers were able to discharge employees without cause (and employees could quit at any time) under the _____ doctrine.

3.   Most of the cases that limit at-will employment rule that the employer has violated _____.

4.   Private employers generally are prohibited from screening job applicants with the polygraph because of the _____ Act.

5.   Employers sometimes protect themselves from unjustified lawsuits from employees through maintaining detailed documentation of unsatisfactory job performance called the _____.

6.   The process by which labor and management negotiate and reach agreements is termed _____.

7.   Yellow-dog contracts under which employees agreed not to join unions were prohibited by the _____ Act.

8.   The 1935 statute creating the NLRB was the _____ Act, also known as the _____ Act.

9.   Forbidden acts by employers and employees are called _____.

10. The 1947 statute that provided for an 80-day cooling off period was the _____ Act.

TRUE-FALSE SELECTIONS

1.   _____   Under labor law the decision to whom the employer will sell a product is a compulsory bargaining issue.

2.   _____   The Taft-Hartley Act outlaws (prohibits) the closed shop.

3.   _____   It is illegal in most states for an employer to agree to require new employees as a condition of employment to join a union.

4.   _____   In states that have adopted right to work laws, the union shop agreement is prohibited.

5.   _____   The Taft-Hartley Act made jurisdictional strikes illegal.

6.   _____   The Wagner Act provides for the union members' "bill of rights."

7.   _____   The Landrum-Griffin Act makes the hot-cargo contract an unfair labor practice.

8.   _____   Featherbedding as an unfair labor practice is not of much importance today.

9.   _____   Labor law forbids an employer to agree with a union to stop doing business with any other employer.

10. ____ When a union-shop agreement is in effect, the law limits the size of union initiation fees and dues.

MULTIPLE CHOICE PROBLEMS

1. Select the most *incorrect* statement:

   a. In many states it is against public policy to fire an employee for whistleblowing.
   b. Under federal law, employers may use the polygraph to test suspected employees.
   c. Current federal law prohibits private employers from random drug testing.
   d. Many courts have ruled that statements in personnel handbooks create contracts between employers and employees regarding employee treatment.

2. The Norris-LaGuardia Act generally prohibited federal (but not state) courts from enjoining all of the following, *except*:

   a. Non-violent striking by employees.
   b. Non-violent picketing by employees.
   c. Employers' refusal to recognize unions.
   d. Payment of strike benefits.

3. Select the most *incorrect* statement about certification of the union as bargaining agent:

   a. Before an employer must deal with a union, the union must be certified by the NLRB to represent the employees.
   b. The NLRB conducts secret certification elections upon receipt of a petition signed by at least 30 percent of the employees.
   c. The NLRB determines the unit of employees appropriate for bargaining purposes (and thus also for voting).
   d. An employer must recognize the union as bargaining agent if more than 50 percent of the employees in an appropriate unit sign cards unequivocally authorizing the union to bargain for them.

4. Under the Wagner Act, all of the following are unfair labor practices by employers, *except*:

   a. Threatening to fire employees who support the union.
   b. Refusing to bargain over a decision to automate a plant and discharge its workers.
   c. Favoring one union over another leading up to a union certification election.
   d. Going partially out of business when a particular unit of workers has unionized.

5. Under the Taft-Hartley Act, all of the following are unfair labor practices by unions *except*:

    a. Threatening employees unless they join the union.
    b. Setting up picket lines around a work site common to several employers when a labor dispute is with only one of them.
    c. Bargaining in a non-right-to-work state to get an employer to require all employees to join the union.
    d. Picketing a supplier of the union members' employer to get the supplier to put pressure on the employer regarding a labor matter.

DISCUSSION ANALYSIS

The philosopher John Locke wrote that people have property in themselves and their efforts. Discuss the organization of workers into a union as a property arrangement. Compare and contrast it to the organization of a corporation as a property arrangement.

Chapter
15

Discrimination in Employment

Laws prohibiting discrimination exist at both the federal and state levels. This chapter focuses on the principal such law, the Civil Rights Act of 1964, and its amendments. This law prohibits certain discrimination based on race, sex, color, religion, and national origin.

The chapter also covers other important anti-discrimination laws. It concludes with a discussion of trends in employment discrimination litigation and a short essay on employment discrimination, corporate governance, and the broad sense of property.

THE CIVIL RIGHTS ACT OF 1964

Historically, common law permitted employers to hire and fire virtually **at will** unless restrained by contract or statute. Under this system, white males came to dominate the job market. The most important statute regulating discriminatory employment practices today is the federal Civil Rights Act of 1964, as amended by the Equal Employment Opportunity Act of 1972 and the Civil Rights Act of 1991.

I.   The provisions of **Title VII** of the Civil Rights Act of 1964 apply to employers with 15 or more employees, to unions, and to employment agencies.

    A.   These laws prohibit discrimination based on race, color, religion, sex, or national origin.

    B.   The types of employer action in which discrimination is prohibited include:

        1.   Discharge
        2.   Refusal to hire
        3.   Compensation
        4.   Terms, conditions, or privileges of employment

    C.   Employers, unions, and employment agencies are prohibited from discrimination in their hiring and referral practices.

    D.   Employers, unions, and employment agencies are also prohibited from discriminating against an employee, applicant, or union member because he or she has made a charge under the act or otherwise opposed any unlawful practice. Such discrimination is referred to as **retaliation**. Many Title VII lawsuits by employees are based on retaliation.

II.   The Civil Rights Act of 1964 created the Equal Employment Opportunity Commission (**EEOC**), which has the primary responsibility of enforcing the provisions of the act.

    A.   Under the Equal Employment Opportunity Act of 1972, the EEOC can file a civil suit in federal district court and represent a person charging a violation of the act, after first exhausting efforts to settle the claim.

    B.   Remedies that may be obtained in court include reinstatement, back pay, and injunctions against future violations of the act by the defendant.

    C.   Since discrimination complaints can take years to litigate and may involve large employee classes, the size of awards and settlements is sometimes many millions of dollars.

    D.   In 1991 Congress amended the Civil Rights Act *to allow compensatory and punitive damages in addition to back pay*, but *only* when employers are guilty of *intentional* discrimination.

    E.   In enacting Title VII of the Civil Rights Act of 1964, Congress made it clear that it did not intend to preempt states' fair employment laws.

    F.   To win a Title VII civil action, a plaintiff must generally prove either disparate treatment or disparate impact.

        1.   In proving **disparate treatment**, the plaintiff must convince the court that the employer *intentionally* discriminated against the plaintiff. If discrimination is intentional, it is illegal, even though other factors, such as customer preference, also contributed.

            a.   Disparate treatment is permitted if the employer can prove a bona fide occupational qualification (**BFOQ**).
            b.   To prove a BFOQ the employer must prove that all or substantially all of the class (e.g., women) discriminated against *cannot* perform the job.

        2.   In a **disparate impact** case the plaintiff must prove that the employer's policies had a discriminatory effect on a group protected by Title VII.

            a.   The employer can defeat the plaintiff's claim by proving the **business necessity defense**, that is that the policies used are job related and based on business necessity.

b.   The plaintiff can still establish a violation by showing that other policies would serve business necessity without having undesirable discriminatory effects.

G.   The 1991 amendments state that the showing of a statistically imbalanced workforce is not enough *in itself* to establish violation of Title VII.

III.   The primary objective of the Civil Rights Act of 1964 is the integration of African Americans into the mainstream of American society.   Title VII, which deals with employment practices, is the key legal regulation for achieving this goal.

A.   Title VII prohibits discriminatory employment practices, either intentional or with disparate impact, based on race or color.

1.   Discrimination is prohibited in activities that involve *recruiting*, *hiring*, and *promotion* of employees.
2.   The law also prohibits discrimination in *employment conditions* and *benefits*.

B.   Title VII prohibits employment discrimination against members of all races.

IV.   Title VII's prohibition against national origin discrimination protects various ethnic groups in the workplace.

A.   Discrimination concerning the speaking of a native language frequently causes national-origin lawsuits under Title VII.

B.   Title VII provisions apply equally to foreign companies operating in the United States.

V.   Under Title VII, employers cannot discriminate on the basis of religion.

A.   Religious corporations, associations, or societies can discriminate in all their employment practices on the basis of religion, but not on the basis of race, color, sex, or national origin.

B.   Other employers cannot discriminate on the basis of religion, and they must make **reasonable accommodation** to the religious needs of their employees if it does not result in undue hardship to them or their employees.

C.   Since 1990, Title VII complaints filed annually based on religious discrimination have more than doubled. Between 2002-03 alone, EEOC religious discrimination filings rose 21 percent. Since the 9/11 bombings, religious discrimination against Muslim employees has risen also.

VI. State statutes designed to "protect" women are not a defense to a claim of intentional sex discrimination under Title VII. The only legitimate defense is a bona fide occupational qualification. Sex must be provably relevant to job performance.

A. A common type of illegal sex discrimination in the workplace is **sexual harassment**. Under Title VII, an employer is liable for the sexual harassment of an employee by his or her supervisor. Commonly, this involves a promise of benefits or threat of loss if sexual favors are not granted the supervisor. Such harassment is sometimes called "quid pro quo" (this for that).

B. A related type of sexual harassment is the **hostile work environment**, one in which coworkers make offensive sexual comments or propositions, engage in suggestive touching, show nude pictures, or draw sexual graffiti. Any harassment reasonably perceived as "hostile and abusive" is illegal when it seriously effects conditions of employment.

   1. An employer is liable to a plaintiff employee for a hostile working environment created by fellow employees *only when the employer knows of the problem and fails to take prompt and reasonable steps to correct it.*
   2. An employer can defend itself by proving:

      a. That the employer exercised reasonable care to prevent and correct promptly any sexually harassing behavior

      and

      b. That the plaintiff employee unreasonably failed to take advantage of any preventive or corrective opportunities provided by the employer or to avoid harm otherwise.

C. In *Oncale v. Sundowner Offshore Services, Inc.*, the U.S. Supreme Court ruled that "same-sex sexual harassment is actionable under Title VII...." In other words, employers must protect employees when males harass males or females harass females *because* of their gender.

D. The Pregnancy Discrimination Act amended the Civil Rights Act in 1978. Under it, employers can no longer discriminate against women workers who become pregnant or give birth.

E. Sex discrimination in employment compensation is prohibited under both Title VII and the Equal Pay Act of 1963.

F. The Equal Pay Act prohibits an employer from discriminating on the basis of sex in the payment of wages for equal work performed. *Equal* does not mean *identical*; it means *substantially* equal.

G. Discrimination in pay is allowed if it arises from a seniority system, a merit system, a piecework production system, or any factor other than sex.

H. The courts have not interpreted Title VII to prohibit discrimination against employees based on their sexual orientation. They have defined the word *sex* to refer only to gender. Many cities and states, however, do forbid discrimination based on sexual orientation. Thousands of companies have also begun offering domestic partner benefits to all employees. Increasingly, state or local anti-discrimination laws also protect employees following transgender medical procedures.

EMPLOYMENT PRACTICES THAT MAY BE CHALLENGED

There are several specific employment practices that employees or job applicants may challenge as discriminatory. These practices include:

1. Setting testing and educational requirements
2. Having height and weight requirements for physical labor
3. Maintaining appearance requirements
4. Practicing affirmative action
5. Using seniority systems

VII. To help them find the right person for the right job, employers use questionnaires, interviews, references minimum educational requirements, and personnel tests, among other tools. However, employers must be extremely careful not to use tools that illegally discriminate.

A. Personnel tests can have a *disparate impact* on job applicants, as can educational standards, unless they are job related and necessary for business (business necessity defense).

B. The practice of *race norming* tests is the practice of setting two different cutoff test scores for employment based on race or one of the other Title VII categories. The Civil Rights Act amendments of 1991 specifically prohibit the race norming of employment tests.

VIII. Minimum or maximum height or weight job requirements apply equally to all job applicants, but if they have the effect of screening out applicants on the basis of race, national origin, or sex, the employer must demonstrate that such requirements are validly related to the ability to perform the work in question (business necessity defense).

IX. It is unclear whether appearance and grooming standards are legal or illegal. There have been rulings both ways, depending on whether or not a court believed that the business necessity defense applied to the standard involved.

X. Since the 1940s, a series of presidential executive orders have promoted nondiscrimination and **affirmative action** by employers who contract with federal government. The affirmative action requirement means that federally contracting employers must actively recruit members of minority groups being underused in the workforce.

    A. The Labor Department administers executive orders through its Office of Federal Contract Compliance Programs (OFCCP) to advance affirmative action in firms that do business with the federal government.

    B. Some affirmative action programs are voluntarily adopted by businesses or are the result of contracts negotiated with unions. Voluntarily adopted programs have sometimes subjected employers to charges of **reverse discrimination** when minorities or women with lower qualifications or less seniority than white males are given preference in employment or training. However, affirmative action is usually legal when it is designed to overcome historic under representation in the workforce and is implemented for a limited time.

    C. The 1991 Civil Rights Act amendments prohibit the setting of *quotas* for various groups in employment. Quotas exist when employers determine that a set percentage of the workforce must be of a certain gender, race, etc.

    D. The EEOC has issued guidelines intended to protect employers who set up affirmative action plans.

    E. Government-imposed affirmative action plans are subject to *strict judicial scrutiny*. To be constitutional under the equal protection clause, such plans must be supported by a *compelling interest*.

XI. **Seniority systems** give priority to those employees who have worked longer for a particular employer or in a particular line of employment of the employer. In a union shop, seniority systems are usually the result of collective bargaining. It is not an unlawful employment practice for an employer to apply different employment standards under a bona fide (good-faith) seniority system if the differences are not the result of an *intention* to discriminate.

OTHER STATUTES AND DISCRIMINATION IN EMPLOYMENT

The Civil Rights Act of 1964 is the most widely used anti-discrimination statute, but there are other important anti-discrimination laws. The following sections examine the Civil Rights Act of 1866, the Age Discrimination in Employment Act, the Americans with Disabilities Act, and various state and local laws.

XII. **Section 1981** of the Civil Rights Act of 1866 provides that "all persons ... shall have the same right to make and enforce contracts ... as enjoyed by white citizens." Courts have interpreted this section as banning racial discrimination in employment relationships.

    A. Often, plaintiffs alleging racial discrimination sue under both Title VII and under Section 1981; but there are at least two advantages to filing suit under Section 1981:

        1. There are no procedural requirements for bringing a suit under Section 1981, whereas there are a number of requirements plaintiffs must follow before bringing a private suit under Title VII of the Civil Rights Act of 1964.

        2. Under Section 1981, *courts can award unlimited compensatory and punitive damages*; there are no caps, as there are under Title VII.

    B. Section 1981 does not cover discrimination based on sex, religion, national origin, age, or handicap. It applies only to the hiring or firing of employees based on race and to protections against hostile workplace environments.

    C. Because the concept of race was quite broad in the nineteenth century, when the law was passed, courts have stated that the law applies to the descendants of a particular "family, tribe, people, or nation," a rather broad definition of race that includes ethnic origin.

XIII. Neither the Civil Rights Act nor the Equal Employment Opportunity Act forbids discrimination based on age. However, the Age Discrimination in Employment Act (**ADEA**) does.

    A. The ADEA prohibits employment discrimination against employees ages 40 and older, and prohibits the mandatory retirement of these employees. Only bona fide executives and high policy makers of private companies can be forced into early retirement.

    B. It is illegal to engage in disparate treatment (intentional discrimination) against employees on the basis of age, unless age is a bond fide occupational qualification. Job-related physical requirements are also allowed on a case-by-case basis, depending on business necessity.

C. Some courts, though not all, award damages for the psychological trauma of being illegally fired or forced to resign. *Willful* violations of the act entitle discrimination victims to *double damages*.

D. In *Reeves v. Sanderson Plumbing Products, Inc.* the U.S. Supreme Court ruled that it was appropriate for a jury to impose liability on an employer for age discrimination when the only discriminatory comments made by the employer did not occur in the actual termination context. The employee had convinced the jury that the nondiscriminatory reasons given for the firing were merely a pretext.

XIV. Most disabled people who want to work are not working. In 1990, Congress passed the Americans with Disabilities Act (**ADA**) to prohibit employment discrimination against the disabled and help them get work.

A. The ADA prohibits employers from asking about medical history or requiring medical exams prior to the offer of a job.

B. Under the ADA, **disability** is defined as "any physical or mental impairment that substantially limits one or more of an individual's major life activities."

C. The ADA prohibits employer discrimination against job applicants or employees based on:

1. Their having a disability
2. Their having had a disability in the past
3. Their being regarded as having a disability

D. Persons with AIDS are considered disabled for the purposes of the ADA, but homosexuality, sexual behavior disorders, compulsive gambling, kleptomania, and disorders resulting from *current* drug or alcohol use are not. Those recovering from drug or alcohol disabilities are protected under the ADA.

E. Employers of 15 or more employees, unions of 15 or more, and employment agencies are prohibited from discriminating against the qualified disabled. **Qualified disabled** are defined as those with a disability who, with or without reasonable accommodation, can perform the essential functions of a particular job position.

F. **Reasonable accommodation** is the required process of adjusting a job or work environment to fit the needs of disabled employees. An employer can plead *undue hardship*, defined as "an action requiring significant difficulty or expense," as a reason for not accommodating the needs of disabled employees.

G. In *U.S. Airways, Inc. v. Barnett*, the U.S. Supreme Court decided that an employer would ordinarily not have to reassign an employee who had become disabled *in violation of seniority rules* unless the employee could prove "special circumstances" showing the reassignment to be "reasonable."

H. Businesses must also reasonably accommodate not only employees for their disabilities under the ADA *but also customers and others who use the business's public facilities.*

I. Remedies under the ADA are basically the same remedies available under the Civil Rights Act.

XV. In 1997, Congress passed the Health Insurance Portability and Accountability Act (HIPAA). This act prohibits group health plans and health insurance issuers from discriminating against employees based on the employee's health status, medical condition or history, genetic information, or disability.

A. The main impact of the act is to prevent discrimination against individual employees in small businesses. Prior to the act, insurers were reluctant to cover individual employees whose medical condition might produce large claims.

B. HIPAA also guarantees that insured employees who leave their old employer are able to continue their health coverage, either through self-pay or by transferring to a new employer's health plan.

C. HIPAA's anti-discrimination provisions do not apply to individuals who purchase individual health insurance.

XVI. There is additional federal legislation that deals with employment discrimination.

A. The National Labor Relations Act of 1936 covers union certification, which can be revoked for discrimination, as well as labor-management negotiations in which discrimination is considered a mandatory bargaining issue.

B. Various other federal agencies may prohibit discriminatory employment practices under their authorizing statutes.

XVII. *Federal law specifically permits state legislatures to pass laws imposing additional duties and liabilities in the area of equal employment opportunity*, and many have done so.

A. State acts usually set up an administrative body, generally known as the Fair Employment Practices Commission, which as the power to make rules and regulations and hear and decide charges of violations filed by complainants.

B.   State acts sometimes protect categories of persons not protected by federal law, such as those exposed to discrimination on account of weight or sexual preference.

C.   Discrimination plaintiffs can also sue employers under various state common law causes of action and can usually receive unlimited compensatory and punitive damages. Greater numbers of plaintiffs seem to be suing under common law, such as battery and intentional infliction of mental distress.

XVIII. There are several trends in employment discrimination and litigation worth noting.

A.   More and more complaints are surfacing about discriminatory e-mail in the workplace. Companies should develop formal policies regarding acceptable e-mail use to protect themselves from hostile environment discrimination lawsuits.

B.   Private lawsuits alleging discrimination in employment has surged in recent years, more than tripling.

C.   The success of the Human Genome Project presents the possibility of using genetic testing to discriminate on the basis of genetic conditions. Some states have already prohibited employers from using genetic testing to evaluate employees, but more inclusive laws, and legislation at the federal level may be forthcoming.

D.   As arbitration clauses become more common in contracts, many employers have also begun placing arbitration clauses in employment contracts. The EEOC has issued a policy statement concluding that "agreements that mandate binding arbitration of discrimination claims as a condition of employment are contrary to the fundamental principles" of anti-discrimination laws. Nevertheless, the Supreme Court has upheld arbitration clauses in certain employment discrimination cases, and there are steps employers can take to eliminate many objections to the arbitration process.

E.   Employers are beginning to ask for and to get employment practices liability insurance, a type of insurance aimed specifically at discrimination claims. Some states, however, do not permit companies to insure against intentional discrimination claims.

IX.   Words often have both specific and broader meanings. In a discussion of employment discrimination, the terms *corporate governance* and *property* can both be appropriately used.

A.   In a broad sense, corporate governance refers to the general public regulation of businesses. In this sense, the regulation of the employer-employee relationship through nondiscrimination laws also deserves the name corporate governance.

B. In its larger sense, as set forth by James Madison, property embraces everything to which someone may attach a value and have a right. In this "larger and juster meaning," property applies to whether the employer has a right to discriminate or whether the employee/job applicant has the right not to be discriminated against.

1. Prior to enactment of anti-discrimination laws, employers had the right to exclude job applicants and employees from their businesses on the basis of race, sex, color, religion, national origin, age, and disability. This use of their businesses, and their right to exclude others from interfering with it was a type of property right, in the Madisonian sense.

2. Title VII and other anti-discrimination laws took this property right away from the employer and reassigned it to job applicants and employees. Under the law, these people now possess an exclusionary right not to have employers discriminate against them in the employment relationship.

3. The exclusionary right of property produces the potential for resource development, and resources represent not only physical things but also the conditions for human action. Therefore, the shift in the right of property, from the right of employers to discriminate to the right of employees to nondiscrimination, produces more nondiscrimination in the employer-employee relationship.

4. Note that the "Madisonian" sense of property is not property as current legal expression usually uses it. But for ethical analysis and theoretical understanding of law, this "larger and juster meaning" of property helps you understand that a basic exclusionary right applied to very many situations is at the heart of law and the maximum conditions for the production of many things.

COMPLETION EXERCISES

1. The primary anti-discrimination provision of the Civil Rights Act of 1964 is known as _____.

2. For an employer to discriminate against an employee for filing a discrimination claim against the employer is itself an illegal act called _____.

3. For an employer intentionally to discriminate against an employee on the basis of race, sex, color, religion, or national origin is called disparate _____.

4. When employer's policies unintentionally discriminate against employees on the basis of race, sex, color, religion, or national origin, it is called disparate _____.

5. When an employer's policies discriminate unintentionally, the employer can defend by proving _____.

6.   Even if an employer's policies intentionally discriminate, the employer can successfully defend by proving the classification is a(an) _____.

7.   If it does not result in undue hardship to employers, they must make _____ to the religious needs and practices of employees.

8.   For coworkers to create an abusive and discriminatory workplace for an employee based on race, sex, color, religion, or national origin is commonly known as a(an) _____ environment.

9.   Under the Equal Pay Act "equal" does not mean identical; it means _____ equal.

10.   The section of the Civil Rights Act of 1866 that prohibits racial discrimination in the making of contracts is known as _____.

TRUE-FALSE SELECTIONS

1.   ____   Under Section 1981, courts can award unlimited compensatory and punitive damages.

2.   ____   Willful violations of the ADEA entitle discrimination victims to triple damages.

3.   ____   The ADA prohibits employers from asking about a job applicant's medical history or requiring medical exams prior to the offer of a job.

4.   ____   The ADA prohibits discrimination only against the "qualified" disabled.

5.   ____   Union certification can be revoked if the union discriminates on the basis of race, sex, color, religion, national origin, age, or disability.

6.   ____   Many employers have begun placing arbitration clauses in employment contracts to cover, among other things, discrimination claims.

7.   ____   In its broader application, "corporate governance" includes prohibitions against employment discrimination.

8.   ____   Historically, common law permitted employers to hire and fire at will.

9.   ____   Title VII only applies to employers with 25 or more employees.

10.   ____   Under the 1964 Civil Rights Act as amended, plaintiffs can recover compensatory and punitive damages against their employers for illegal discrimination, but only when employers are guilty of intentional discrimination.

MULTIPLE CHOICE PROBLEMS

1. Select the most *incorrect* statement about Title VII:

    a. Title VII prohibits discrimination against employees because they are white.
    b. A statistically imbalanced workforce is enough by itself to prove a Title VII violation.
    c. Title VII applies to foreign companies operating in the U.S.
    d. Churches can legally discriminate under Title VII by hiring only members of their own faiths to work maintenance in their buildings.

2. Select the most *incorrect* statement against affirmative action:

    a. The OFCCP can require affirmative action of certain employers who do business with the federal government.
    b. Government-imposed affirmative action is constitutionally subject to strict judicial scrutiny and must be supported by compelling state interest.
    c. Affirmative action permits the setting of racial and gender quotas.
    d. Voluntarily adopted affirmative action has subjected employers to reverse discrimination lawsuits.

3. None of the following groups are considered "disabled" under the ADA, *except*:

    a. Those with sexual behavior disorders.
    b. Homosexuals.
    c. Those with prior histories of alcoholism or drug abuse.
    d. Those who currently use drugs or alcohol.

4. Arcog Inc. requires all of its employees to speak fluent English. Several Hispanics and Asians who are denied jobs due to their lack of English fluency sue under Title VII. Select the most *correct* answer based on the facts given.

    a. Arcog has violated Title VII.
    b. Arcog has not violated Title VII.
    c. Arcog has not violated Title VII if it can prove business necessity.
    d. If found liable under Title VII, Arcog will have to pay compensatory and punitive damages.

5.   Select the most *incorrect* statement about sexual harassment liability.

   a.   A promise of benefits or threat of loss if sexual favors are not granted a supervisor is called quid pro quo discrimination.
   b.   Hostile work environment discrimination is illegal only when it seriously affects conditions of employment.
   c.   An employer is liable for a hostile work environment only when it knows of the discrimination and fails to take prompt, reasonable steps to correct it.
   d.   An employer is liable for quid pro quo discrimination only when it knows of the discrimination and fails to take prompt, reasonable steps to correct it.

DISCUSSION ANALYSIS

Fredrique's of Holiwould, Inc. is a lingerie shop that hires only women to work as sales personnel in its shop. Does this policy violate Title VII? Discuss.

Chapter 16

Securities Regulations

The regulation of securities began as part of the program to help the United States overcome the great depression of the early 1930's. Although federal securities laws are now more than seventy years old, their application is at the heart of corporate governance during the first years of the 21st century.

A clear understanding of securities regulations and legal issues is essential if managers are to avoid the liability, both civil and criminal, discussed in this chapter. This chapter also acquaints investors with the laws designed to protect them.

INTRODUCTION

The following sections examine the broad legal meaning given to the word "security." Federal and state securities laws are also discussed. Such laws at the federal level regulate the sale of securities in interstate commerce as well as the operation of national securities exchanges. These sections should give you an understanding of two major federal securities laws – the *Securities Act of 1933* and the *Securities Exchange Act of 1934* – and significant recent legislation such as the *Sarbanes-Oxley Act*.

I. The term **security** has a very broad definition, because the objective of securities laws is to protect uninformed people from investing their money without sufficient information. The Supreme Court has held that a *security exists when one person invests money and looks to others to manage the money for profit*. There are three questions that must be answered affirmatively for a security to be involved:

   A. Is the investment in a common business activity?

   B. Is the investment based on a reasonable expectation of profits?

   C. Will these profits be earned through the efforts of someone other than the investor?

II. The **Securities and Exchange Commission (SEC)** is an administrative agency created in 1934 that is responsible for administering the federal securities laws.

A. The SEC consists of five commissioners appointed by the president as well as staff personnel.

B. The SEC has both quasi-legislative and quasi-judicial powers.

THE SECURITIES ACT OF 1933: GOING PUBLIC

The **Securities Act of 1933** is a disclosure law with respect to the *initial sale of securities to the public*. It requires disclosure of certain financial information to potential investors. The information must not be untrue or even misleading.

The act recognizes three sanctions for violations:

1. Criminal punishment
2. Civil liability
3. Injunction

Proof of an intentional violation usually is required before criminal or civil sanctions are imposed. Proof of negligence will, however, support an injunction.

III. Anyone who is involved with or promotes the initial sale of securities is subject to regulation under the Securities Act of 1933. Parties who must comply with the act's disclosure requirements are:

A. An **issuer**, the individual or business organization offering a security for sale to the public

B. An **underwriter**, anyone who participates in the original distribution of securities by selling such securities for the issuer or by guaranteeing their sale

C. A **controlling person**, one who controls or is controlled by the issuer, such as a major stockholder of a corporation

D. A **seller**, anyone who contracts with a purchaser or who is a motivating influence that causes the purchase transaction to occur

IV. The Securities Act of 1933 is viewed as a *disclosure* law. An issuer of securities who complies with the federal law must prepare, prior to any sale, a registration statement and a prospectus, which are disclosure documents.

A. A **registration statement** must be filed with the SEC. The statement includes *a detailed disclosure of financial and other information about the issuer and the controlling individuals* involved in the offering. The law describes selling activities permitted at the various stages of the registration process. There are three registration periods:

1. During the **prefiling period**, it is legal for the issuer of a security to engage in preliminary negotiations and agreements with underwriters. It is illegal to sell or even to offer to sell or to buy securities during this period.

2. After the registration statement is filed, a **waiting period** begins, typically lasting twenty days. During this time the SEC staff investigates the accuracy of the registration statement. It is still illegal during this waiting period *to sell* the securities; *however offers may be solicited and made*, though offers may not yet be accepted.

    a. Many solicitations during the waiting period are made in advertisements called **tombstone ads**. These are brief announcements identifying the security, its price, by whom orders will be executed and from whom to obtain a prospectus.

    b. During the waiting period solicitations may also be made by use of a statistical summary, a summary prospectus, or a preliminary prospectus.

3. The end of the waiting period is the beginning of the **posteffective period**. During this period, securities are sold. A **prospectus** must be furnished to any interested investor. This document contains the same essential information contained in the registration statement. Its purpose is to supply the investor with sufficient facts to make an intelligent investment decision. The law, however, does not prohibit the sale of worthless securities, nor prevent foolish investments.

V. Under the Securities Act of 1933, both civil and criminal liability may be imposed for violations. Criminal liability results from a *willful violation* of the act or from *fraud* in any offer or sale of securities, such as *when a material fact is omitted*. Three sections of the act apply directly to civil liability:

A. *Section 11 deals with registration statements.* It imposes liability on every person who signed the statement, who is named as a director or partner, who assists in the preparation, certification, or underwriting of the statement.

1. The above persons are liable if, as of the date the registration statement becomes effective, it:

    a. *Contains untrue statements of material facts*
    b. *Omits material facts* required by statute or regulation
    c. *Omits information that if not given makes the facts stated misleading,* such as half-truth

2. A plaintiff-purchaser need not prove reliance on a false registration statement to recover the investment amount.

3. Knowledge of the falsity by a defendant need not be proved, but reliance on an expert is. The reliance exception does not apply to the issuer, since the issuer provides information to the expert.

B. Section 12 of the Securities Act of 1933 is divided into two parts:

1. The first subsection of *Section 12 imposes liability on those who offer or sell securities that are not registered with the SEC.* Liability may be imposed regardless of the intent or conduct of the violators. However, in *Pinter v. Dahl*, the U.S. Supreme Court indicated that if the plaintiff had substantially equal responsibility for failing to file oil and gas securities, the defendant could raise this as a defense (the *in pari delicto defense*), and thus there would not be strict liability against the defendant for failing to register the securities.

2. The second subsection of *Section 12 imposes liability on sellers who use a prospectus or make communications that contain untrue or misleading statements of material fact.*

3. As under Subsection 11, the plaintiff does not have to prove reliance on the false or misleading prospectus or communication, nor does the plaintiff have to establish that the defendant intended the deception.

4. Plaintiffs may sue for their actual damages. A refund of the purchase price may also be available.

C. *Section 17* of the Securities Act of 1933 *prohibits the use of any instrument of interstate communication* if the offer or sale of any securities *when the result is*:

1. *To defraud.* In this case, the plaintiff must prove the defendant-seller's intent (**scienter**) to deceive or mislead.

2. *To obtain money or property by means of an untrue or misleading statement.* No proof of the defendant's intent is required.

3. To engage in a business transaction or practice that may operate to defraud or deceive a purchaser. No proof of intent is required.

VI. The Securities Act of 1933 recognizes several *defenses* that may be used to avoid civil liability. Among the most important are:

A. *Lack of materiality.* If the false or misleading information is not *material*, it should not have had an impact on the purchaser's decision-making process. A material fact is one that if correctly stated or disclosed would have deterred or tended to deter the average prudent investor from purchasing the securities in question.

B. *Expiration of the statute of limitations.* The basic period is one year from the discovery of the untrue statement or omission, or the time such a discovery would have been made with reasonable diligence, but not more than three years after the sale.

C. An important defense for experts, such as accountants, is the **due diligence defense**. To establish this defense, *the expert must prove* that a reasonable investigation of the financial statements of the issuer and controlling persons was conducted, that he or she was not guilty of fraud or negligence. The standard of *reasonableness* is that required of a prudent person in the management of his or her own resources. The burden of proof is on the expert.

SECURITIES EXCHANGE ACT OF 1934: BEING PUBLIC

The **Securities Exchange Act of 1934** *regulates transfers of securities after the initial sale.* The act, which created the Securities and Exchange Commission, also deals with the regulation of securities exchanges, brokers, and dealers in securities.

The Securities Exchange Act of 1934 *makes it illegal to sell a security on a national exchange unless a registration is effective for the security.*

The Securities Exchange Act also requires stockbrokers and dealers in interstate commerce to be registered and to keep detailed records of their activities and file annual reports with the SEC.

VII. Section 10(b) and Rule 10b-5 of the Securities Exchange Act of 1934 declare that *it is unlawful to use the mails or an instrumentality of interstate commerce or any national securities exchange to defraud any person in connection with the purchase or sale of any security.* Most of the litigation under the act is brought under this section and rule. Courts have interpreted Section 10(b) and Rule 10b-5 as implicitly providing a private cause of action for the benefit of defrauded investors. Issues include:

A. Who is liable?

1. Defendants tend to fall into four general categories:

a. Insiders
b. Broker-dealers
c. Corporations whose stock is purchased or sold by plaintiffs
d. Those, such as accountants, who aid and abet or conspire with a party who falls into one of the first three categories
e. In *SEC v. Zandford*, the U.S. Supreme Court ruled that the defendant broker's misappropriation of investment funds deposited with him was "in connection with the purchase or sale of a security" and thus was subject to civil liability under Rule 10b-5.

2. The statute and its rule require those standing in a fiduciary relationship (one of highest loyalty and good faith) to *disclose all material facts* before entering into transactions. Failure to do so is, in effect, fraudulent.

3. An accountant is liable for errors in financial statements contained in a filed report even though he or she only performed an unaudited write-up, if there are errors the accountant knew or should have known because of suspicious circumstances.

4. In essence, there is no federal statute of limitations for private actions under Section 10(b) of the 1934 Act. The statute of limitations is "the limitation period provided by the laws applicable in the jurisdiction" where the case arises.

B. What can be recovered by the plaintiff, and does the defendant have the right to seek contribution from third parties?

1. A plaintiff in a suit under Rule 10b-5 must prove damages.

2. The damages of a defrauded purchaser are actual losses or the excess of what was paid over the value of what was received. Courts sometimes use the *benefit of the bargain* measure of damages and award the buyer the difference between what was paid and what the security was represented to be worth.

3. A defrauded seller's damages are more difficult to compute. The seller's damages are the difference between the fair value of all that the seller received and the fair value of what would have been received had there been no fraud. If the defendant received more than the seller's loss, the seller is entitled to the defendant's profit as well.

4. Plaintiffs under Rule 10b-5 are also entitled to consequential damages, including lost dividends, brokerage fees, and taxes. Punitive damages are not permitted.

5. In *Musick, Peeler & Garrett v. Wausau Ins.*, the Supreme Court ruled that a defendant who is liable under Section 10(b) can seek contribution from third parties.

C. When is information *material* to the transaction?

1. Materiality under the 1934 act is the same as materiality under the 1933 act; however, liability under Rule 10b-5 requires proof of the defendant's intent to deceive. Section 10(b) and Rule 10b-5 are usually referred to as the *antifraud provisions* of the act.

2. The concept of fraud under Section 10(b) encompasses the half-truth that misleads. It also includes failure to correct a misleading impression already made as well as silence where there is a duty to speak.

VIII. Section 16, one of the most important provisions of the Securities Exchange Act of 1934, concerns insider transactions. *Insiders are prohibited from trading for profit so that they cannot make use of information that is available to them but not to the general public.*

A.   An **insider** is any person who:

   1.   *Owns more than 10 percent of any security.*
   2.   *Is a director or an officer of the issuer of the security.*

   a. In 1991, the SEC adopted rules defining an officer for insider trading purposes as the executive officers, accounting officer, chief financial officers, and controllers.
   b. The SEC examines the individual investor's function within the company rather than the title of the position held.

B.   Insiders must file with the SEC a statement of the amount of issues of which they are the owners. The filings must be revised upon any changes in ownership.

C.   Section 16 creates a presumption that *any profit by an insider made within a six-month time period is illegal.* The profits are referred to as **short-swing profits**, and they are absolutely prohibited and not dependent on any misuse of information. However, the SEC does not enforce the provisions of Section 16. It is enforced by civil actions filed by the issuer of the security (for example, a corporation) *or by a person who owns a security of the issuer* (for example, a shareholder).

IX.   The users of nonpublic information under the 1934 Act are treated like insiders if they can be classified as tippees.

A.   A **tippee** *is a person who learns of nonpublic information from an insider*, in other words, a temporary insider.

B.   If the tipper communicated nonpublic information for reasons other than personal gain, and no fiduciary was breached, neither the tipper nor the tippee is liable for a securities violation.

C.   The SEC has successfully argued that a person should be considered to be a temporary insider if that person conveys nonpublic information that was to have been kept confidential, e.g., a printer who learns such information by reading the non-public documents being printed. This is the **misappropriation theory** of *insider trading.* In *U.S. v. O'Hagan* the U.S. Supreme Court determined that a lawyer whose client was considering a tender offer (offering to buy the stock of a company from its investors) for Pillsbury Co. could be criminally liable under the misappropriation theory for buying Pillsbury stock.

D.   *The civil penalty for gaining illegal profits with nonpublic information is three times the profits gained.* Controlling persons who fail to prevent these violations by employees may be civilly liable for the greater amount of triple damages or $1,000,000.

E.   The *Insider Trading and Securities Fraud Enforcement Act of 1988* increased the penalties to their current level and also provided that suits alleging the illegal use of nonpublic information may be filed within a five-year period after the wrongful transaction. This is substantially longer than the limitation periods for other federal securities violations.

X.   In 1990, Congress passed the Securities Enforcement Remedies Act. This act added to the civil penalties provided by the 1933 and 1934 securities acts, as previously discussed.

A.   The Securities Enforcement Remedies Act provides that civil fines of up to $500,000 per organization and $100,000 per individual may be imposed and collected by the courts, and that *an individual found to have violated the securities laws may be prohibited by the court from serving as an officer or director of a business organization*.

B.   Under Section 18 of the Securities Exchange Act of 1934, both purchasers and sellers can be held liable for making false or misleading statements of material fact. Plaintiffs must prove three things:

1.   The defendant knowingly made a false statement
2.   Reliance on the false or misleading statement
3.   Damage

XI.   In 2002, Congress increased the criminal penalties for violating the Securities Exchange Act of 1934.

A.   An individual found guilty of filing false or misleading documents with the SEC *may be fined up to $5,000,000 and imprisoned for up to 20 years*. A business organization found guilty may be subject to a fine up to $25,000,000.

B.   An individual guilty of securities fraud may face a prison sentence of up to 25 years.

C.   Failure to file the required reports and documents makes the issuer subject to a $100 forfeiture per day. Lack of knowledge of a statute is no defense.

D.   Accountants, as well as officers and directors, may be found guilty of a crime for failure to disclose important facts to shareholder-investors.

1.   The critical issue for accountants is whether the financial statements as a whole fairly present the financial condition of the company.
2.   If they do not, the second issue is whether the accountant operated in good faith.

3. Accused accountants usually admit mistakes or even negligence but deny any criminal wrongdoing. Proof of motive is not required, however.

TRENDS IN SECURITIES LAWS

Federal statutes do not preempt states from imposing their own regulation of securities. Every person dealing with the issuance of securities should be familiar with the applicable state's securities regulations, as the intrastate aspects of the transaction are governed by the state. It is also important to make sure you are familiar with recent developments in securities law.

XII. In 2002, Congress passed the **Sarbanes-Oxley Act**. The act:

A. Increases the SEC budget significantly.

B. Creates a Public Company Accounting Oversight Board. Both the SEC chairman and the first chairman of the new Board have resigned as a result of controversy over the fact that *the Board reports to the SEC*, rather than having its own standing as an administrative agency.

C. *Requires that board members of corporate audit committees, which are responsible for the financial integrity of corporations, must be independent*, i.e., they must be outsiders who are not officers or employees of the company. This is generally seen as a positive step, but the ways in which it will change the oversight exhibited by CEOs and other key members of management teams remains to be seen.

D. *Mandates that CEOs certify financial statements*. This aspect of the act works in conjunction with the new requirements for corporate audit committees. It makes CEOs legally responsible for misrepresentations in these statements.

E. Increases criminal penalties (as discussed in Section XI).

XIII. As previously noted, *federal securities laws do not preempt the existence of state securities laws* or **blue sky laws**, so called because they were intended to protect the investor from buying "a piece of the attractive blue sky" (worthless or risky securities). In 1956, the Uniform Securities Act was proposed for adoption by all states, to bring state laws into closer alignment. Since that time, a majority of states have used the uniform proposal as a guideline; however state laws still vary a great deal.

A. Some states require *registration by notification*; others require *registration by qualification*.

1. Registration by *notification* allows issuers to offer securities for sale automatically after a stated period expires unless the administrative agency takes action to prevent the offering.

2. Registration by *qualification* usually requires a more detailed disclosure by the issuer. A security cannot be offered for sale until the administrative agency grants the issuer a license or certificate to sell securities.

B. The Uniform Securities Act also created a third procedure – *registration by coordination*. For those issuers of securities who must register with the SEC, duplicate documents are filed with the state's administrative agency. Unless a state official objects, the state registration becomes effective automatically when the federal registration statement is deemed effective.

C. Further compounding the confusion about blue sky laws, *various exemptions have been adopted by the states*. Every state likely has enacted at least one and perhaps a combination of four basic exemptions:

1. For an isolated transaction
2. For an offer or sale to a limited number of offerees or purchasers within a stated time period. This is probably the most common exemption, as it is part of the Uniform Securities Act, although states vary as to the maximum number of such offerees or purchaser involved, usually between five and thirty-five. The time period also may vary, with twelve months being the most common.
3. For a private offering
4. For a sale if the number of holders after the sale does not exceed a specified number

D. Although blue sky laws may cause confusion due to their variation, ignorance of the state legal requirements is no defense. Any person involved in issuing or transferring securities should consult with lawyers and accountants as well as other experts who have a working knowledge of securities regulations.

COMPLETION EXERCISES

1. The administrative agency that administers the federal securities laws is the _____.

2. When one person invests money and looks to others to manage the money for profit, the investment is termed a(an) _____.

3. The Securities Act of 1933 regulates the _____ of securities to the public.

4. The person offering a security for sale to the public is the _____.

5. One who sells initial securities offerings for the issuer or who guarantees their sale is called a(an) _____.

6.   The Securities Act of 1933 requires that a(an) _____ be filed with the SEC.

7.   After their initial sale, securities transfers are regulated under the _____.

8.   _____ and _____ make it unlawful to use the mail or other "instrumentality of interstate commerce to defraud any person in connection with the purchase or sale of a security."

9.   One who owns more than 10 percent of any security or who is a director or officer of the issuer of the security is known as a(an) _____.

10.   Illegal profits by insiders made within a six-month time period are known as _____.

TRUE-FALSE SELECTIONS

1.   _____   Tippees are treated as temporary insiders under securities law.

2.   _____   An accountant, lawyer, or a printer can be considered insiders under misappropriation theory.

3.   _____   An individual guilty of securities fraud faces a prison sentence up to 5 years.

4.   _____   The Sarbanes-Oxley Act decreased the SEC's budget significantly.

5.   _____   State securities laws are called "blue sky laws."

6.   _____   Ignorance of state blue sky laws is a defense to their violation.

7.   _____   Federal securities laws give a narrow meaning to the word "security."

8.   _____   The SEC has both quasi-legislative and quasi-judicial powers.

9.   _____   The Securities Act of 1933 is a disclosure law.

10.   _____   During the prefiling period, the issuer may offer to sell the security.

MULTIPLE CHOICE PROBLEMS

1. Linda Chen, CEO of Softwear, Inc. a publicly traded clothing company, bought Softwear stock on January 15 and sold Softwear stock on May 1 for a profit of $50,000. She has likely violated:

    a. Section 11 of the Securities Act of 1933.
    b. Section 12 of the Securities Act of 1933.
    c. Section 10(b) of the Securities Exchange Act of 1934.
    d. Section 16 of the Securities Exchange Act of 1934.

2. David Rausch owns 51 percent of Rausch industries, a publicly traded company. From this fact, which one of the following terms likely describes him most correctly?

    a. Issuer.
    b. Underwriter.
    c. Controlling person.
    d. Seller

3. The Securities Act of 1933 imposes liability on every person who signs a registration statement (select the *incorrect* statement).

    a. If it contains untrue statements of material fact.
    b. If it seeks to register a worthless security.
    c. If it omits material required facts.
    d. If it contains material half-truths.

4. The Securities Act of 1933 differs from the Securities Act of 1934 in that the former law:

    a. Applies only to initial offerings of securities.
    b. Applies only to fraud in the sale of securities.
    c. Does not contain a scienter requirement.
    d. Does not permit the due diligence defense.

5. Tombstone ads are securities solicitations that take place generally during:

    a. The prefiling period.
    b. The waiting period.
    c. The posteffective period.
    d. The prospective period.

DISCUSSION ANALYSIS

Explain and give examples of how the securities laws contribute to corporate governance.

Chapter
17

Environmental Laws and Pollution Control

Environmental regulation remains the single most expensive area of government's regulation of the business community. Environmental and pollution-control laws govern regulation on three levels:

1. Government's regulation of itself
2. Government's regulation of business
3. Suits by private individuals

GOVERNMENT'S REGULATION OF ITSELF

The modern environmental movement began in the 1960s. It generated political pressure that forced government to reassess its role in environmental issues.

I. **The National Environmental Policy Act (NEPA)** imposes specific "action-forcing" requirements on federal agencies. These requirements have a significant impact on the business community. The most important requirement demands that all federal agencies prepare an **environmental impact statement (EIS)** prior to taking certain actions. The EIS is a "detailed statement" that estimates the environmental impact of the proposed action.

   A. An EIS must be included by a federal agency "*in every recommendation or report on proposals for legislation and other major federal actions significantly affecting the quality of the human environment.*"

   B. The EIS must contain information on *adverse environmental effects that cannot be avoided, any irreversible use of resources necessary*, and *available alternatives to the action*. In *Metropolitan Edison Co. v. People Against Nuclear Energy*, the U.S. Supreme Court ruled that the Nuclear Regulatory Commission did not have to consider in an EIS the "psychological harm" that reopening a nuclear power plant might do to the community.

   C. One regulatory guideline that makes the EIS more useful directs federal agencies to engage in **scooping**. Scooping requires that even before preparing an EIS, agencies must designate which environmental issues of a contemplated action are most

209

significant. This encourages impact statements to focus on more substantial environmental concerns and reduce the attention devoted to trivial issues.

D. Another guideline requires that EISs be "clear, to the point, and written in plain English." This requirement helps those reading impact statements to understand them.

II. NEPA *does not require federal agencies to follow the conclusions of an EIS*; although if the environmental costs of a project outweigh the benefits, the project will likely be abandoned. Critics have several problems with the present EIS process:

A. Some critics point out that the present process fails to consider the economic injury caused by abandoning or delaying projects.

B. Others maintain that most impact statements are too descriptive and not sufficiently analytical. They fear the EIS is "a document of compliance rather than a decision-making tool."

C. A general criticism of the EIS process notes the limits of its usefulness. Environmental factors are often so complex that projections concerning environmental effects amount to little more than guesswork.

D. Many states have enacted legislation similar to the NEPA. Because states lack the resources and expertise of the federal government, state EISs are often even less helpful than those prepared by federal agencies.

GOVERNMENT'S REGULATION ON BUSINESS

The national commitment to a cleaner environment is here to stay. Over the past 25 years, the federal government has enacted a series of laws regulating the impact of private enterprise on the environment. More and more companies are hiring environmental managers to deal with environmental compliance issues.

III. One of the first steps taken at the federal level is response to concerns about the environment was the establishment of the **Environmental Protection Agency (EPA)** in 1970. The EPA coordinates public control of private action as it affects the environment. The EPA administers federal laws that concern pollution of the air and water, solid waste and toxic substance disposal, pesticide regulation, and radiation. The EPA:

A. Conducts research on the harmful impact of pollution

B. Gathers information about present pollution problems

C. Assists states and local governments in controlling pollution through grants, technical advice, and other means

D. Advises the Council on Environmental Quality about new policies needed for protection of the environment

E. Administers federal pollution laws

IV. The key federal legislation for controlling air pollution is the **Clean Air Act**. It directs the EPA administrator to establish air quality standards and to see that these standards are achieved according to a definite timetable.

A. The administrator has set *primary* and *secondary* air quality standards for particulates (pollution in particle form), carbon monoxide, sulfur dioxide, nitrogen dioxide, hydrocarbons, and lead.

1. **Primary air quality standards** are those necessary to protect public health.
2. **Secondary air quality standards** guard the public from other adverse air pollution effects such as injury to property, vegetation, and climate and damage to aesthetic values.
3. In *Whitman v. American Trucking Associations, Inc.*, the U.S. Supreme Court ruled that air quality standards did not have to take implementation costs into account under the language of the Clean Air Act.

B. The states bear principal responsibility for *enforcing* the Clean Air Act, with the EPA providing *standard-setting*, *coordinating*, and *supervisory* functions. However, the EPA *may also participate in enforcement*.

C. Various criminal and civil penalties and fines back up the Clean Air Act. The EPA may also order industries that do not obey cleanup orders to pay amounts to the EPA that equal the economic savings the industries realize from their failure to install and operate proper antipollution equipment.

D. In 1990, Congress passed amendments to the Clean Air Act. These amendments require cities to meet clean air standards. If they do not, businesses in these areas must install pollution-control equipment and tailpipe emissions for cars and trucks must be reduced. Utility power plant emissions also must be reduced nationwide. The amendments divide air pollution sources into two categories, *stationary source* and *mobile source*:

1. Stationary polluters, such as steel mills and polluters must follow timetables and schedules in complying with emission requirements. They must install the best system of emission reduction that has been adequately demonstrated.
2. Mobile source polluters (transportation) also have a timetable of air pollution standards, for which control technology may not yet exist. This is a

technology-forcing aspect of the amendments to the Clean Air Act, and it is unique to the history of governmental regulation of business. Because technology-forcing does not always succeed, the EPA may grant *compliance waivers* and *variances* from its standards.

V. The EPA has moved to make its regulatory practices more economically efficient. All new pollution control rules are now subjected to cost-benefit analysis, and the EPA has developed specific policies to achieve air pollution control in an economically efficient manner.

A. Traditionally the EPA regulated each individual pollution emission **point source**, such as a smokestack within a complex. Now the EPA encourages the states to adopt an approach called the **bubble concept**, in which the plant complex is treated as if it were encased in a bubble. The pollution of the complex as a whole is the focus of regulation, and a business may suggest its own plan for cleaning up multiple sources of pollution within the complex, as long as the total pollution emitted does not exceed certain limits. This permits flexibility and provides businesses with economic incentives to discover new methods of control.

B. A number of states have developed EPA-approved plans for **emissions reduction banking**. Businesses can cut pollution beyond what the law requires and "bank" these reductions for their own future use or to sell to other companies as emission offsets.

1. Utility companies are allowed, under the 1990 amendments, to engage in emission reduction banking and trading. The EPA believes that this trading accounts for reduced sulfur dioxide emissions from electric utilities and a simultaneous increase in electricity generation.

2. Emissions reduction banking and trading is rapidly growing and extending beyond the Clean Air Act. In 2003 the Chicago Climate Exchange became the first U.S. program of voluntary property-based market step to cut greenhouse gases (GHG), like carbon dioxide. The European Union plans to implement full-scale GHG emissions trading markets by 2005. These markets are based on the principle of **cap and trade**, in which the government issues a limited number of pollution permits, capping GHG pollution; and a company may sell the unused amount of a permit on the market.

C. Another important policy of the Clean Air Act is the **prevention of significant deterioration**, under which pollution emission is controlled, even in areas where the air is cleaner than air quality standards require.

1. Before a business can construct new pollution emission sources, it must endure the delay and red tape of the *permitting process*. Both the EPA and Congress are considering ways to streamline the permitting process.

2. The EPA is experimenting with allowing states to issue "smart permits" to air polluters. These permits eliminate the expensive delays of previous permitting processes.

D. Although the Clean Air Act does not currently apply to indoor pollution, its applications could be extended in the future. While the overall air quality in the United States is improving, some studies have found that indoor levels of certain pollutants far exceed outdoor levels, at home and at work. Tobacco smoke is a particularly significant indoor pollution problem, and workplace smoking is banned or regulated by many businesses and local governments.

VI. The principal federal law regulating water pollution is the **Clean Water Act**, passed by Congress in 1972. This act sets goals to eliminate water pollution in all navigable waterways, intrastate as well as interstate.

A. Business enterprise is a major source of water pollution in the United States. Almost one-half of all water used in this country is used for cooling and condensing purposes in connection with industrial activities. Industry also discharges chemical and other effluents into the nation's waterways.

B. The Clean Water Act is administered primarily by the states in accordance with EPA standards. If the states do not fulfill their responsibilities, the EPA can step in and enforce the law.

C. The Clean Water Act sets strict deadlines and strong enforcement provisions, which industry, municipalities, and other water polluters must follow. Enforcement revolves around the act's permit discharge system.

1. Without being subject to criminal penalties, no polluter can discharge pollutants from any *point source* (such as a pipe) without a permit. Since the act applies only to "navigable waterways," the *criminal penalties apply only to the unpermitted point-source pollution of navigable waterways.* In *Solid Waste Agency v. U.S. Army Corps of Engineers*, the U.S. Supreme Court determined that isolated ponds, some only seasonally (only filled at certain times of the year) were not navigable waterways under the Clean Water Act.

2. The Clean Water Act requires industries to adopt a two-step sequence for cleanup of industrial wastes:

a. Polluters must first install *best practicable technology (BPT)*.
b. The second step demands installation of *best available technology (BAT)*.

3. The EPA administers two other acts related to water pollution control.

a. The Marine Protection, Research, and Sanctuaries Act of 1972 requires a permit system for the discharge or dumping of various material into the seas.

b. The Safe Water Drinking Act of 1974 has forced the EPA to set maximum drinking water contaminant levels for certain organic and inorganic chemicals, pesticides, and microbiological pollutants.

4. *Non-point source pollution*, which comes from runoffs into streams and rivers, is not reached by the Clean Water Act and other current statutes. The National Non-Point Source Pollution Program was authorized by Congress to study the problem. In 2000 the EPA issued a rule requiring states to impose antipollution standards for about twenty thousand bodies of water within five years. Congress, however, required the EPA to conduct further studies of the rule's impact before implementing it; and that is ongoing as of this writing.

VII. In 1973, Congress passed the Endangered Species Act (ESA), the world's toughest law protecting animals and plants and, perhaps, the country's most controversial environmental standard.

A. The ESA is designed to protect species listed as "endangered" or "threatened" by the Secretary of the Interior.

1. In addition to considering factors of endangerment, the secretary must consider the destruction of habitat, disease or predation, commercial and recreational activity, and "other natural or manmade factors."

2. Within a year of listing a species as endangered or threatened, the Secretary of the Interior must determine the "critical habitat," which is the area with the biological or physical features necessary to species survival.

B. *No federal agency* can take any action that is likely to jeopardize an endangered species, but it is *the ESA's application to private business activity* that has caused the greater debate in recent years.

1. Section 9 of the ESA prohibits any person from transporting or trading in any endangered species of fish or wildlife or from "*taking any such species.*"

2. *Taking* a species is defined as "harass, harm, pursue, hunt, shoot, wound, kill, trap, capture, or collect, or attempt to engage in any such conduct." *The Secretary of the Interior has defined "harm" to include damage to the habitats of endangered species.* It is this definition that has been the subject of much litigation.

3. In *Babbitt v. Sweet Home Chapter*, the U.S. Supreme Court upheld the Secretary of the Interior's decision under the ESA that "harm" included "significant habitat modification or degradation that actually kills or injures [endangered] wildlife."

C. *The ESA does not permit courts or regulators to take economic factors into consideration in applying its provisions.* There has been much criticism of the act, and Congress has established a review board that can grant exemptions for certain important federal projects. *Exemptions do not apply to private activities, however.*

VIII. Pesticides have been wisely used in the United States to control the damage caused to crops by insect pests. The widespread, continual use of pesticides creates environmental problems, however. Federal regulation of pesticides is accomplished primarily through two statutes: the **Federal Insecticide, Fungicide, and Rodenticide Act of 1947**, as amended, and the **Federal Environmental Pesticide Control Act of 1972 (FEPCA)**. Both statutes require the registration and labeling of pesticides, and FEPCA coverage extends to the application of pesticides as well.

A. Under the acts, the administrator of the EPA registers pesticides that are properly labeled, meet their claims of effectiveness, and will not have *unreasonable adverse effects on the environment*, defined as "any unreasonable risk to man or the environment, taking into account the economic, social, and environmental costs and benefits of the use of any pesticide."

B. The EPA also classifies pesticides for either general use or restricted use. In the second category, the EPA may require application only by a trained applicator or with the approval of a trained consultant. The EPA may also require employers to train employees in pesticide safety, post safety information, and keep workers away from freshly sprayed areas.

C. The EPA has a variety of enforcement powers to ensure that pesticide goals are met, including the power to deny or suspend registration.

D. The EPA also defines what a pesticide can and cannot be used for and may seek penalties against violators.

E. Pesticide control has been attacked by manufacturers, who complain that the required testing procedures are expensive, inhibit research, and delay useful pesticides from reaching the market. Environmentalists, on the other hand, contend that it is hypocritical to not apply the FEPCA to U.S. manufacturer's shipments of pesticides to foreign countries.

IX. Disposal of solid waste can potentially create air pollution, water pollution, or noise pollution. The **Solid Waste Disposal Act**, passed in 1965, represents the primary federal effort ion solid waste control.

A. Congress recognized in this act that the main responsibility for nontoxic waste management *rests with regional, state, and local governments*. The federal role is limited mainly to promoting research and providing technical and financial assistance to the states.

B.   State and local governments have taken a variety of approaches to solid waste disposal problems, including developing sanitary landfills, requiring the separation into categories of solid waste, and granting tax breaks for industries using recycled materials. Thousands of cities and towns recycle solid wastes, usually at the household level.

X.   In the last several years, *regulation of toxic and hazardous waste has been expanding rapidly*. Public control of private action in this area can be divided into three categories: Regulation of the use of toxic chemicals, regulation of toxic and hazardous waste disposal, and regulation of toxic and hazardous waste cleanup.

A.   Toxic substances are potentially the most serious environmental problem we face. To meet these problems, Congress in 1976 enacted the **Toxic Substances Control Act (TSCA)**. The primary purpose of the TSCA is to force an early evaluation of suspect chemicals before they become economically important.

1.   Under TSCA, the EPA can require manufacturers to test their chemicals for possible harmful effects. *To date, however, only a small fraction of the 70,000 chemicals in production used have been safety tested.*

2.   The TSCA also requires manufacturers and distributors to report to the EPA any information they possess that indicates a chemical substance presents a *substantial risk* of injury to health or the environment.

3.   Under TSCA, manufacturers must give the EPA advance notice of the manufacture of a new substance or processing for a significant new use of any substance. The EPA may choose, after a review, to stop or limit introduction of new chemicals if they threaten human health or the environment with unreasonable risks. Congress directed the EPA, through the TSCA, *to consider the economic and social impact of its decisions*, as well as the environmental impact.

B.   A major environmental problem has been how to ensure that the generators of toxic wastes dispose of them safely. *To help ensure proper handling and disposal of hazardous and toxic wastes*, Congress in 1976 amended the Solid Waste Disposal Act by the **Resource Conservation and Recovery Act (RCRA)**.

1.   Under the RCRA, a generator of wastes has two primary obligations:

a.   To determine whether its wastes qualify as hazardous under RCRA
b.   To see that such wastes are properly transported to a disposal facility that has an EPA permit or license

2. The RCRA accomplishes proper disposal of hazardous wastes through the **manifest system**. A generator of hazardous waste prepares a manifest document that designates a licensed facility for disposal purposes and gives copies of the manifest to the transporter of the waste. After receiving the wastes, the disposal facility must return a copy of the manifest to the generator, confirming proper disposal of the waste. *If the generator does not receive this copy, it must notify the EPA.*

3. The EPA has investigatory powers, and there are penalties, including criminal fines and imprisonment, for violating RCRA's provisions.

4. As amended in 1986, the RCRA is moving the handling of toxic wastes away from burial on land to treatments that destroy or permanently detoxify wastes. Proper toxic waste disposal, however, is expensive.

C. After passage of the TSCA and RCRA in 1976, regulation of toxic and hazardous substances was still incomplete, as these acts did not deal with problems of the cleanup costs of *unsafe hazardous waste dumps or spills*. In 1980, Congress created the **Comprehensive Environmental Response, Compensation, and Liability Act (CERCLA)**, known as **Superfund**, *to address these problems.*

1. The act requires anyone who releases unauthorized amounts of hazardous substances into the environment to notify the government. The government has the power to order those responsible to clean up such releases, whether or not they complied with the notification requirement. Refusal to comply can result in a suit for cleanup cost reimbursement plus punitive damages of up to triple cleanup costs.

2. The government can also recover damages for injury done to natural resources. Liability includes the costs of **remediation**, which are the costs of restoring land to its previous condition.

3. No negligence need be proved to establish liability. Responsible parties include:

a. Those who currently or formerly operate or own waste disposal sites (though CERCLA gives no definition of *operator* and *owner*). In *U.S. v. Bestfoods*, the U.S. Supreme Court ruled that a parent corporation that exercised control over the operations of a subsidiary corporation could be held responsible under CERCLA as an "operator" who generated hazardous waste.

b. Those who arrange for disposal of wastes

c. Those who transport wastes

4. The law makes current as well as former landowners liable for hazardous wastes. The purchaser may escape liability by proving that it is innocent of knowledge of the wastes and has used *due diligence* in checking the land for toxic hazards. This can be both costly and difficult to prove, however.

5. *Lenders can become responsible parties if they exert control over borrowers' contaminated land or assume ownership of it. Insurers may also be required*

to cover cleanup costs if policies insure against *damages* arising from an *occurrence*, which includes *accidental* discharge of pollutants.

6. The business community has proposed various reforms to the Superfund law, which is very unpopular with industry due to its costs. It may cost as much as $500 billion over the next 50 years to clean up the nation's hazardous waste sites. Since 2000, however, the pace of cleanups has declined substantially.

D. No single piece of legislation comprehensively controls radiation pollution, and no one agency is responsible for administering legislation in this technologically complex area. Overall responsibility for control of radiation pollution, however, rests with the Nuclear Regulatory Commission. The EPA conducts testing and provides technical assistance. The Clean Air Act and the Clean Water Act also contain sections applicable to radiation discharges into the air and water.

SUITS BY PRIVATE INDIVIDUALS

XI. Citizen Enforcement

A. Many environmental laws such as the Clean Air Act and the Clean Water Act contain *citizen enforcement provisions*, allowing private persons to sue to enforce environmental laws.

B. Both the EPA and private companies can be sued under these provisions.

C. As well as individuals, public interest groups can sue to enforce environmental laws. These groups must show how their members are directly affected by what the defendants have done, i.e., they need to show *standing to sue*.

XII. Tort Theories

A. Various tort theories are used by those whose health or resources are harmed by the pollution of others.

B. Public and private nuisance doctrines are often used against polluters (see Chapter 7).

C. Trespass, negligence, and ultrahazardous activity theories are also used (see Chapter 8) against polluters.

TRENDS IN ENVIRONMENTAL REGULATION

Public and business awareness of environmental issues has significantly increased. A strong majority of the public favors more government regulation of the environment. At the World

Economic Forum, 650 business and government leaders ranked the environment as the greatest challenge facing business.

XIII. For every claim of pollution-caused environmental harm, there is a countertheory. Lack of scientific opinion on many environmental issues reveals a key controversy at the heart of the environmental regulation: *How much certainty of harm is required to justify regulatory intervention?*

    A. In 1992, a report signed by 1,575 scientists, including 100 Nobel Prize winners warned that if not checked, many of our current practices jeopardize both plant and animal kingdoms and may so alter our living world that it will be unable to sustain life as we know it.

    B. In 1990, 59 countries agreed to stop producing certain chemicals that destroy the earth's *ozone layer*, which protects the earth's surface from harmful radiation from the sun that causes cataracts, skin cancer, and unknown serious damage to animals and plants.

    C. An even greater source of concern than ozone destruction is the *greenhouse effect*. Burning of fossil fuels, such as oil and coal, creates carbon dioxide, which lingers in the atmosphere and leads to warmer global temperatures. Changing climatic patterns and rising sea levels are possible results of the greenhouse effect.

        1. In 1997, delegates from 150 nations reached a treaty (the Kyoto Protocol) to reduce emission of various greenhouse gases such as carbon dioxide. The United States, however, has not ratified the treaty, a step necessary for it to become law in this country.

        2. The United States represents only 5 percent of the world's population, yet it consumes more than 20 percent of the world's energy production, much of it in fossil fuels. Developing countries, under the Kyoto Protocol, are not required to reduce greenhouse gas emissions, so a debate rages over whether it is fair for the United States to alter its standard of living while developing countries use cheap fossil fuels as their economies grow.

    D. Concerns about pollution, climate change, and even food production are magnified by population growth, yet birth control raises controversial cultural and religious issues.

XIV. Some environmentally concerned investors are turning to corporate governance as a way to make polluting industries more environmentally sensitive. Increasingly, shareholders are presenting resolutions at the annual meetings of corporations to encourage the directors and manager of polluting industries to analyze and report on environmental issues. As of 2003, these resolutions are failing to pass, but support for them among shareholders is gaining rapidly.

XV. Theory and practice suggest that improper use of *common* resources causes more environmental problems than does improper use of *private* resources. People tend to be more careful with their own private resources than with resources that are common to all, such as air, water and public land. There are exceptions, however, and environmental regulations exist to prevent, for example, the dumping of toxic substances on privately owned land.

A. Some landowners have challenged environmental regulation and zoning as a governmental "taking" of private property without "just compensation," which the Fifth Amendment expressly prohibits. The Supreme Court has ruled that land regulation is not a taking that must be compensated as long as an owner is allowed a "reasonable" use of the land. In a strong property system, owners cannot use their land or other resources in ways that harm the resources of others, including the resource that others have in their health.

B. The emissions trading approach to pollution management is a property approach, using the exclusionary right of property to achieve goals for the common good. The world is heading toward increased emissions trading.

COMPLETION EXERCISES

1. The most important requirement of NEPA demands that all federal agencies prepare a(an) _____ prior to taking certain actions.

2. Even before preparing an EIS, federal agencies must designate the most important environmental issues in a process known as _____.

3. The public agency that coordinates public control of private action as it affects the environment is the _____.

4. _____ air quality standards are those necessary to protect public health from air pollution.

5. _____ air quality standards are those necessary to protect the climate, vegetation, and the resources of owners.

6. Treating an air polluting plant as a whole instead of various point sources is called the _____.

7. Plans that allow businesses to reduce pollution below that required and to use the difference in the future, or to sell it, are called by the term _____.

8. A policy that controls air pollution in areas where the air is cleaner than air quality standards require is known as the _____.

9. "Best practicable technology" must be installed by polluters under the _____ Act,

10. CERCLA is also known as the _____.

TRUE-FALSE SELECTIONS

1. _____ The cost of restoring mined or polluted land to its previous condition is called "remediation."

2. _____ The RCRA accomplishes proper disposal of hazardous wastes through the "manifest system."

3. _____ Under the Superfund, lenders can become liable if they exert control over borrowers contaminated land or assume ownership of it.

4. _____ Private persons lack standing to sue to enforce the Clean Air Act and Clean Water Act.

5. _____ Theory and practice suggest that improper use of common resources causes more environmental problems than does improper use of private resources.

6. _____ The emissions trading approach to pollution management is a property approach.

7. _____ The EIS must be included when the Nuclear Regulatory Commission proposes new legislation for Congress to consider.

8. _____ NEPA requires federal agencies to follow conclusions of an EIS.

9. _____ Under the Clean Air Act, air quality standards are set for dozens of pollution categories.

10. _____ The Clean Air Act and Clean Water Act contain civil but not criminal sanctions.

MULTIPLE CHOICE PROBLEMS

1.   Select the most *correct* statement. Under the Clean Water Act:

    a.   Enforcement applies to all waterways.
    b.   Enforcement applies to non-point source water pollution.
    c.   Enforcement does *not* apply to runoffs from pesticide use.
    d.   Polluters must first install "best available technology."

2.   The most controversial provision of the ESA prohibits persons from:

    a.   Trading endangered species.
    b.   Hunting endangered species.
    c.   Harming the habitats of endangered species.
    d.   Transporting endangered species across state lines for immoral purposes.

3.   The Act that allows the EPA to require manufacturers to test chemicals for possible harmful effects is the:

    a.   Solid Waste Disposal Act
    b.   TSCA
    c.   RCRA
    d.   CERCLA

4.   Under the RCRA who must notify the EPA if it does not receive a copy of the manifest?

    a.   The generator of toxic wastes.
    b.   The transporter of toxic wastes.
    c.   The disposer of toxic wastes.
    d.   Any lender who finances the parties in (a), (b), and (c) above.

5.   Poultry, Inc. builds a chicken processing plant one-half mile from Fernbrook Estates, a residential development. When the wind is out of the north, the smell is overwhelming. Many residents feel ill. If the residents sue Poultry, what would be their most successful legal cause of action?

    a.   Trespass.
    b.   Private nuisance.
    c.   Intentional infliction of mental distress.
    d.   Ultrahazardous activity.

DISCUSSION ANALYSIS

If private property and the market effectively eliminate many problems of overpollution, why is there any need for the government to regulate environmental pollution? Discuss.

Chapter 18

International Law

Law is fundamental to business in the United States and throughout the globe. The protection of the exclusionary property right and the transfer of an owner's resources through contract is critical for governing the exchange of resources in the global market. Nations enter into treaties and agreements with other countries that govern competition and the way goods and technology are sold from one country to the next. Every country is interested in developing rules that make its products and services more competitive in the global market.

National economies rely upon their ability to export products and services abroad to create jobs and economic growth at home. The United States continues to run a huge trade deficit as it buys more than it sells abroad. This chapter focuses on issues important to management decision making by examining the methods and risks of transacting international business. The chapter also considers the role and impact of international organizations and agreements on business and the effect of foreign competition on American business at home.

INTERNATIONAL LAW AND ORGANIZATIONS

Unfortunately, international law does not consist of a cohesive body of uniform principles. Nonetheless, international law can be found in a variety of sources from U.S. domestic law to the law of other countries to international agreements and treaties and even in customary international principles found in the general practice of civilized nations. The Supreme Court has held that "international law is part of our law, and must be ascertained and administered by the courts of justice of appropriate jurisdiction as often as questions of right depending upon it are duly presented for their determination."

I.   Generally, international law is classified as either public international law or private international law.

A.   **Public international law** examines relationships between nations and uses rules that are binding on all countries in the international community. Article 38 of the **International Court of Justice (ICJ)** is the traditional source for ascertaining what is public international law. However, the decisions made by the ICJ, the World Court, *do not create binding rules of law or precedent in future cases.*

1. The ICJ is the judicial branch of the United Nations and sits at The Hague in the Netherlands. It consists of 15 judges representing all of the world's major legal systems. No more than one judge may be a national of any country.

2. The ICJ has *not* been a major force in settling disputes, rendering, on average, only one contested decision per year and one advisory opinion every two years since its inception in 1946. There are several reasons for the widespread reluctance to resolve disputes in the ICJ:

   a. Only countries, *not private parties*, have access to the Court.
   b. Only countries that have submitted to the Court's jurisdiction may be parties, and a country may choose to accept the Court's jurisdiction only when that may suit its own interests.
   c. The ICJ *has no enforcement authority* and must rely on diplomacy or economic sanctions against countries that breach international law.

3. Deciding whether international law has been violated can be difficult. Article 38 sets the order of importance for determining what is international law in a given case. In descending order, the ICJ looks at:

   a. *International Conventions*, which are similar to legislation or statutes and represent formal agreements between nations;
   b. *International Custom*, or common legal practices followed by nations in working with each other over a long period of time;
   c. *The General Principles of Law*, which may be found in national rules common to the countries in a dispute;
   d. *Judicial Decisions and the Teaching of the Most Highly Qualified Publicists* of various nations, which, although not binding, may be used as a means of determining the rules of law to use for guidance in resolving a dispute.

B. **Private international law**, which is of principal concern to the business manager, examines relationships created by commercial transactions and utilizes international agreements and the individual laws of nations to resolve business disputes. Even in purely domestic business deals, the law is rarely predictable or certain. In international business, the situation can become quite unstable, as a single transaction often involves several firms with operations in different nations. In the case of a dispute, the outcome depends on two determinations, which may be difficult to make:

1. *Which nation's law controls the transaction.*
2. *Which nation's court may hear the case.*

II. Several international organizations and agreements play important roles in the development of political, economic, and legal rules for the conduct of international business.

A. The **United Nations** was established after World War II and has grown to include almost every nation in the world. The Charter of the United Nations sets forth as its primary goal "to save succeeding generations from the scourge of war," and authorizes measures to prevent and to suppress threats to the peace.

   1. The General Assembly of the United Nations is composed of every nation represented in the United Nations and permits each country to cast one vote.

   2. The real power in the United Nations rests in the Security Council, which is composed of 15 member states. The council has the power to authorize military action and to sever diplomatic relations with other nations. The five permanent members of the Council (United States, Russia, China, France, and United Kingdom) have veto power over any action proposed in the council.

   3. A number of organizations affiliated with the United Nations have authority over activities that directly affect international business.

      a. The United Nations Commission on International Trade Law (UNCITRAL) was created in 1966 in an effort to develop standardized commercial practices and agreements. UNCITRAL has no authority to force any country to adopt any of the conventions or agreements that it proposes, such as the Convention on the International Sale of Goods.

      b. The United Nations Conference on Trade and Development (UNCTAD) was created in 1964 to deal with international trade reform and the redistribution of income through trading with developing countries. It has drafted the Transfer of Technology Code and the Restrictive Business Practices Code, both largely ignored by most nations.

      c. At the Bretton Woods Conference of 1944, two important agencies were also created under the auspices of the United Nations:

         i. The International Monetary Fund (IMF) *encourages international trade by maintaining stable foreign exchange rates and works closely with commercial banks to promote orderly exchange policies.*

         ii. The World Bank *promotes economic development in poor countries by making loans to finance necessary development projects and programs.*

B. The **General Agreement on Tariffs and Trade (GATT)**, signed by 23 countries after World War II, represented those nations' desires to liberalize trade through reduced tariffs and free markets. It has undergone eight major revisions and added a number of countries.

C. The 1994 Uruguay Round of GATT talks culminated in the creation of the **World Trade Organization (WTO)** as an umbrella organization to regulate world trade. It was signed by 125 countries, and its primary purpose is to resolve trade disputes among member nations. The WTO administers the GATT, and it can sanction nations that ignore its rulings.

    1.   The WTO has several benefits:

        a. The WTO helps promote peace.
        b. Disputes are handled constructively.
        c. Free trade cuts the costs of living.
        d. Trade stimulates economic growth.
        e. WTO encourages good government.

    2.   Criticisms of the WTO have also increased, as everyone, from states to business firms, question the benefits of globalization.

        a. The United States has criticized the lack of appreciation for competition and antitrust enforcement in WTO rulings.
        b. Environmentalists have protested WTO's ability to undercut U.S. environmental policies that impact free trade.
        c. Other WTO critics are concerned about the effect of globalization on developing countries.

D.   The **Convention on the International Sale of Goods (CISG)** outlines standard international practices for the sale of goods. It represents the cumulative work of over 60 nations and international groups, work which required many compromises. It has become widely accepted around the globe.

    1.   The CISG applies to contracts for the commercial sale of goods between parties whose businesses are located in different nations, provided that those nations have adopted the convention.
    2.   A significant degree of freedom is provided for the individual parties in an international contract. *Parties may even opt out of the CISG entirely.*
    3.   Contracts for the sale of goods need not be in writing.
    4.   As international transactions typically involved sophisticated parties, the CISG makes it easier to disclaim warranties on goods than under traditional U.S. law.
    5.   *Parties are still subject to local laws and customs,* making international agreements complex and tricky to negotiate.

III.   Probably the most significant development affecting international business was the signing in 1957 of the Treaty of Rome, which created the European Community. Now known as the **European Union (EU)**, it has grown to include fifteen countries. The combined gross national product (GNP) of the top five of these countries is very significant when compared to that of either Japan or the United States. Over the past fifteen years, the EU has passed a number of reforms aimed at eliminating barriers between member nations.

A.   The *Single European Act of 1987* mandated the removal of many physical, technical, and tax barriers to the free movement of persons, goods, services, and capital.

B.   In 1992, the *Maastricht Treaty* created common foreign and defense policies, established a joint central bank, required member countries to reduce government deficits, and *established a single currency*. Trade barriers between member states are essentially being eliminated under a system *similar to the trading policy between states in the United States*.

C.   The *Nice Summit of 2000* laid the groundwork for admitting 12 more countries to the EU.

D.   The major institutions of the EU are:

1.   The Council of Ministers, one representative from each member state, coordinates the policies of the member states in a variety of areas.
2.   The Commission, which carries out many of the executive functions of the Union, and consists of individuals who represent the will of the entire Union, rather than national concerns.
3.   The Parliament, which elects representatives from each state, and is divided into political factions that often create coalitions across national borders.
4.   The Court of Justice, which decides the nature and parameters of EU law. Justices are appointed by the Council, and each member nation has a justice seated on the Court.

IV.   The **North American Free Trade Agreement (NAFTA)**, passed in 1993, aims to increase free trade and eventually eliminate tariffs and other barriers to business among the United States, Mexico, and Canada. It also provides a mechanism that makes it easier to resolve trade disputes among the countries. Side agreements also were reached to improve labor rights and environmental protection in Mexico. NAFTA has expanded U.S. exports and imports to and from Mexico and Canada.

METHODS OF TRANSACTING INTERNATIONAL BUSINESS

Choosing a method of doing business in foreign countries not only requires understanding the factors normally involved in selecting an organization and operating a business domestically but also demands an appreciation of the international trade perspective. Depending upon the country, type of export, and amount of export involved in a particular transaction, international trade may involve direct foreign sales, licensing agreement, franchise agreements, or direct foreign investment.

V.   Foreign sales, the sale of goods directly to buyers in other countries, is the most common approach for a manufacturer trying to penetrate foreign markets. *Increased uncertainty over ability to enforce the buyer's promise to pay often requires that more complex arrangements for payment be made.* International sales involve many risky legal issues.

   A.   Commonly, an **irrevocable letter of credit** is used to ensure payment. This arrangement involves the buyer, the seller, and two banks, one in each country.

      1.   The buyer obtains from an *issuing bank* in the buyer's country a commitment to advance (pay) a specified amount (the price of the goods) upon receipt from the carrier, of a **bill of lading**, stating that the goods have been shipped.
      2.   The issuing bank's commitment to pay is given, not to the seller directly, but to a *confirming bank* located in the seller's country, from which the seller obtains payment.
      3.   The confirming bank forwards the bill of lading to the issuing bank in order to obtain reimbursement of the funds that have been paid to the seller.
      4.   The issuing bank releases the bill of lading to the buyer after it has been paid, and with the bill of lading the buyer is able to obtain the goods from the carrier.
      5.   The issuing and confirming banks are paid fees for their roles in letters of credit.

   B.   In *Voest-Alpine Trading v. Bank of China*, the federal Fifth Circuit ruled that the law requires an issuing bank to "give notice of refusal to the beneficiary no later than the close of the seventh banking day following the day of receipt of the presentation documents." As the issuing bank noted "discrepancies" in the documents but did not specifically refuse to pay the letter of credit within the seven banking days, the bank had to honor the letter (pay it).

VI.   The **license** or **franchise** contract is the typical method for controlling transfers of information. A domestic firm may choose to grant a foreign firm the means to produce and sell its product. Intangible property rights, such as patents, copyrights, trademarks, or manufacturing processes, are transferred in exchange for royalties in the foreign country.

   A.   A licensing arrangement allows the international business to enter a foreign market without any direct foreign investment. It is a way to expand the company's market without the need for substantial capital.

   B.   *Licensing and franchise agreements must follow the local laws where they operate.*

   C.   The licensor must take care to restrict the use of the product or technology geographically and must take adequate steps to protect the confidential information so that third parties cannot exploit it.

VII.   As a business increases its level of international trade, it may find that creation of a **foreign subsidiary** is necessary, e.g., a manufacturing plant in another country. Most countries will permit a foreign firm to conduct business only if a national of the host country is designated as its legal representative.

    A.   The usual practice for multinational corporations is to create a foreign subsidiary in the host country. The form of subsidiary most closely resembling a U.S. corporation is known as a *societe anonyme (S.A.)*, or in German-speaking countries, an *Aktiengesellschaft (AG)*.

    B.   *Creation of a foreign subsidiary may pose considerable risk to the domestic parent firm by subjecting it to foreign laws and the jurisdiction of foreign courts.*

    C.   In many instances the only legal or political means a firm has to invest directly in a foreign country is to engage in a **joint venture** with an entity from the host country. Many foreign countries favor joint ventures because they allow local participation and discourage foreign domination of local industry.

RISKS INVOLVED IN INTERNATIONAL TRADE

Among the risks involved in international trade are expropriation and nationalization, export controls, pressures for bribes, and ill will resulting from U.S. antitrust laws.

VIII.   A domestic firm that locates assets in a foreign country may be subject to the ultimate legal and political risk of international business activity – expropriation.

    A.   **Expropriation**, as used in the context of international law, *is the seizure of a foreign-owner's resources by a government.* When the owners are not fairly compensated, the expropriation is also considered to be a *confiscation* of an owner's resources.

    B.   Usually, the expropriating government itself assumes ownership of the resources, so the process includes **nationalization** as well. In the United States, the counterpart of expropriation is called the *power of eminent domain*.

    C.   While the power of a government to take an owner's private resources is regarded as inherent, it is subject to restraints upon its exercise. The extent of such restraints, however, varies widely from country to country.

    D.   The "modern traditional theory," that governments may expropriate the resources of foreign owners only when accompanied by *"prompt, adequate and effective compensation,"* is accepted by most nations as the international standard.

IX.   Another risk involved in doing business abroad is **export controls** placed on the sale of U.S. strategic products and technology abroad. Controlling the export of such items has been the cornerstone of Western policy since the end of World War II; although with the end of the Cold War, the policy rationale behind export controls came into question.

    A.   In 1994, the Coordinating Committee for Multilateral Export Controls (COCOM), an organization created by the major Western nations and Japan to control exports, came to an end.

    B.   A new organization known as the *Wassanaar Arrangement* has come into existence to help control the spread of both military and dual-use technology to unstable areas of the world, so that regional and international security is not compromised. The 2002 plenary meeting of the Wassanaar Arrangement resulted in several significant initiatives aimed at intensifying cooperation to prevent terrorist groups and individuals from acquiring arms and strategic goods and technologies.

    C.   The U.S. export control system is regulated by the Department of State and the Department of Commerce under authority provided by the Export Administration Act and the Arms Export Control Act. The Department of Defense and the U.S. Customs Service also play roles. Significant criminal and administrative sanctions may be imposed upon corporations and individuals convicted of violating the law.

    D.   In *U.S. v. Reyes*, the federal Seventh Circuit ruled that the shipping overseas of military aircraft parts without a license "provided more than sufficient grounds for the jury's finding of a willful violation of the AECA" when the parts ended up in Iran to which shipment of such parts was illegal.

X.   The **Foreign Corrupt Practices Act (FCPA)** of 1977 is designed to stop the formerly widespread practice by American firms of bribing and making payments to foreign officials for the purpose of obtaining business. Prior to passage of the act, it was common for businesses to account for bribes as commission payments or other normal business expenses and illegally deduct the payments on income tax returns.

    A.   The FCPA has two principal requirements:

        1.   Financial records and accounts must be kept "which, in reasonable detail, accurately and fairly reflect the transactions and dispositions of assets" of the business.

        2.   The business must "devise and maintain a system of internal accounting controls sufficient to provide reasonable assurances" that transactions are being carried out in accordance with management's authorization.

    B.   The U.S. prohibition of under-the-table payments has caused discrimination against U.S. businesses in nations where such payments to government officials are customary and expected. It has also caused resentment in those countries, where it is seen as an attempt to impose U.S. standards of morality in other parts of the world.

C.   After intensive lobbying by the U.S. business community, Congress amended the FCPA in 1988. The amendments establish clearer standard for firms to follow in overseas operations and limit criminal liability for violations of accounting standards to those who "knowingly" circumvent accounting controls or falsify records.

D.   A new type of payment called "offsets" has taken the place of bribes in international business. Offsets are legal, though officially discouraged, and can be *any form of aid, such as direct investments or pacts to use more foreign components*. There are several other types of payments that are legal under the FCPA.

     1.   Any payments permitted under the written laws of a foreign country;
     2.   Travel expenses of a foreign official for purposes of seeing demonstration of a product;
     3.   "Grease" payments (small bribes) to foreign customs officials to speed goods through customs;
     4.   Other small payments for "routine" government action such as obtaining visas, work permits, or police protection.

E.   Basically, what the FCPA prohibits is *the bribing of foreign governmental officials in order to obtain the business of their governments*.

XI.   To protect the welfare of the U.S. consumer, the government may apply our antitrust laws to foreign commerce, under the Foreign Trade Antitrust Improvements Act (**FTAIA**), where the action has a "direct, substantial, and reasonably foreseeable effect" on U.S. commerce. This application has generated much recent controversy and ill will abroad. The government's enforcement efforts, however, sometimes must reach foreign defendants as a means of ensuring open and free markets.

A.   The Department of Justice and the Federal Trade Commission have issued guidelines delineating the U.S. government's policy on enforcement of federal antitrust law in the international arena. The guidelines provide that:

     1.   Anticompetitive conduct, regardless of where such conduct occurs in the world or the nationality of the parties involved, may be prosecuted *if it affects U.S. domestic or foreign commerce*.
     2.   *Imports intended for sale in the United States by definition affect the U.S. market* directly and will, therefore, invariably be subject to control.
     3.   In *U.S. v. Nippon Paper*, the federal First Circuit ruled that price fixing that occurred entirely outside the United States (in Japan) could be criminally prosecuted in the U.S.

B. Business regulation and enforcement efforts in many Asian, European, and Latin American countries are, by comparison to ours, very weak. Such investigative and enforcement lapses could undermine growth and confidence in world markets.

XII. The doctrine of **sovereign immunity** *provides that a foreign sovereign is immune from suit in the United States, based on its status as a state.*

A. Until 1952, the notion of sovereign immunity was absolute.

B. From 1952 until 1976, U.S. courts adhered to a *restrictive theory* under which immunity existed with regard to sovereign or public acts but not with regard to private or commercial acts.

C. In 1976, Congress enacted the **Foreign Sovereign Immunities Act (FSIA)**, which codifies this restrictive theory and rejects immunity for *commercial acts* carried on in the United States or having direct effects in this country. *When governments act in a private or commercial capacity, they will be subjected to the same rules of law as are applicable to private individuals.* A nationalization of assets probably will be considered an act in the "public interest" and immune from suit under the FSIA.

D. In *Dole Food Co. v. Dead Sea Bromine Co.*, the U.S. Supreme Court ruled that "a foreign state must itself own a majority of the shares of a corporation if the corporation is to be deemed an instrumentality of the state under the provisions of the FSIA...." Thus, the protections given to sovereign states and their instrumentalities under the FSIA did not apply where the nation of Israel no longer owned the company sued.

XIII. In order to sue a foreign firm in the United States, a plaintiff must:

A. Establish *"minimum contacts"* between the foreign defendant and the forum court, that is, demonstrate that exercise of personal jurisdiction over the defendant "does not offend traditional notions of fair play and substantial justice."

B. Comply with the terms of the Hague Service Convention when serving the foreign defendant notice of the lawsuit. *Many countries, including the United States, have approved the convention*, which was formulated "to provide a simpler way to serve process abroad, to assure that defendants sued in foreign jurisdictions would receive actual and timely notice of suit, and to facilitate proof of service abroad." *Under the convention, each nation establishes a central authority to process requests for service of documents from other countries and to serve the documents.*

C.   In *Morelli v. Cedel* the federal Second Circuit ruled that "in determining whether Cedel (the defendant) satisfies the ADEA's 20-employee threshold, employees cannot be ignored merely because they work overseas.

XIV.   International businesses are focusing on the need for new methods of international commercial disputes, and *are increasingly resorting to the use of arbitration.* The advantages of arbitration, discussed in Chapter 5, are even more pronounced in international transactions, where litigation costs are higher.

A.   The United Nations Convention on the Recognition and Enforcement of Foreign Arbitral Awards of 1958 (New York Convention) *has been adopted in more than 50 countries.* It encourages the use of arbitration in commercial agreements made by companies in the signatory countries. The convention makes it easier to compel arbitration, where previously agreed upon by the parties, and to enforce the arbitrator's award once a decision has been reached.

B.   Once the parties to an international transaction have agreed to arbitrate disputes between them, the U.S. courts are reluctant to disturb that agreement.

C.   There are many advantages to arbitrating international disputes. For example:

1.   The arbitration process likely will be more streamlined and easier for the parties to understand than litigating the dispute in a foreign court.
2.   Parties can avoid the publicity that often results from open court proceedings.
3.   Parties can agree, before the dispute even arises, on a neutral and objective third party to act as the arbitrator. Several organizations provide arbitration services for international disputes.

COMPLETION EXERCISES

1.   The ICJ is the judicial branch of the _____, and it sits at the _____.

2.   _____ uses international agreements and laws of individual nations to resolve business disputes.

3.   The _____ administers the General Agreement of Tariffs and Trade (GATT).

4.   The _____ outlines standard international practices for the sale of goods.

5.   The Treaty of Rome has led to what is now known as the _____.

6.   The agreement encouraging free trade among the United States, Mexico, and Canada is the _____.

7. The document issued by an "issuing bank" is the _____.

8. _____ is the seizure of a foreign owner's resources by a government.

9. The statute designed to control bribery by American companies is the _____.

10. Often taking the place of bribes in international transactions is a new type of technically legal payment called _____.

TRUE-FALSE SELECTIONS

1. _____ Decisions of the ICJ create binding precedents for future cases.

2. _____ The ICJ enforces its decisions.

3. _____ The International Monetary Fund helps maintain stable international exchange rates of currencies.

4. _____ Parties to international contracts may opt out of the rules of the Convention on the International Sale of Goods.

5. _____ The EU's Council of Ministers are elected according to the relative population sizes of the member nations.

6. _____ In a letter of credit transaction, the seller obtains payment from the issuing bank.

7. _____ Expropriation of a foreign company's assets is not acceptable according to the "modern traditional theory."

8. _____ Grease payments to a custom official or a licensing official are illegal under the FCPA.

9. _____ A principal enforcement requirement of the FCPA is the required maintenance of internal accounting controls.

10. _____ The doctrine of sovereign immunity makes a foreign government immune from lawsuit in the U.S. based on that government's state policies.

MULTIPLE CHOICE PROBLEMS

1. To obtain the goods in a letter of credit transaction, the buyer will have to present what to the shipper?

   a. Letter of credit.
   b. Bill of lading.
   c. Proof of insurance.
   d. Contract.

2. All of the following concepts belong together, *except*:

   a. Expropriation.
   b. Nationalization.
   c. Eminent domain.
   d. Extrication.

3. Which one of the following international acts and treaties does not belong with the others?

   a. Treaty of Rome
   b. Maastrich Treaty
   c. Bretton Woods Treaty
   d. Single European Act

4. Select the most *incorrect* statement about the reach of U.S. antitrust laws in international business transactions.

   a. Price fixing that occurs entirely outside the United States cannot be prosecuted.
   b. Imports intended for sale in the United States are subject to U.S. antitrust regulation.
   c. Sovereign immunity prevents the application of U.S. antitrust policy to OPEC's oil limitations.
   d. The Department of Justice and the FTC have issued antitrust guidelines applying to international commerce.

5. Select the most *incorrect* statement about a plaintiff suing a foreign company in the U.S.:

   a. The plaintiff must comply with the Hague Service Convention.
   b. The plaintiff must show minimum contacts between the foreign defendant and the U.S. court.
   c. Personal jurisdiction over the foreign defendant must not offend notions of fair play and substantial justice.
   d. The plaintiff cannot sue if the foreign company does not have an American subsidiary.

DISCUSSION ANALYSIS

Discuss at least three ways that domestic companies do business internationally.

Appendix

Solutions to Problems

A word about your desired approach to the problems. The completion exercises, true-false selections, multiple-choice problems, and the discussion illustrate not ideal exam style but, rather, a review of the most significant points of the chapters. To this end, the multiple-choice problems in particular were written to cover as many correct statements as possible, and this is why many of them ask for you to identify the "incorrect" statement. Your work, then, does not end merely with identifying the incorrect statement of the problem, but also includes carefully thinking about why the correct statements are correct. Likewise in answering the True-False Selections, do not stop with answering a selection "T" or "F." Consider how the statement could be qualified to change the answer. And the solution to the Discussion problem is only suggested. You may be able to come up with additional insights yourself. Good luck!

CHAPTER 1

COMPLETION EXERCISES	TRUE-FALSE SELECTIONS	MULTIPLE-CHOICE PROBLEMS
1. Law	1. T	1. b
2. Property	2. T	2. a
3. Common law, civil law	3. T	3. c
4. Civil law	4. F	4. a
5. private law	5. F	5. b
6. Procedural law	6. T	
7. constitutions	7. T	
8. stare decisis	8. T	
9. tort	9. T	
10. corporate governance	10. F	

DISCUSSION

Your answer should discuss dependency theory, technology, education, natural resources, cultural values, and a property-based legal system, with emphasis on the last reason.

CHAPTER 2

COMPLETION EXERCISES	TRUE-FALSE SELECTIONS	MULTIPLE-CHOICE PROBLEMS
1. morals	1. T	1. b
2. deontology, teleology	2. T	2. b
3. formalistic	3. F	3. c
4. Categorical imperative	4. F	4. b
5. results	5. T	5. a
6. utilitarianism	6. T	
7. stakeholder	7. T	
8. professional responsibility	8. T	
9. conflict of interest	9. F	
10. good faith	10. T	

DISCUSSION

Your answer should define deontology and teleology, discuss the categorical imperative and utilitarianism, and ask yourself the questions to evaluate your own personal morality.

CHAPTER 3

COMPLETION EXERCISES	TRUE-FALSE SELECTIONS	MULTIPLE-CHOICE PROBLEMS
1. laws, facts	1. T	1. b
2. judicial immunity	2. F	2. d
3. petit jury	3. F	3. b
4 court of appeals, supreme court	4. F	4. d
5. federal questions	5. T	5. c
6. diversity of citizenship	6. T	
7. judicial review	7. T	
8. writ of certiorari	8. T	
9. constitutional relativity	9. F	
10. logic	10. T	

DISCUSSION

Your answer should identify the various issues that federal courts do have jurisdiction over and contrast federal courts with state courts that have jurisdiction over all types of issues.

CHAPTER 4

COMPLETION EXERCISES	TRUE-FALSE SELECTIONS	MULTIPLE-CHOICE PROBLEMS
1. litigation	1. T	1. b
2. plaintiff	2. T	2. d
3. defendant	3. F	3. d
4. counterclaim	4. T	4. b
5. appellant	5. T	5. d
6. respondent	6. T	
7. standing to sue	7. F	
8. cross claim	8. F	
9. jurisdiction	9. T	
10. summons	10. F	

DISCUSSION

Your answer should define judicial activism, judicial restraint, and judicial review; then it should observe that judicial activists are more likely than judicial restraintists to use judicial review to hold unconstitutional a decision of one of the other branches of government.

CHAPTER 5

COMPLETION EXERCISES	TRUE-FALSE SELECTIONS	MULTIPLE-CHOICE PROBLEMS
1. litigation	1. T	1. a
2. negotiation	2. F	2. b
3. mediation	3. F	3. d
4. mediator	4. T	4. c
5. arbitrator	5. T	5. b
6. Voluntary	6. F	
7. court order	7. T	
8. Federal Arbitration Act	8. T	
9. mandatory	9. T	
10. award	10. T	

DISCUSSION

Your answer should point out that arbitration is usually faster, cheaper, and less public than litigation but that litigation usually offers greater opportunity for discovery and to correct errors of decision-makers.

Appendix

CHAPTER 6

COMPLETION EXERCISES	TRUE-FALSE SELECTIONS	MULTIPLE-CHOICE PROBLEMS
1. federalism	1. F	1. a
2. Supremacy Clause	2. T	2. d
3. Commerce Clause	3. T	3. c
4. apportionment	4. F	4. a
5. prior restraints	5. T	5. c
6. actual malice	6. T	
7. due process	7. F	
8. due process, Fourteenth Amendment	8. F	
9. strict scrutiny	9. T	
10. minimum rationality	10. T	

DISCUSSION

Your discussion should explain the equal protection clause and the minimum rationality test as it applies to state action that discriminates. Justifying arguments that meet minimum rationality include public health and safety reasons for the discrimination.

CHAPTER 7

COMPLETION EXERCISES	TRUE-FALSE SELECTIONS	MULTIPLE-CHOICE PROBLEMS
1. private property	1. T	1. d
2. personal property, real property	2. T	2. c
3. fixture	3. T	3. d
4. Contract	4. T	4. a
5. adverse possession	5. F	5. d
6. confusion	6. F	
7. lease	7. T	
8. eminent domain	8. F	
9. deed	9. F	
10. nuisance	10. T	

DISCUSSION

Your answer should discuss how the exclusionary right of property gives incentive to the maximum production of resources. Property provides the certainty and stability of resources necessary to the modern private market. Observe that contract law concerns how owners exchange resources in the private market.

CHAPTER 8

COMPLETION EXERCISES	TRUE-FALSE SELECTIONS	MULTIPLE-CHOICE PROBLEMS
1. resources	1. F	1. c
2. goods	2. T	2. b
3. law, quasi-	3. T	3. d
4. executory	4. T	4. c
5. specific performance	5. F	5. c
6. legal purpose	6. T	
7. U.C.C.	7. T	
8. Consideration	8. T	
9. Capacity	9. F	
10. legal purpose	10. T	

DISCUSSION

Your answer should discuss the different levels of contractual performance and their legal implications. Only if the failure to fence is considered a material breach of the contract would Arrow be discharged and the contract terminated.

CHAPTER 9

COMPLETION EXERCISES	TRUE-FALSE SELECTIONS	MULTIPLE-CHOICE PROBLEMS
1. tort	1. T	1. b
2. intent	2. F	2. c
3. intentional torts, negligence, strict liability torts	3. T 4. F	3. d 4. d
4. battery	5. T	5. a
5. crime	6. F	
6. defamation of character	7. F	
7. Fraud	8. T	
8. negligence	9. T	
9. malpractice	10. F	
10. ultrahazardous activity		

DISCUSSION

Your answer should discuss litigation costs, punitive damages, products liability, medical malpractice, and various proposals for changing them.

CHAPTER 10

COMPLETION EXERCISES	TRUE-FALSE SELECTIONS	MULTIPLE-CHOICE PROBLEMS
1. $100 billion	1. F	1. d
2. felonies, misdemeanors	2. T	2. a
3. no contest	3. T	3. c
4. grand jury	4. T	4. c
5. conspiracy	5. F	5. c
6. accessory	6. T	
7. Fourth	7. T	
8. Fifth	8. T	
9. Sixth	9. T	
10. obstruction of justice	10. F	

DISCUSSION

Your answer should discuss how various people in an organization may know of a crime being committed but be reluctant to give information to the authorities, how the authorities may not know exactly who participated in the crime, and how easy it is to charge everyone with conspiracy or aiding and abetting and then plea bargain or drop charges when those not seriously involved give evidence against those who are.

CHAPTER 11

COMPLETION EXERCISES	TRUE-FALSE SELECTIONS	MULTIPLE-CHOICE PROBLEMS
1. corporate governance	1. F	1. c
2. corporate governance	2. T	2. d
3. closely held	3. T	3. a
4. publicly held	4. T	4. c
5. taxation	5. F	5. b
6. sole proprietorship	6. T	
7. partnership	7. T	
8. shareholders	8. F	
9. fiduciary	9. T	
10. Subchapter S	10. T	

DISCUSSION

Your discussion should focus on the basic legal concerns of business organizations (ease of creation, liability, taxation, control, and continuity) and apply them to the facts of this problem. Forming an LLG will likely be best for John and Mary. Except for potential liability problems for the general partner (Mary), a limited partnership would also work.

CHAPTER 12

COMPLETION EXERCISES		TRUE-FALSE SELECTIONS		MULTIPLE-CHOICE PROBLEMS	
1.	agency	1.	F	1.	c
2.	quasi-legislative	2.	T	2.	d
3.	Equal Access to Justice Act	3.	F	3.	d
4.	Cease and desist order	4.	F	4.	a
5.	Administrative law judges	5.	F	5.	d
6.	adoption	6.	T		
7.	standing to sue	7.	F		
8.	due process	8.	F		
9.	exhausted remedies	9.	T		
10.	primary jurisdiction	10.	T		

DISCUSSION

Your memorandum should discuss how regulation is a form of taxation with burdensome paperwork, often faulty or absent cost-benefit analysis, and the frequent inhibition of competition and innovation.

CHAPTER 13

COMPLETION EXERCISES		TRUE-FALSE SELECTIONS		MULTIPLE-CHOICE PROBLEMS	
1.	trust	1.	F	1.	a
2.	Sherman Act	2.	T	2.	d
3.	Clayton Act	3.	T	3.	c
4.	Federal Trade Commission	4.	F	4.	a
5.	price fixing	5.	T	5.	d
6.	monopoly	6.	F		
7.	per se	7.	T		
8.	triple (treble)	8.	T		
9.	resale price maintenance or vertical price fixing	9.	F		
10.	good faith	10.	F		

DISCUSSION

Your answer should discuss the requirements to establish price discrimination illegality, namely, that the sale involve a "commodity," of "like grade or quality," that the buyers be competitors, that the sale "may lessen competition substantially," and that one of the sales must cross a state line.

CHAPTER 14

COMPLETION EXERCISES		TRUE-FALSE SELECTIONS		MULTIPLE-CHOICE PROBLEMS	
1.	Fair Labor Standards Act	1.	F	1.	c
2.	employment at will	2.	T	2.	c
3.	public policy	3.	F	3.	d
4.	Employee Polygraph Protection Act	4.	T	4.	b
5.	paper fortress	5.	T	5.	c
6.	collective bargaining	6.	F		
7.	Norris-LaGuardia	7.	T		
8.	National Labor Relations, Wagner	8.	T		
9.	unfair labor practices	9.	T		
10.	Taft-Hartley	10.	T		

DISCUSSION

The organization of resources gives power to those who control them. Employers are often highly organized and powerful. Unions represent a similar organization by employees. Your answer should observe that if the property system permits employers to organize, employees should likewise be able to organize their resources (themselves).

CHAPTER 15

COMPLETION EXERCISES		TRUE-FALSE SELECTIONS		MULTIPLE-CHOICE PROBLEMS	
1.	Title VII	1.	T	1.	b
2.	retaliation	2.	F	2.	c
3.	treatment	3.	T	3.	c
4.	impact	4.	T	4.	c
5.	business necessity	5.	T	5.	d
6.	bona fide occupational qualification (BFOQ)	6.	T		
		7.	T		
7.	reasonable accommodation	8.	T		
8.	hostile working environment	9.	F		
9.	substantially	10.	T		
10.	Section 1981				

DISCUSSION

Your discussion should observe that since the employer's action constitutes disparate treatment the only defense is that hiring only women is a BFOQ. Discuss BFOQ.

CHAPTER 16

COMPLETION EXERCISES	TRUE-FALSE SELECTIONS	MULTIPLE-CHOICE PROBLEMS
1. Securities and Exchange Commission	1. T	1. d
2. security	2. T	2. c
3. initial sale	3. F	3. b
4. issuer	4. F	4. a
5. underwriter	5. T	5. b
6. registration statement	6. F	
7. Securities Exchange Act	7. F	
8. Section 10(b), Rule 10b-5	8. T	
9. controlling person	9. T	
10. short-swing profits	10. F	

DISCUSSION

Your answer should define corporate governance as regulating the relationship between directors/officers and owners of corporations. Securities regulations help control various frauds against corporate owners. Discuss Rule 10b-5, the registration process under the 1933 Act, etc.

CHAPTER 17

COMPLETION EXERCISES	TRUE-FALSE SELECTIONS	MULTIPLE-CHOICE PROBLEMS
1. environmental impact statement	1. T	1. c
2. scoping	2. T	2. c
3. Environmental Protection Agency	3. T	3. b
4. Primary	4. F	4. a
5. Secondary	5 T	5. b
6. bubble concept	6. T	
7. emissions trading	7. T	
8. prevention of significant deterioration	8. F	
9. Clean Water Act	9. F	
10. Superfund	10. F	

DISCUSSION

Your answer should explain that many resources like the air and certain waterways are not subject to private property. It should also address the fact that many subtle problems of environmental pollution are not easily addressed by private litigation and thus require public regulation.

CHAPTER 18

COMPLETION EXERCISES	TRUE-FALSE SELECTIONS	MULTIPLE-CHOICE PROBLEMS
1. United Nations, Hague	1. F	1. b
2. Private international law	2. F	2. d
3. World Trade Organization	3. T	3. c
4. Convention on the International	4. T	4. a
Sale of Goods	5. F	5. d
5. European Union	6. F	
6. North American Free Trade Agreement	7. F	
7. letter of credit	8. F	
8. Expropriation	9. T	
9. Foreign Corrupt Practices Act	10. T	
10. offsets		

DISCUSSION

Your answer should discuss foreign direct sales and the irrevocable letter of credit, licensing and franchising, and the foreign subsidiary.